PAUL NIZAN: COMMUNIST NOVELIST

Also by Michael Scriven

SARTRE'S EXISTENTIAL BIOGRAPHIES

Paul Nizan:
Communist Novelist

MICHAEL SCRIVEN
Lecturer in French
University of Bath

St. Martin's Press   New York

First published in the United States of America in 1988

Printed in Hong Kong

ISBN 0–312–01692–1

Library of Congress Cataloging-in-Publication Data
Scriven, Michael, 1947–
Paul Nizan: Communist novelist / by Michael Scriven.
p.   cm.
Bibliography: p.
Includes index.
ISBN 0–312–01692–1: $40.00 (est.)
1. Nizan, Paul.   2. Communism in literature.   3. Novelists,
French—20th century—Biography.   4. Communists—France—Biography. 87–32140 CIP
I. Title
PQ2627.I95Z87 1988
843'.912—dc19
[B]

For Jonathan and Sara

Some people deal in diplomatic dispatches, but what really matters is the city morgue

Paul Nizan

Contents

Preface

There exist many images of Paul Nizan, but one has assumed hegemonic cultural dominance. When Sartre published the preface to *Aden Arabie* in 1960, he not only triggered off a long-overdue re-evaluation of Nizan's life and work, he also created at the same time a potent and dramatic image of Nizan which has exercised a hypnotic fascination over an entire generation. The rebellious, icono-clastic, uncompromising Nizan embodied in the text of *Aden Arabie* coincided exactly with the spirit of the times: oppositional, youthful, optimistic.

However, time passes, circumstances alter, opinions evolve. The radical optimism of the 1960s has given way to the pragmatic realism of the 1980s with the result that the intellectual and emotional thread of this book is in many ways a critique of this potent Sartrean image, an image which no longer coincides with the spirit of the present time. Nizan, in short, still captures the imagination, but in a different way.

My interest in Nizan has consequently evolved from the lyrical to the realistic, from the literary to the political. A genuine sympathy for the anarchistic and critically destructive tendencies of Nizan's early work, which so clearly forms the texture of the Sartrean image of Nizan, has over a period of time been replaced by a growing respect for the more constructive, politically oriented aspects of Nizan's life and writings.

In this sense, the Nizan–Sartre comparison has again been instruc-tive. Sartre's generous rehabilitation of Nizan necessitates inevitably a reassessment of Sartre himself. It is difficult at one level to be convinced by Sartre's postwar appeal for a committed literature fully integrated in the social and political concerns of the contem-porary world, and to ignore at another level the fact that it was Nizan, not Sartre, who produced such a literature in the prewar period. Nizan's full-blooded literary commitment at a time of historic socio-political change, with the rise of fascism, the advent of the Popular Front, the tragic unfolding of the Spanish Civil War, and the ensuing drift to Munich and the Second World War, highlights the inadequacy of Sartre's lack-lustre, apolitical abstentionism during the same period. Anyone genuinely convinced by Sartre's own postwar arguments on committed literature must surely be impressed by Nizan's prewar involvement in the political and social issues of his time, and by his efforts to produce revolutionary literature addressing itself to contemporary social and political concerns. This progressively more politicised image of Nizan which has gradually supplanted in my own mind the emotionally charged Sartrean image is, in effect, the primary reason for my interest in Nizan's life and work. A growing preoccupation with French left-wing politics and socialist realist literature, has brought me to a realisation of the highly original status of Paul Nizan. The intriguingly ambiguous situation of the communist writer engaged in the production of imaginative literature, entrusted with the task of fusing an ideologically 'correct' political content within an artistically satisfying literary form, finds exemplary illustration in the political literature of Nizan. There is a sense in which the literary production of the communist novelist Nizan in the 1930s stands as an ever-present interrogation to the critical evaluation of the existentialist theoretician Sartre in the 1940s. To the extent that I believe that Nizan goes a long way to achieving a literary goal that Sartre himself declares to be theoretically, politically and artistically unattainable, work on Nizan became for me the natural prolongation of work on Sartre.

To write a book on Nizan as a *sequel* to a book on Sartre is consequently not a purely arbitrary development. The logic underlying this decision is that there is something important, something unique in the work of Nizan which is absent from the work of Sartre and which needs to be given prominence. The reason for this book is therefore not simply academic: a desire to highlight once again the rather obvious point that both intellectually and artistically Sartre and Nizan are linked, and that they must therefore necessarily be understood in relation to one another. Nor is the reason purely subjective: a pretext for foregrounding a personal development towards the political and away from the literary sphere. On the contrary, the reason is itself political: a decision to give prominence to the view that if a genuinely revolutionary literature is possible, then the example of Sartre is interesting, but that the example of Nizan is crucial, seminal. To examine the life and work of Paul Nizan is to explore the possibility of an authentically left-wing political literature.

The full responsibility for the ideas expressed in the following pages is mine alone. However, I should like to take this opportunity to thank a number of friends and colleagues who, directly or indirectly, have been instrumental in the production of this book. I feel especially indebted to all members of the Socialist Realism Research Group in the School of Modern Languages at the University of Bath, particularly Dennis Tate and David Gillespie who were both of great assistance in providing a broader European cross-cultural reference system for my ideas. I should also like to thank Jolyon Howorth, whose comments on French political culture frequently catalysed my thoughts on Nizan's life and work. Thanks are also in order for Chris Williams and Nigel Lewis for their enduring patience in solving my word-processing problems, and for all colleagues in the French section of the School of Modern Languages without whose co-operation I would not have found the necessary research time for the completion of this project. Finally, I should like to record my gratitude to the library staff at the University of Bath. Without the untiring assistance of the Inter-Library Loans Section, the writing of this book would not have been possible.

M.S.

Acknowledgements

The author and publishers wish to thank the following who have kindly given permission for the use of copyright material: Editions Grasset, for the extracts from *Antoine Bloyé*, and Editions Gallimard, for the extracts from *Le Cheval de Troie* and *La Conspiration*.

All translations are my own.

1
Problems and Method

Critical opinion remains divided over Paul Nizan. Hardly surprising, no doubt, since the entire thrust of Nizan's work was aimed at disrupting what he perceived as the hypocritical serenity and intolerable indifference of an unjust world. Nizan generally spoke his mind and refused to pull his punches. In the process he made many enemies. Few who have confronted his writings remain serenely indifferent. The quite extraordinarily polarised assessments of his life and work are perhaps the ultimate tribute to the enduring potency of his political and literary activities. Throughout his life he remained an enigmatic figure. Perceptions of Nizan's character are widely diverging: 'arrogant, thin-skinned, secretive, fond of wealth, ambitious, a tactician delighting in outmanœuvring opponents, honest, gentle, generous, brusque, cheerful, tormented, astute, surprisingly uncompromising'.[1]

Since his death the enigma has been compounded by the obliteration of the reality of his existence beneath conflicting cultural images, the product of ideological warfare in a changing socio-political context. Although it is clearly the case that the Nizan that is currently available in the cultural supermarket is predominantly Sartrean, the precise contours of Nizan's existence have become blurred. Between the negative Stalinist image of 'cowardly police spy', and the positive Sartrean image of 'perennially youthful iconoclast', coexist a multitude of images of a less violent hue. Caught up in this complex network of conflicting cultural images, Nizan's life and work are today the site of confusion, myth-making and uncertainty.

To study Nizan it is therefore necessary to abandon cultural images. It is necessary to attempt to disclose the *reality* of a communist writer's existence. It is necessary, in other words, to establish a clear distinction between an existence as it was lived in the prewar period, and an existence as it was mythically reproduced in a postwar period. Only then will it be possible to reach a comprehensive assessment of Nizan's life and work.

At the heart of an analysis entitled *Paul Nizan: Communist Novelist*,

1

lie two fundamental questions:

(1) What is the nature of Nizan's commitment to and insertion in the French communist party? ('Paul Nizan: Novel Communist')
(2) Is it possible to reconcile an ideological commitment to the French communist party with the literary integrity of Nizan the writer? ('Paul Nizan: Communist Novelist')

The focus of analysis in this book is consequently the relationship between ideology and literature. Is it the case, as Sartre maintains,[2] that communism and the novel are incompatible? Or, on the contrary, is it the case, as Nizan maintains,[3] that communism and the novel are ultimately reconcilable?

Globally, the issue at stake is the complex relationship between Marxism and literature as exemplified in the life and work of a specific interwar French intellectual.

The nature of this enterprise must therefore be understood within this frame of reference. This is not an attempt to unearth every detail of Nizan's contingent existence in order to provide an exhaustive inventory of Nizan's life.[4] Nor is it an attempt to engage in extended analysis of Nizan's texts as self-justifying autonomous products. The aim, by contrast, is to *focus on the dynamic interaction between a chosen mode of political existence and a chosen mode of literary production*.

Given the mythology surrounding Nizan's life and work, it is essential to establish at the outset the full range and scope of Nizan's activities in order to highlight the very real intellectual and literary qualities of the man himself. Although he died in 1940 at the age of 35, he had in the space of very few years produced a quite prodigious range of political and literary texts. Between 1931 and 1939 – that is to say between the ages of 26 and 34 – Nizan published two polemical essays, *Aden Arabie* (1931) and *Les Chiens de garde* (1932), three novels, *Antoine Bloyé* (1933), *Le Cheval de Troie* (1935) and *La Conspiration* (1938),[5] one historical text, *Chronique de septembre* (1939), an adaptation of a Greek anti-war play by Aristophanes, *Les Acharniens* (1937), an edition of Greek materialist philosophy, *Les Matérialistes de l'antiquité* (1938), an edition of Marx, *Morceaux choisis de Marx* (1934), and two translations of extensive and important contemporary texts on America and the Soviet Union, *L'Amérique tragique* (1933) by T. Dreiser, and *Les Soviets dans les affaires mondiales* (1933) by L. Fischer. At the same time he produced a wide range of political, cultural and literary articles for publication in journals such as *Europe, Monde, Commune, La Littérature internationale, Vendredi, Clarté* and *Cahiers du bolchevisme*, he was co-scriptwriter of a film *Visages de la France* (1937), and he contributed regularly in his capacity as foreign-affairs correspondent for *L'Humanité* between 1935 and 1937, and *Ce Soir* between 1937 and 1939.

It is not appropriate in these initial remarks to offer any sweeping value-judgements of Nizan's writings, but two points need stressing:

First, to understand the full complexity of Nizan's life and work, it is important to take account of all aspects of his writing activity. Far too often misleading views arise because an excessively selective approach has been adopted in order to further the cause of a particular ideological viewpoint; and here Sartre is as guilty as the hostile Stalinist hatchet-men.

Secondly, the quality and quantity of Nizan's output must be judged bearing in mind not only the ideological but also the practical implications of his membership of the French communist party during the 1930s. This is not to advocate that Nizan should be judged solely by criteria acceptable to Nizan individually or the communist party as a whole, but it is to put forward the idea that Nizan's situation as a *communist* writer in interwar France needs to be given prominence in any assessment. It is not an exaggeration to maintain that the fundamental determining factor in Nizan's global experience was his encounter with Marxism and his deep personal involvement in the French communist party. Nizan' communist allegiances cannot consequently be glossed over, however signifi cant his ultimate break from the party might be. They are the guiding principle in his life and work and must be clearly visible in any evaluation.

The first part of this work will accordingly be aimed at elucidating the totality of Nizan's experience as a communist writer/intellectual in the political and historical context of interwar French society. A subsequent and subsidiary task in this part will be to examine the symbolic fascination exercised on French intellectual life by the posthumous Nizan in the postwar period, a moment of cultural reproduction when Nizan in many ways becomes a touchstone of the political conscience of the French left.

The second part of this work will be aimed at disclosing initially the original set of political, historical and cultural circumstances in which Nizan's literature was produced. This initial historical con-textualisation will prepare the ground for a detailed textual analysis in which the focus will be not only the original moment of production of the text, but also, and by implication, its subsequent moments of reproduction in differing historical circumstances.

In this way the fully historical nature of the literary act is articulated in its progressive unfolding. Literature is not reduced to a spectral series of disembodied texts, but is seen to be a point of mediation in a developing dialectical process. Only a resolutely historical critical approach such as this can begin to do justice to the life and work of Paul Nizan, inextricably enmeshed as it is in the illusions, deceits, hopes, aspirations, successes and failures of its time.

To study the life and literature of Paul Nizan is to be thrown abruptly into the cultural history of contemporary France. To shrink from examining this broad historical and cultural reference system is to shrink from reality. As Nizan himself pointedly remarked in 1935, 'All reactionary literatures dread reality; they either avoid it or conceal it. They are the expression of those societies with something to hide. This is the very definition of idealism. Revolutionaries have nothing to hide: they mark a return to reality. They describe it in such a way that it finally appears as it is, that is to say intolerable.'[6]

My analysis will be in two principal parts, the first entitled 'Paul Nizan: Novel Communist', the second entitled 'Paul Nizan: Communist Novelist'.

In Part One, I shall offer a dual biography of Nizan's existence. Initially (Chapter 2), I shall trace the progressive development of Nizan's life and work between 1905 and 1939 by focusing on the three formative structural influences that shaped his existence: the family unit, the schooling system and the communist party. I shall attempt to display the complex and divergent possibilities in Nizan's life, but shall stress throughout the importance of the stabilising effect, both politically and emotionally, afforded by the French communist party. Secondly (Chapter 3), I shall examine not only Nizan's resignation from the party and his subsequent death, but also his dramatic afterlife, a moment of political, ideological and cultural reproduction in which the complexity of his existence is obliterated beneath politically advantageous stereotypes: traitor, police spy, rebel, anti-hero.

In Part Two, I shall analyse Nizan's literary output with specific reference to his three published novels, *Antoine Bloyé*, *Le Cheval de Troie* and *La Conspiration*, as well as his unfinished and unpublished final novel *La Soirée à Somosierra*. I shall preface this textual analysis with an account of the cultural politics of the period 1927–40 (Chapter 5), and a theoretical and ideological assessment of interwar socialist realism (Chapter 6). My examination of Nizan's communist novels (Chapter 7) will be directed at accomplishing two tasks: first, to examine the processes whereby each of three texts is produced and reproduced in successively different historical situations; here, particular emphasis will be given to the idea that each text is not a perfectly finished artistic product but the narrative site of ideological and literary contradictions. Secondly, to explore the formal and ideological parameters and ambitions of the three published novels with a view to assessing the efficacy of a revolutionary literature; here, attention will be focused specifically on the tensions arising from the injection of a communist and hence anti-bourgeois political content within an archetypal bourgeois literary form.

Overall, the objective is not only to give prominence to the life and work of a highly original and much underrated communist intellectual and novelist, but also to scrutinise the example of Nizan as a guiding principle for action in the present. If a genuinely revolutionary literature is desirable and possible, then the example of Nizan is instructive to the degree that his life and work are an illustration of both the limits and the potential of politically dissident literature in a contemporary western democracy.

final novel in Soviet Romania. I shall preface this textual analysis with an account of the cultural politics of the period 1921–30, narratives and theories, and ideological assessment (theory of influences) and Chapter 6, *Myth-construction of literary communist models (narrative)*, will be directed at exploring these two issues. First I will examine the processes whereby each of these texts is produced and reproduced in a given literary-historical matrix. Here a particular emphasis will be given to the idea that each text is never a perfectly finished artefact, hinged both to the narrative and to ideological and literary conjunctures. Secondly, to explore the internal and ideological tensions and ambitions of the three published novels within a view to assessing the influence of a revolutionary literature here; attention will be focused specifically on the tensions of being firstly the construction of a communist literature about post-revolutionary content within an already established literary norm.

Overall, the objective is not only to give prominence to the fact that works of a highly oriental and general order than the communist literary and novelist, but also to set out time, the example of how an abiding principle for action in the present. It a genuine revolutionary, the nature is desirable and possible. Then the example of Gaan is that to give the degree that his life and work are not unaware of both the limits and the potential for political and cultural literature in a contemporary western democracy.

Part One
Paul Nizan:
Novel Communist

Any Ethic which does not explicitly profess that it is impossible today *contributes to the mystification and alienation of men. The ethical 'problem' arises from the fact that Ethics is* for us *inevitable and at the same time impossible.*

Sartre

Introduction

Biography is of necessity a false narrative. Not only does it invert the natural sequence of events in a given life by interpreting origins and development in the light of conclusions (teleological falsification); it also selects particular ideas, events and utterances for interpretation within the framework of a preferred intellectual system (ideological falsification).

Ultimately, there is no way to avoid this. Biography, like all other cultural products, is the result of a process of cultural reproduction in which the past is continuously reinterpreted from the vantage point of the present. The past exists, in short, as the terrain to be rediscovered by contemporary consciousness.[1] The underlying premise of biography is consequently an unresolved tension between fact and fiction, truth and deception. Paradoxically, the manner in which a given biographical narrative chooses to be false determines the extent to which it can make claims to truth.

The ensuing 'false' enquiry is itself underwritten by one global assumption of both a teleological and ideological nature; the belief that the truth of Nizan's contingent existence is most effectively disclosed by locating the significance of his insertion within the French communist party; that is to say, the reasons why he joined the party, the image that he created of himself and of the party whilst he was a member, and the reasons why he left the party.

In order to reveal the global significance of Nizan's existence, analysis will be organised around the three dominant structural influences in his life: the family unit, the schooling system and the communist party. The existential problems of isolation, uncertainty and disorientation that Nizan encounters initially in his family situation and subsequently in the French schooling system are ultimately resolved within the ranks of revolutionary political party.

2

Enter the Party

Paul Nizan died on 23 May 1940, aged 35. It would seem appropriate, given the centrality of the theme of death in Nizan's life and work, to begin a biography of Nizan by focusing on the moment at which he died.

To understand Nizan it is necessary first to register the fact that he died young. There is nothing particularly commendable about that in itself, but it does assist in making sense of Nizan's emotional, intellectual and political development. Unlike Sartre, Nizan was not given the opportunity to grow old and reflect serenely on his past life. His life was short and eventful. His actions and ideas were those of a young man with a clear perception of what he considered to be right and wrong, and a clear understanding of what he judged to be the sources of oppression in the world. Whether such clear-sightedness is dismissed as the naïveté of youth, or extolled as exemplary moral integrity untainted by the compromises of old age, does not concern us at this stage. What is important to stress is that Nizan's life and work must be seen in the context of his *youth*. His major work was produced between 1931 and 1939, between the ages of 26 and 34.

To understand Nizan it is necessary, secondly, to root his personal experience firmly in its socio-political and historical context. To have died in 1940 at the age of 35 is to have experienced in different ways the dramatic historical upheavals of the interwar period, and in particular in Nizan's case, the post-revolutionary development of the Soviet Union and the growth of the French communist party. It is necessary, in other words, to recognise that Nizan's itinerary as a communist intellectual, his understanding of the Soviet experience, must be placed in the context of the interwar period. However advantageous it may be either ideologically or strategically to view Nizan's communist itinerary from a post-Stalinist perspective, the result of such perceptions is merely to obliterate the reality of Nizan's lived experience beneath contemporary images and stereotypes.

To understand Nizan, it is necessary, thirdly, to highlight the fact that the story of Paul Nizan is the story of division: division within his family, division within his class, division within his party. Throughout his life Nizan never quite succeeded in reconciling the division between a public image of ideological certainty and a private image of recurring *angst* and self-doubt. Nizan never quite managed to come to terms with the childhood traumas originating in a family divided through crisis and noncommunication. Nizan failed to resolve the problems arising from his divided class origins. Educated in one class, politically affiliated to another, Nizan was ultimately swallowed up in the no man's land situated between both. Nizan was unsuccessful in his attempts to allay the suspicion that he did not really belong to the French communist party. His petty-bourgeois family background, his status as an intellectual conversant with the rites of bourgeois education, values and culture, his sophisticated literary and critical talents as a writer, all conspired to set him apart from the communist party leadership and rank and file members alike.

In many ways, the originality of Paul Nizan is to be located precisely in this divided status. A man divided cannot allow himself the luxury of complacency. A man convinced that the world is a trap, that existence is plagued by death, can ill afford to have complete faith in the established order, whether of the Right or the Left.

To understand Nizan it is necessary, finally and perhaps most importantly, to recognise the fact that Nizan was an intellectual *in search of moral integrity*. In 1930 Nizan noted 'I dislike the philosophy of oppressors because I feel that I have been the victim of oppression; reconciliation with oppression does not strike me as a victory for freedom, but rather as a death sentence.'[1] Nizan's personal need to combat an oppressive bourgeois philosophy with the liberating intellectual system of Marxism could not be more starkly expressed. In these words are echoed the spirit of moral crusade and sense of justice that Nizan, in his status as a communist intellectual in the 1930s, came to associate automatically with Marxism. Marxism was not primarily a scientific method designed to uncover the mechanisms of the capitalist economy. It was above all else a moral philosophy, the means by which the oppressed members of society came to understand the source of their oppression and worked towards its overthrow. Marxism as a philosophical system, and the French communist party as the political expression of that system, represented in Nizan's eyes the prime agents of moral regeneration and justice in an oppressive society divided by class war.

In a post-Stalinist epoch it is easy to be dismissive of the moral imperative of Marxism as embodied in the Soviet experiment and the French communist party. Yet in the 1930s Nizan's intellectual itinerary was centred on the attempt to reconcile a genuine belief in the moral integrity of Marxism with the practical application of communist party politics, the attempt, in other words, to reconcile intellectual images with political reality. The bitter lesson that Nizan learned to his cost in 1939 was that moral integrity and political reality rarely coincide.

(i) FAMILY CONTRADICTIONS, 1905–16

'We are all born predestined', noted Sartre in 1971. 'The development of our lives is predetermined from the beginning by our family situation and the structure of society at a given moment in time.'[2] To no one does this apply more aptly than to Paul Nizan. Nizan's life chances were clearly and inalterably inscribed in his family situation long before he was born in Tours in February 1905.

In 1931, at the age of 26, Nizan referred to his family as an insubstantial presence resting as lightly on his shoulders as 'the wind and the dust of the dead'.[3] An accurate description, to the extent that it highlights his lack of a cultural, familial tradition weighing him down. 'My grandparents bequeathed me no worldly goods, no duties, no knowledge, no respect. . . . Fifty years ago my ancestors were as anonymous as those of the animal kingdom', he laconically remarked.[4]

Family tradition must not be confused, however, with family situation. Nizan did not inherit a family tradition. By contrast, he did inherit a destructive family situation which weighed heavily on him for the rest of his life. The family tradition was light, but the family situation was heavy. It is this family situation as experienced by the child Nizan which requires detailed commentary, for it is precisely here that the fundamental structure of Nizan's emotional and intellectual outlook was formed, a deep-rooted psychological state which had profound effects on the thoughts and actions of the adult writer.

The destiny of Paul Nizan was to be born into a climate of death. The birth of Paul-Yves at Tours in 1905 could in no sense erase the dark memory of the tragic death of his six-year-old sister, Yvonne, two years previously. Implicitly, unconsciously, subconsciously, the family still grieved the loss of its only daughter. The infant Nizan was nurtured in a manner that betrayed the ever-present possibility of death. If death could steal away a daughter, why not a son as well? Little by little, the overprotective zeal and care of a fearful mother was translated in the infant's psyche as the need to ward off death, an ever-present possibility on the horizon of life.

As long as he lived, Nizan would never escape from the visceral awareness that death could strike suddenly, unexpectedly in the midst of life, that death threatens everybody and everything, that man is truly mortal. It is no exaggeration to maintain that Nizan was weaned on death. As an infant he sucked the milk of death into his very marrow. As a child he was haunted by the absent presence of a dead sister stolen away by the death-dealing forces of an unfathomable universe. The child Nizan grew up in the shadow of death. The adult Nizan was never to escape from it. From these deathly origins Nizan's life span was to proceed in an anguished spiral. Between 1905 and 1916 the fundamental texture of Nizan's psyche was traced out in the drama enacted in the Nizan household by its three principal characters: Clémentine Nizan, née Métour, cast in the role of mother and wife, Pierre Marie-Joseph Nizan, cast in the role of father and husband, Paul Pierre Yves Henri Nizan, cast in the role of only son.

Although born in Tours, Paul Nizan's roots were in Brittany. Both parents were of Breton origin, but of markedly different social backgrounds; Clémentine Métour a product of the urban, commercial bourgeoisie of Nantes, Pierre Nizan a product of the tenant farming rural peasantry of the Basse-Vilaine. Clémentine Métour/Nizan, dominated initially by the overpowering personality of her husband, remained throughout her life a retiring, acquiescent woman both submissive and dutiful. Clémentine fearfully spun the protective web of catholicism, the family and middle-class values around her unenterprising existence, and provided little alternative for her son but to look to his father for inspiration and guidance.

Pierre Marie-Joseph Nizan was undoubtedly the pivotal influence in Paul-Yves's formative years. Driven on by the desire to escape from the hardship of his peasant origins, Pierre Nizan pushed himself ever forward in a process of continual self advancement. Educational success provided him with the means of breaching the barrier of his lowly birth and enabled him to gain access to the lower echelons of the petty bourgeoisie as an engineer in the French railway system. Between 1883 and 1916 Pierre Nizan's life was the story of progressive career advancement, promotion following promotion in a nomadic itinerary from Tours to Aurillac to Montluçon to Limoges to Angers to Tours to Brive to Limoges to Tours to Périgueux to Choisy-Bâches (Paris). There is a self-willed flight forward here, a certain careerist mentality, a belief in the objectives of the company, a sense of purpose and an appetite for work encoded in this trajectory which mirrors the relentless flight forward of the son a generation later.

Already the various structural elements in Nizan's psychology are becoming apparent: a brooding sense of death nurtured in his formative months and years as an infant and as a child; a childhood admiration for the values and life-style of his father, a man exuding certainty, conviction and power, a man involved in the practical problems of everyday existence; a corresponding indifference for the seemingly hollow existence of his mother preoccupied with family duties, social functions and religious rites; an implicit recognition that the path to be followed was to be located somewhere in the dynamic working-class origins of his father rather than in the passive middle-class origins of his mother; a sense of loneliness as a child compensated by a deeply experienced relationship with his father, an idol, the source of knowledge and truth.

The destiny of the father is ultimately the key to the destiny of the son. Prior to 1916 Paul-Yves's life was anchored by the rock-like presence of a reassuring father figure, dominant, capable, sure. In 1916 Pierre Nizan, who had wagered his existence on a career in the railway company, saw his life explode around him. His certainty, his sense of direction, his belief in himself disintegrated alongside his career, and the Nizan household was never the same again. Mother and son alike became the passive, helpless witnesses to the demise, fall and dissolution of a man who had given direction to them both.

The contingent cause of the crisis is not of great significance, a tale of possible sabotage, possible negligence regarding the transport of shells destined for the battle front in late 1915. Whatever the truth of the affair, the consequence was that Pierre Nizan was immediately transferred from Périgueux to Choisy-Bâches in the suburbs of Paris, a demotion which signalled a halt to his professional career and a moment of crisis in his personal and family life.

Assessing his father retrospectively with a mixture of filial compassion and uncompromising lucidity, Nizan remarked:

My father depicted culture as power and wealth, as the one thing that he did not have and without which he could not become a bourgeois. He sensed vaguely that he was inferior, as do the majority of those who are on the threshold of the bourgeoisie but who do not know its inner secrets.[5]

In 1916 Pierre Nizan's efforts to gain full admission to the bourgeoisie were finally dashed. His feelings of inferiority were compounded only by the vague sense of unease that his careerism and social mobility had possibly been misguided from the outset. The years that followed, until his death in 1929, were a prolonged process of disillusionment and despair. A deep and brooding sense of shame and failure led him to turn in upon himself, withdraw from both his wife and his son, and ultimately during 1920 and 1921 to engage in nightly excursions, disappearances designated by Sartre as 'attempted suicides'.[6]

The bewilderment of the child Nizan cannot be overstated. The self-control and lucidity which Nizan displayed as an adult when retrospectively assessing his father, particularly in *Antoine Bloyé*, should not mask the fact that this was a moment of structural crisis in Nizan's development, a moment which coloured his entire existence and shaped his underlying psyche irreversibly. 1916 was a moment of total psychological disruption. Nizan's only stable point of reference in a mysteriously contingent world had been obliterated His father, the visible sign of self-assurance, power and knowledge, whose mere presence had calmed his original *angst* and fearfulness, had forsaken him, a broken man. An unknowable, harsh and cruel society had destroyed his father for no apparent reason. A father's self-confidence and certainty were transformed into disorientation, self-doubt and a morbid contemplation of death. Death firmly re-established its presence in Nizan's life in 1916.

By 1917, the year that he first came into contact with Sartre, the very year that Lenin was establishing a new revolutionary Soviet state, three years before the birth of the French communist party, this future activist of the French Left was in the throes of a major personal crisis brought about by the demise of his father. It was to take a further ten years and another major crisis before he could emerge from despair and find a solution to his *angst* and disorientation in the ranks of the party.

More significantly, what needs to be clearly articulated at this juncture is the fundamental emotional structure of Nizan's personality, the product of his family existence between 1905 and 1916.

His family situation led him to the inescapable conclusion that the world was a hostile, alien environment in which was concealed the terrible presence of death, and in which the hopes, convictions and aspirations of men could be dashed by the unforeseeable and irreversible consequences of a malevolent destiny.

The origins of Nizan's celebrated cynicism are to be located here. Sartre recalls Nizan speaking of his parents in 1916 with 'cynical detachment'.[7] Nizan was clearly showing the first signs of a defensive strategy that he would deploy to great effect throughout the remainder of his life. The ironic, cynical tone that Nizan adopted was the visible sign of an effort to master a situation which was otherwise uncontrollable. Aloofness, detachment, distancing, flippancy, all variations on a theme – a sustained effort to remain *above* and *beyond* a threatening world. Beneath the cynicism, beneath the irony, however, turmoil. Beneath the apparent certainty, a nexus of contradictions and paradoxes. And what this produced was a fundamentally *manichean* view of the world. In an unpredictable, alien world in which all sense of certainty and reliability appeared to have disappeared, there was an urgent need to locate a positive and stable community of interests and values to be defended against the destructive, negative, death-like forces of a hostile universe. Beyond the distancing and perpetual deferment of irony, therefore, Nizan engaged in a quest for stability, certainty, reliability. Such a quest necessarily involved a process of selection and categorisation in which the constituent elements of the world were divided into the forces of Good and the forces of Evil; those working with him, those working against him; those working for one class, those working for another. As long as he lived Nizan clung to this fundamentally manichean view of existence.[8]

It is not surprising that Nizan's gaze eventually alighted on the French communist party, a source of ideological certainty, a small community defending itself by rigid discipline against the fluidity, compromise and unreliability of centrist politics in Third Republic France. It is no exaggeration to maintain that the family drama experienced by the child Nizan between 1905 and 1916 prepared him emotionally and intellectually for entry to the PCF ten years later.

However, it is as yet too early to assess Nizan's integration in the political sphere. Between 1916 and 1927 his quest for intellectual and emotional stability led him to examine another solution: bourgeois culture and bourgeois education.

(ii) EDUCATIONAL DILEMMAS, 1916–27

'I don't like losers', noted Nizan in 1925. 'I am capable of liking only those whom I consider to be my equals.'[9] This is not a serene affirmation of faith by Nizan in his own superiority, a condescending refusal to interact with lesser mortals than himself. It is rather the visible sign of underlying defensiveness and uncertainty. It is symptomatic, in short, of a need both to proclaim his own worth and to keep a threatening world at a distance. This defensiveness, this compelling desire to present himself as *superior* and *different* from common humanity, this tenacious refusal to be a loser, became the driving force in Nizan's psychology after 1916.

There can be little doubt that, in the aftermath of the crisis of 1916–17, Nizan gradually, irreversibly began to perceive his father as a loser; a loser not through any fault of his own, other than a self-confessed lack of bourgeois schooling and culture. The system had simply smashed him.[10] Yet however unjust, whoever was to blame, the result was the same: his father was a broken man. Objective number one, then, in Nizan's mind after 1916 was to avoid the terrible fate of his father. If the only attributable cause of his father's demise was his inadequate mastery of bourgeois culture, the most effective way forward for the son was to aim for total acquisition of the cultural identity that his father manifestly lacked.

Between 1916–17 and 1927 the setting for this particular drama was the bourgeois educational system of the Third Republic. Nizan's strategy was consequently straightforward: to enter fully into the competitive struggle of the state educational system, to conduct an effective campaign of academic self-advancement, to acquire full mastery of bourgeois culture, and in the process avoid the deathly fate of his father. The objective, in other words, was to avoid becoming a loser.[11]

Nizan's schooling extended from 1911 until 1929. In 1911 he was initiated into the schooling process at the École Primaire in Tours. In 1929 he reached the pinnacle of educational success when he passed the *agrégation* at the École Normale Supérieure in the company of Sartre and Simone de Beauvoir. Table 1 provides a chronological outline of Nizan's passage through the French educational system.

Although the formal process of schooling began in 1911 and terminated in 1929, the critical phase was between 1917 and 1927. This formative ten-year period, signalled at the outset by the personal crisis of his father and at its conclusion by his own personal crisis in

TABLE 1.1   Nizan's schooling

Date	Institution	Location
1911–13	École Primaire	Tours
1913–17	(a) École Primaire	Périgueux
	(b) Lycée	
1917–22	Lycée Henri IV	Paris
1922–4	Lycée Louis-le-Grand	Paris
1924–6	École Normale Supérieure	Paris
1926–7	——	Aden
1927–9	École Normale Supérieure	Paris

Aden, was the privileged moment during which the psychological development of Paul Nizan was determined predominantly by the substance and form of the French education system.

Prior to 1916–17, prior to the crisis brought about by the demise of his father, the process of schooling was merely an extension of family life, a childhood means of emulating a successful father, the arena in which to live up to the expectations of a demanding father-figure. From 1917 onwards, however, the educational system became the chosen battle-ground where the child/adolescent Nizan was to struggle for personal identity and stability. 1917: the breaking of the father, the move to Paris, the first encounter with Sartre, the beginning of the struggle. After 1927, following Aden, following the decision to join the PCF, the centre of gravity shifted from the educational to the political domain. Everything that occurred in the educational sphere after 1927 was no more than a 'clearing-up' operation. From 1927 on the struggle became political.

The adult Nizan, the uncompromising communist militant, may quite legitimately be angrily dismissive of the process of schooling to which he was subjected as an adolescent and young man. 'Bourgeois culture is a barrier, a luxury, a corruption of man, an instrument of warfare', he vehemently proclaimed in 1930.[12] This negative, retrospective condemnation of the cultural values encoded in the French middle-class schooling of the time should not, however, divert attention from the fact that in 1916–17 the educational system was perceived by the child Nizan as the only available route to personal salvation and success. Encouraged initially by his father in the belief that the acquisition and mastery of the culture dispensed in the state educational system was a necessary prerequisite to self-advancement, and spurred on by the conviction that to avoid his father's fate he must acquire the one element that his father lacked, Nizan proceeded systematically and relatively uncritically between 1917 and 1924 to immerse himself in bourgeois culture.

His brilliant track record at school is a testimony not only to his academic prowess, but also to his application and determination to succeed. The seven years spent at Henri IV and Louis-le-Grand testify to a relentless pursuit of academic excellence rewarded by numerous prizes across a wide range of disciplines.[13] More specifically, the years from 1920 to 1924 were especially productive, Nizan's inbred appetite to succeed being increased by the competitive presence of Sartre, back from a three-year stint in a provincial lycée in La Rochelle.[14] Sartre's preface to *Aden Arabie* is in fact a moving account of their high personal ambitions whilst at Henri IV, Louis-le-Grand and especially the École Normale Supérieure. Implicit in this emotional narrative is the assumption that their academic success of the time would serve as the platform for future literary achievements, and would lead inevitably to public recognition of their undoubted talents.

A life story is not encapsulated, however, in an academic curriculum vitae. The image of intellectual and emotional self-control and stability projected by Nizan was fragile. Beneath the outward appearance of self-assurance and scholarly success, deep-seated psychological tensions were being set up in Nizan's personality, tensions exacerbated by changes in Nizan's family and educational situation, tensions that were to lead to a personal crisis. To wager one's existence on an educational solution is a viable option as long as individual academic success is forthcoming, and as long as the educational solution itself is perceived as credible. Two factors, one personal, one educational, were to conspire to undermine the credibility of the educational solution in Nizan's mind.

Sartre records that by 1920–21, the personal predicament of Nizan's father had become so desperate that he had taken to disappearing at frequent intervals from the family home at night, disappearances which Sartre interprets as 'attempted suicides'.[15] The effect on Nizan of this progressive deterioration of his father's situation cannot be overestimated. The final moral disintegration of his father was witnessed by the son with a sense of helplessness and incomprehension. Yet the personal tragedy of the father was not only the occasion for the impotent compassion of a bewildered son. It was also a moment of decisive self-scrutiny in which the image of the destiny of the father conjured up an image of the destiny of the son. Was it not his father who had been the prime agent in advocating the educational route to success? Was it not his father who had resolutely argued a case for the necessary acquisition of bourgeois culture in order to succeed? Was it not his father who had implicitly argued a case for the moral uprightness of bourgeois culture and bourgeois education? And yet here was his father on the brink of suicide destroyed by a bourgeois system that he so admired. Could it be that his father had been wrong? Could it be that the bourgeois educational system was flawed?

Nizan's transition to the higher education system in 1924, his first encounter with the fundamentally different educational environment of the École Normale Supérieure, coincided with a drastic reappraisal of the educational solution itself and projected Nizan into a downward spiral of crisis and despair. 'Until coming to the ENS, I developed in a closed system', he noted in 1927.[16] Prior to 1924 Nizan had been enveloped, cocooned, embalmed almost in the reassuring network of social relations on which the process of schooling is founded: hierarchical teaching and administrative structures, institutional discipline, academic discipline. In *La Conspiration* Nizan ironically refers to school life as a barrack-room existence cut off from the reality of the outside world.[17]

Entry to the libertarian, undisciplined and nakedly élitist lifestyle of the École Normale Supérieure inevitably led Nizan to take stock of his situation from an entirely new perspective. For the first time Nizan was forced to confront the social reality of the process of schooling. Schooling was no longer simply a purely autonomous activity, an esoteric if somewhat ruthless exercise in which the objective was to demonstrate superiority over one's peers. Schooling was perceived in its historical, social and political context, as a highly selective process from which the majority of society were excluded. Inevitably, the image of his father, the image of his family, the image of his class, were at the forefront of this searing reappraisal:

> When my father was fifteen years old, he did not go for holidays on beaches, as I did with his money. He used to be working fourteen hours a day in the shipyards of the Loire. At an age when I was having qualms over the philosophy of M. Bergson, he was speaking in a factory yard of the necessity to go on strike.[18]

The contrast between the political and social reality of his father's existence and the political and social reality of his own existence was dramatically brought into focus from the moment that he entered the École Normale Supérieure. For Nizan it was no longer possible to shelter in the protective, disciplined, self-contained environment of school. At the rue d'Ulm he could delude himself no longer about the contradictory nature of his existence. Images of his past, his origins, became blurred by images of his present, his future aspirations, and the result was turmoil. The cosy solution of bourgeois educational success in which the sole objective was not to be a loser, was abruptly shattered by the realisation that the majority of men and women were, like his father, losers, and that to turn one's back on them and on his origins in a strategy of personal self-survival, was an inadequate response.

His intellectual and emotional itinerary between 1924 and 1927 is the record of a deepening crisis brought on by a growing realisation of the political and social dimension of his current lifestyle, an awareness that his pursuit of academic excellence and success had implicated him personally in a way of life that contradicted, subverted and emasculated the values and beliefs of his own social origins. In the space of three years the educational solution was perceived initially as potentially flawed, ultimately as totally bankrupt. The search consequently began for an alternative solution.

At the outset, no doubt, the problem was examined in purely personal terms: on the one hand, the contrast between the life of his father and the life of the intellectual élite of the ENS; on the other, the reluctance to accept the logical outcome of the bourgeois educational system, integration and assimilation within the provincial middle-class teaching profession, a fate considered by Nizan as worse than death, a form of protracted suicide in which an individual is slowly asphyxiated within the drab grey tedium of bourgeois life. Subsequently, however, the problem was perceived from a progressively more politicised perspective, and was ultimately understood in class terms as a violent struggle against a specific form of oppression.

His first two years at the ENS were a period of growing disorientation and extremist experimentation. On the surface Nizan appeared unchanged – distant, aloof, self-controlled, academically industrious and successful. However, in February 1925, only a few months after entry to the rue d'Ulm, he was suffering from nervous depression and planned a trip to a Swiss sanatorium. By the summer of 1925 his growing disillusionment manifested itself in ceaseless role-playing, posing, self-interrogation. The ironic delight that Nizan displayed in presenting an extremist image of himself, whether it be as the arch-conservative, staunch defender of private property and the Church, or as the committed Bolshevik,[19] reached its climax in late 1925 and early 1926. In the space of a few months in late 1925, Nizan joined and left the French fascist movement, Le Faisceau, led by Georges Valois,[20] and in an equally short space of time in early 1926, he joined the French communist party for the first time and subsequently left.[21] The extremist solutions proffered by both fascism and communism fleetingly held Nizan fascinated during this phase of unstable personal development.

Throughout this period what is striking is the perpetual fluctuation between the serious and the humorous, between a desperate situation and an ironical response. The compelling need to experiment with alternative solutions in order to resolve the dilemma of his personal predicament had as its counterpart a light-hearted, seemingly casual participation in role-playing and disguise, techniques of escaping temporarily from an oppressive situation.[22]

Ultimately, none of the readily available solutions – dandyism, literary experimentation,[23] cinematic experimentation,[24] fascism, communism – provided Nizan with anything more than brief respite from an increasingly acute perception of the contradiction lodged at the heart of his existence. The situation became unbearable. In September 1926 he settled for what appeared to be the only remaining solution: escapism. He escaped from the stifling atmosphere of the ENS and fled to Aden.

The Aden episode lasted from September 1926 until May 1927: approximately nine months; a brief period in Nizan's existence but one which had far reaching consequences. However overinflated the Aden myth may subsequently have become, however difficult it might be to disentangle the truth of the episode from the fictionalised version purveyed through romanticised images of tortured adolescence, the exotic Mid-East, the rejection of Western culture, the Rimbaldian quest for personal salvation, and so on, one stark fact remains. Between September 1926 and May 1927 Nizan underwent a profound change in his intellectual and emotional outlook. It was in Aden that the alternative solution was found, and Paul Nizan finally became Paul Nizan.

In the opening sequence of *Le Cheval de Troie* the workers are first seen in the countryside viewing the town of Villefranche, the site of their daily oppression, *at a distance*. The trip to the countryside enables each working man, woman and child to look down upon

Villefranche and place it in perspective. Released from the confine-
ment of their workplace, the workers are offered a global view of
their oppressive working conditions. From afar the class enemy is
finally clearly visible.

There is an analogy to be drawn here with Nizan's trip to Aden. At
a distance from France, Nizan was able to place his own indoctrination
and oppression in perspective. From afar, his class enemies became
clearly visible. In Aden the path forward became clear, the alternative
strategy was revealed.

The tempo of this metamorphis was far from abrupt, however.
On the contrary, this was a slow if deep-rooted change occurring
over many months with many set-backs and reversals. *Aden Arabie*
itself is a text which doubtless overstates the extent of Nizan's
politicisation during 1926 and 1927. It is an angry, retrospective
account of the trip to Aden which coincides more accurately with
Nizan's highly militant frame of mind in 1930 and 1931, than it does
with the Nizan of 1926 and 1927 groping his way slowly towards the
solution of political action. The Aden correspondence,[25] by contrast,
accurately records the ebb and flow of Nizan's intellectual and
emotional state of the time, and graphically records the genesis and
development of a far-reaching emotional and political metamorphosis.

The emotional metamorphosis is pointedly highlighted in his
correspondence with Henriette (Rirette) Alphen, his future wife and
privileged companion. In the space of several months, Nizan was
progressively captivated by the refreshingly candid, lively and
astute personality of Rirette. The crucial importance of the stabilising
influence of Rirette in Nizan's personal development cannot be
overstated, and there are certainly grounds for drawing a parallel
between, on the one hand, the blossoming at a distance of Nizan's
love and affection for Rirette, with the consequent calming of
personal anxieties, and on the other, the burgeoning at a distance of
his hatred and hostility for those political, social and cultural forces
in French society which he considered to have led him to the brink of
suicide and despair.

The progressive intensification of Nizan's anger in Aden needs to
be registered. Although in November 1926 he could still refer quite
positively to 'this freemasonary of humanists, this international
body of people who can exchange passwords such as Latin verses
and the sentences of Plato',[26] his underlying assessment of Europe,
particularly European culture, was becoming decidedly more critical: 'I
am judging Europe; it is my sole preoccupation. It is an activity

which becomes more straightforward with every mile that takes me further away', he noted on 4 December.[27] By 4 January 1927, the full force of Nizan's anger, repressed for so many years, could no longer be held in check:

> The effect of the solitude at Aden is that I am storing up a violence that was unknown to me. . . . I used sometimes to have to make an effort to be cheerful, but I have never had to restrain myself from bursting into violence and anger. . . . But that's just how I was until the age of twelve, I recognise myself. The expression of the eighteen year old was the expression of a stranger.[28]

Only six months earlier, on 18 August 1926, Nizan had lamented: 'I am even incapable of getting angry. People with strong emotions to control . . . are extremely fortunate.'[29] The contrast could not be more striking. In Aden Nizan rediscovered his emotional strength, rediscovered, in short, the personality that he had relinquished at the age of twelve, at the moment of his father's personal crisis. By April 1927 Nizan could justifiably claim: 'My life has a direction.'[30]

The political solution was neither definitively adopted, nor even clearly formulated in Nizan's mind at this stage. His final letters from Aden, for example, although highlighting his fascination with 'bolshevik mysticism',[31] record at the same time his growing interest in another potential outlet for his talents and energies – a business/entrepreneurial career in the shipping line of Antonin Besse, his erstwhile benefactor in Aden.[32] Yet such a solution would appear to be the last stage in the process of experimentation/disguise previously discussed. In the final analysis the entrepreneurial solution would have been no more than an evasion of the underlying causes of Nizan's personal crisis of 1926–7.[33] His emotional and intellectual development in Aden was such that it was to lead him inevitably back to France, back to emotional security with Rirette, and back to the political and social struggle from which he had escaped in a state of total disorientation a few months earlier.

The experience of Aden had enabled Nizan to come to terms with his own personal development by providing him with the opportunity to understand more completely the political, social and cultural causes of his psychological disorientation. Three years after his return from Aden, Nizan got to the heart of his dilemma when he proclaimed:

I came very close to being a bourgeois. . . . I swallowed your culture wholesale. . . . You almost had me believing that your family secrets were in future to be mine. I know your passwords and your allusions. . . . My father who was not conversant with your rituals, was judged by you to be common; but you consider me to be your equal at the very moment that I am in a position to look down upon my father who was common, and to be ashamed of my grandfather who was working-class. You expect me to detach myself from my non-bourgeois essence . . . to honour your gods, your fathers, your Revolution. . . . Why should I dress myself up in clothes that are not mine? They are a poor disguise. Your initiation rites do not conceal your destitution. You have failed in your attempt to convince me of the coincidence between the bourgeois and the human.[34]

A statement such as this is the ultimate product of Aden. In Aden Nizan had learned a simple and never-to-be-forgotten lesson: that to live one's life, as he had since the age of twelve, with the sole objective of not being a loser was an inadequate response, since it failed to take account of the political and social structures which determined the real significance of such a project. For someone of Nizan's background, not being a loser in the educational system of the French Third Republic necessitated the annihilation of his own class origins. The result was either docile acquiescence to the hegemony of bourgeois culture or schizophrenia.

The experience of Aden was therefore precious in that it revealed the only alternative to acquiescence or schizophrenia: *the political struggle*. From 1927 onwards, the objective was no longer solely not to be a loser by achieving bourgeois academic success. The objective henceforward became not to be a loser by using the benefits of a bourgeois education to fight the cause of all those losers in the world who, like his father, had been smashed by the bourgeois system itself. The task, in short, was to use bourgeois culture against the bourgeoisie.

On his return from Aden the French communist party was unequivocally beckoning Paul Nizan.

(iii) POLITICAL SOLUTIONS, 1927–39

Whatever reasons an intellectual might have for joining the French communist party, whether they be ideological, moral or emotional, this original commitment, as Merleau-Ponty wryly remarks,[35] is inexorably transformed by the pressure of historical events into a commitment of an entirely different nature. And this transformed commitment places such enormous pressures on the individual concerned that continued membership oscillates constantly between genuine belief, self-deluding bad faith and suppressed rebellion. Between 1928 and 1939 Nizan was to experience the bitter reality of communist party membership, the ever-present difficulty of reconciling intellectually coherent and genuinely held beliefs with the tactical manoeuvring and politically expedient policies of a party attempting to survive the twists and turns of history in a highly unpredictable socio-political climate.

To highlight the problematical nature of membership of the PCF, however, is not to seek to discredit membership of the party itself. It is essential to establish at the outset the *correct* relationship between Nizan and the communist party. All too frequently Nizan's highly publicised resignation from the PCF in September 1939 is interpreted by contemporary liberal critics imbued with a visceral hostility to communism as the visible sign that his allegiance to the party was flawed from the beginning. Expressed crudely, advocates of this approach tend to locate the essential Nizan in the act of resignation itself and proceed to interpret his allegiance to communism in the light of the events of September 1939. This is to turn the problem on its head. It is not Nizan's allegiance to communism which must be interpreted in the light of his resignation from the party. It is his resignation from the party which must be interpreted in the light of his allegiance to communism.

It is as inadequate to argue, for example, that the PCF was simply the institutional terrain in which Nizan pursued a carefully orchestrated campaign of political and literary self-advancement and careerism, as it is to argue that for the majority of the ten years that he spent in the PCF Nizan remained unaware of the imperfections of Stalinist Soviet communism. In both cases, the strategic objective is to distance Nizan from too great an involvement in the communist party itself. In the first instance this is achieved by projecting the image of a cynical Nizan attempting, though usually not succeeding, to manipulate the institutional party apparatus to his own personal ends. In the second instance this is achieved by projecting the image of the naïve Nizan systematically manipulated by the ruthless bureaucrats of the party machine. In both cases Nizan is carefully detached from any real ideological involvement in the party, with the result that he can be conveniently presented as a precursor of a non-communist New Left, in opposition either strategically or naïvely to the totalitarian oppression of the party itself.

There is no doubt an element of truth in such arguments, but it is important not be be blind to the fact that temperamentally and ideologically Nizan was ideally suited for membership of the party. It was in a very real sense his natural home, particularly during the initial stages of his membership when the anger and hatred nurtured by Nizan against bourgeois existence and bourgeois culture found sustenance within the counter-culture of a highly sectarian communist party. Consequently, rather than viewing the totalitarian structure of the PCF as a source of oppression, it is more productive to view it as the chosen institution within which Nizan found not only political asylum but also emotional and moral equilibrium, a refuge in short which provided him with a necessary disciplined working environment.

Paradoxically, this view would appear to be corroborated by the blatantly anti-communist theses of Nizan's own grandson, Emmanuel Todd. Todd's contention is that the psychological tensions and traumas generated by the process of selection into winners and losers in 'brutally individualist, egoist, competitive and aggressive societies' such as France, where the working class has assimilated the ambitious, success-seeking ideology of the petty bourgeoisie, are so intense that the creation of a communist party, a form of asylum and counter-culture, becomes imperative.[36] When Todd refers to the party as 'a cosy totalitarian institution', when he remarks that 'fear and dread of the reality of the world imprison communist militants far more than the statutes',[37] he doubtless overstates his case. Yet there can be little doubt that Nizan himself certainly did perceive the party in terms similar to this when he joined its ranks in late 1927. In Nizan's eyes the party assumed the status of an alternative social group, a sanctuary in which psychological and ideological contradictions could be resolved; the perfect site in short from which to launch a counter-ideology in texts such as *Aden Arabie* and *Les Chiens de garde*, angry denunciations of the oppression of bourgeois cultural practices. Hence the need to stress at the outset that Nizan's adult development can be correctly understood only as a deep involvement in the communist party, a process of attraction-repulsion in which Nizan was both deeply committed to and deeply compromised by the party itself.

Nizan joined the PCF in late 1927. He spent 1934 in the Soviet

Union. He resigned from the party on 25 September 1939. During this period the PCF was to undergo major changes and reversals brought about by dramatic socio-political events. From the late 1920s the PCF progressed from sectarian isolationism (1927–33) to Popular Front co-operation (1934–8) to illegality (1939–41). Nizan's individual fate within the party was determined almost exclusively by the vagaries of the national and international politics of the time. It would consequently seem appropriate to assess Nizan's intellectual and emotional itinerary in these crucial years in three consecutive phases: (a) 1927–33, (b) 1934, (c) 1935–9.

1927–33: Sectarian Simplicity

When Nizan joined the PCF in late 1927, it was, as David Caute remarks, 'a curious period. . . . One generation had come to understand the trends within the International and the meaning of Stalinism, while another was ready to disregard such questions in an attempt to find a social solution to essentially personal problems'.[38] *La Conspiration*, Nizan's last published novel, centred on the lifestyles of a group of young, naïve revolutionaries in the late 1920s, certainly bears this out. Nizan's generation was not primarily concerned with the fate of international communism, nor with the true nature of Stalinism. It was preoccupied above all else with the 'attempt to find a social solution to essentially personal problems': family conflicts, class origins, emotional traumas.

The specific nature of Nizan's personal anxieties and problems have already been articulated. In late 1927 the PCF offered Nizan sanctuary from what he perceived as the alienation of bourgeois society. Only in the bosom of the PCF could Nizan breathe freely, could he begin to function effectively. 'Life is possible only within a movement which calls the world into question', he was to note later in *Le Cheval de Troie*.[39]

Yet, at first glance, and for reasons located primarily in the International movement, 1927 would not appear to be an opportune moment for Nizan to join the party. In October of that year the executive committee of the International recommended that the PCF adopt a 'class against class' political strategy. This tactical change, confirmed at the ninth full session of the Communist International in February 1928, and aimed, according to Georges Cogniot, at creating in France a working-class front against the combined bloc of social democracy and the bourgeoisie, was none the less interpreted by many in the PCF primarily as the need to intensify the struggle against social democracy.[40] The overtly sectarian, aggressively anti-intellectual tactics of the party between 1928 and 1931 are well documented.[41] In particular, the period from 1929 to 1931, when the PCF was dominated by the unrelentingly sectarian leadership of Barbé and Célor, seemingly obsessed with the sole task of eliminating devationists from the party line, with all the catastrophic consequences that this entailed (reduced party membership, loss of electoral support, reduced sales of *L'Humanité*), represents a dark period in the history of the party itself.

Although, with the elimination of Barbé and Célor from the leadership in August 1931, and with the increasing prominence given by Maurice Thorez and Jacques Duclos in 1932 to a popular front approach,[42] the ferocity of sectarian politics abated somewhat between 1931 and 1933, nevertheless the period from 1927 to 1933, during which Nizan was initiated into communist party politics, was characterised above all by what is perhaps most accurately described as 'sectarian simplicity'. Extremist doctrinal rigidity and aggressiveness were preferred to constructive attempts to confront real issues, with the result that the practical reality of politics was simply obliterated beneath a series of purely arbitrary images and myths.

Paradoxically, this extremist, sectarian phase of PCF development constituted an entirely suitable moment for Nizan to enter the party. Nizan's fundamentally manichean personality, his realisation after his return from Aden in 1927 that he had been duped by the alienating structures of the bourgeois educational system, his visceral hatred of a bourgeois class suddenly targeted as the principal enemy, the source of his own alienation ('I must no longer be afraid to hate. I must no longer be ashamed to be fanatical. I owe them the worst: they all but destroyed me'[43]), all this made Nizan an obvious candidate for a highly sectarian, aggressive, isolationist communist party.[44] Nizan was undoubtedly ripe for the PCF in 1927. The internal structures and emotional attitudes of the party at this time coincided exactly with his own mental state, and provided him with intellectual strength and emotional security.

The emotional and political stability afforded to Nizan by his entry to the PCF in 1927 needs to be examined in the light of other factors influencing his personal development at this time. Nizan's entry to the party coincided with his marriage to Henriette Alphen.[45] There can be little doubt that his commitment to family life with Rirette was a factor of equal, if not greater, significance to Nizan's personal stability as his entry to the PCF itself. The immediate post-Aden period, 1927–30, was in many ways a period of momentous change in Nizan's life-style, a moment when his individual existence stabilised, a moment of transition when a line was drawn between his bourgeois past and his communist future: 1928, the birth of his daughter, Ann-Marie; 1929, the death of his father; 1930, the birth of his son, Patrick; 1929, the passing of the *agrégation* and the consequent termination of his formal education; 1929–30, collaboration in *La Revue marxiste*. By 1930, at the height of this stridently sectarian phase of PCF development, Nizan had established a firm emotional base with Rirette, had symbolically liquidated his links with the bourgeois state and had begun his apprenticeship in the party.

The apprenticeship was not to prove easy. Although the uncompromising aggressiveness and sectarian mentality of the PCF coincided with his own emotional state at that time, Nizan's pettybourgeois origins, his accomplished bourgeois educational track record inevitably worked to his disadvantage in a party obsessively preoccupied with a working-class/proletarian ethic. Nizan's development between 1927 and 1933 was consequently paradoxical. At one level, he finally found a spiritual home, a sanctuary from which he could vent his spleen on the oppressive bourgeois institutions which had duped him. At another level, he found integration within his new environment difficult. The party may readily have accepted his assistance in attacking common enemies, but it nonetheless remained suspicious of refugees from the other side of the class divide. Nizan's apprenticeship was a testing time.

From the beginning Nizan was quite clearly convinced of the necessity to adopt a strictly orthodox party line. Recognition of his own lack of political experience, allied to a natural sympathy for the vitriolic, sectarian stance of the PCF made Nizan a willing recruit to party orthodoxy. In a letter to Nizan written in August 1929, Georges Politzer summed up their mutual position: 'Inexperienced as we are as militants and as theoreticians, we must place our trust in the party.'[46]

The various strands in Nizan's communist personality at this time are implicit in Politzer's statement: tactical naïveté, trust in the party, willingness to apply to the letter rigid sectarian orthodoxy, and a consequent obsession with ideological myth-making rather than concrete reality. Nizan's writings of this period are charged with the destructive dynamism of the newly converted. Negative, extremist, in them are fused sectarian party orthodoxy and individual self-deliverance. They are vivid, aggressive, occasionally fanatical expressions of anti-bourgeois hatred applied to his own particular experiences.

This fusing of party orthodoxy and personal alienation in Nizan's writings at this time needs to be stressed. It is tempting to be cynical when reading texts such as 'Secrets de famille' (1930), 'Notes-programme sur la philosophie' (1930), *Aden Arabie* (1931), *Les Chiens de garde* (1932), 'Littérature révolutionnaire en France' (1932), and 'Les Conséquences du refus' (1932). It is easy to dismiss them as the strategic outpourings of a new recruit trying to impress the party machine. The truth of the matter is that this sectarian phase of PCF development coincided precisely with a highly sectarian phase in Nizan's personal development. Nizan felt an urgent need to liquidate his bourgeois past, to engage in a frontal attack on the source of his own alienation. Communist party orthodoxy presented him with a unique opportunity to voice his frustration and anger.

When Nizan aggressively proclaimed: 'The time for destruction has returned. . . . Let bourgeois philosophy be cudgelled and smashed by the Revolution',[47] when he uncompromisingly asserted: 'Let us have the courage to be crude: let the spirit of subtlety be swept down the sewer. . . . There are only two human species left and the only bond between them is hatred: the one that crushes and the one that refuses to be crushed',[48] when he pointedly remarked: 'In a world brutally divided into those who rule and those who serve, the philosopher must finally acknowledge a long-concealed secret alliance with those who govern or else declare his solidarity with those who are governed. Scholarly impartiality is no longer possible. In future the only option is partisan struggle',[49] Nizan was not simply playing the role of orthodox sectarian militant. There is a directness, a genuine sense of conviction in these words which extend far beyond strategic posing. The militancy of sectarian party orthodoxy is fused with the militancy of rebellion against personal oppression.

Curiously, the party response to his 'sectarian' writings was not entirely uncritical. Although acknowledging the courage and sincerity of Nizan's outspoken attacks on bourgeois class oppression, the party continued to view his literary production sceptically, suspiciously. Both *Aden Arabie* and *Les Chiens de garde* were judged to be essentially lightweight literary texts, lacking in substantive Marxist analysis, excessively centred on a purely verbal, abstract revolt, and having little relevance to the contemporary class struggle.[50]

Despite Nizan's unswerving commitment to the communist orthodoxy of the period, the image of the petty bourgeois intellectual
remained. He was still seen as tied to the ranks of the bourgeoisie by
an umbilical cord that he had failed to sever.

The image of an umbilical cord linking Nizan to the bourgeoisie is
pertinent when assessing his practical political difficulties and daily
working life during this period. Between 1927 and 1933 Nizan was
clearly in a contradictory situation: at one level committed to sectarian
communist ideology, at another level implicated in bourgeois careerism. Expressed simply, Nizan was still forced to earn his living by
conventional means such as teaching, yet his overriding objective
was full integration in the ranks of the French communist party.
This tense relationship between bourgeois careerism and communist
party political commitment was at the root of the accusation that
during this period Nizan had not entirely succeeded in severing his
links with his bourgeois past.

Although Nizan's writings of the period are suffused with acerbic
communist ideology, although he was chosen as communist party
candidate in Bourg-en-Bresse for the general election of 1932, although
he participated fully in the Université Ouvrière from its opening in
1932, during the same period he was also involved in finalising his
bourgeois education (1927–9), he was also a philosophy teacher at
the Lycée Lalande in Bourg-en-Bresse (1931–2). These diverging
tendencies in Nizan's life-style, on the one hand a genuine aspiration
towards a communist future, on the other hand a residual implication
in a bourgeois past, were symptomatic of a 'tension' in Nizan's life
and work at this time, a 'tension' that was resolved only in late 1932
and early 1933, when he became a permanent official entrusted with
the task of compiling the weekly 'notes de lecture' in *L'Humanité*,
and of supervising the party newspaper's bookshop located at 120
rue Lafayette.

The reluctance of the party to embrace unconditionally the activities of bourgeois intellectuals during this period was doubtless the
result of the highly sectarian and consequently suspicious attitude
with which the party viewed cultural activity at this time. Although,
for example, Nizan and Politzer unquestionably made the correct
tactical decision in 1929 in siding with Rappoport and the party
against the other less orthodox members of the editorial board of *La
Revue marxiste*,[51] and although the party itself was doubtless justified in harbouring misgivings regarding an 'independent' Marxist
journal, the incident itself highlighted the inevitably tense relationship

between a disciplined revolutionary party and its intellectual membership and fellow-travellers.

In 1929 Nizan's acquiescence to party discipline did not prevent him from exploring the possibility of working for the party at the edge of the class divide. His successful infiltration of the journal *Bifur* between 1930 and 1931, and his unsuccessful attempt in 1931 to influence the editorial policy of Barbusse's journal, *Monde*,[52] were striking examples of Nizan's attempt to develop a sectarian communist cultural policy within the sphere of bourgeois publishing houses.

This effort on Nizan's part to promote orthodox sectarian communist party ideology within a bourgeois context found no greater expression than during the year he spent in Bourg-en-Bresse, when he was at one and the same time philosophy teacher at the Lycée Lalande and communist party candidate at the general election of 1932.[53] Arguably, this public proclamation of secretarian communist beliefs during the election campaign, alerting as it did the bourgeois authorities to the subversive political activities of this 'Red Messiah',[54] and resulting in Nizan's transfer to Auch, precipitated his decision to become a fully integrated member of the PCF.

By 1933 Nizan was a permanent official of the PCF. He was writing regularly for *L'Humanité*, and had secretarial responsibilities with Aragon for the journal *Commune*. His intellectual itinerary within the communist party had begun in earnest. However, although at this stage the inner reaches of PCF life, the practical realities of daily party cultural work, were slowly revealing themselves to Nizan, his intellectual and ideological development was still very much dominated by sectarian rhetoric and abstract, idealised images of a better future destined to arise from the overthrow of capitalism. In December 1932 Nizan referred unequivocally to the 'new life' and 'new culture' to be instigated by the proletariat in post-revolutionary society, and to the 'heroic social project being undertaken in the USSR'.[55] In 1934 Nizan was given the opportunity to examine this 'heroic project' at grass roots level.

1934: Soviet Scrutiny

There can be little doubt that Nizan departed for the Soviet Union in January 1934 in a crusading spirit. His writings prior to departure make it abundantly clear that the image of the USSR firmly implanted in his mind was that of a country in full post-revolutionary expansion engaged in the construction of a new society, a new culture and a new man, a country in which social relations were no longer based on human exploitation, and in which the deathly oppression of an exploiting class had been eradicated. The question to resolve is the extent to which Nizan's practical experience of the USSR confirmed or altered these preconceptions.[56]

Simone de Beauvoir was convinced that Nizan's confrontation with the reality of the Soviet experiment had been a profoundly disorientating experience for him: 'Nizan was deeply disturbed to discover that out there, as here, everyone died alone and knew it', she noted.[57] This view was corroborated by Brice-Parain: 'Nizan returned as orthodox as ever. He chose to remain close to Marxism, but my impression is that he was shifting his ground. . . . His conversations with me centred on Heidegger and death'.[58] In a similar vein, Clara Malraux who spent several months in the company of Nizan in Moscow in 1934, recalls that Nizan's hopes for the creation of 'new values', a 'new man' in Soviet society were not fulfilled: 'It seemed to us that the new man had not yet emerged'.[59]

Recollections such as these provide excellent ammunition for arguing a case for Nizan's growing disenchantment with the Soviet experiment and communism in 1934. Yet they must be viewed with circumspection. First, retrospective assessments of this kind are of necessity highly coloured by Nizan's ultimate break with the party in 1939. The break in 1939 invites speculation at every point in Nizan's development regarding his commitment to communism. Secondly, all these comments stress not a disavowal of communism, but rather a heightening of metaphysical *angst* once the reality of Soviet society was disclosed.

Unquestionably, the illusion of a glorious Soviet Utopia, an abstract image with which Nizan had chosen to delude himself between 1928 and 1933, was shattered.[60] It is a big step, however, to proceed from the thesis of heightened metaphysical anguish engendered by confrontation with the practical reality of Soviet society, to the thesis of disavowal of the Soviet communist cause itself. Clara Malraux offers an instructive assessment of Nizan's psychology at this juncture:

> I think that Nizan was capable of living with the faults. He had to relegate his criticisms to a position of secondary importance for the sake of his allegiance to the communist party. . . . *His criticisms never implied a lack of commitment*'.[61] (My italics)

The 1934 experience would consequently appear to represent a watershed in Nizan's political development to the extent that the facile picture of an idealised Soviet society engaged in a harmonious process of social construction was unquestionably supplanted in Nizan's mind by a picture of Soviet men and women struggling together, but ultimately alone and prey to thoughts of death and solitude, for the advancement of the great socialist endeavour. In this sense it is possible to speak of disenchantment on Nizan's part. Reality had not lived up to expectations. Soviet socialist construction was under way, but the new man had not yet emerged. The 'New Greece' that was to emerge from the heroic social project had been postponed until a future date.

Rather than speaking of the seeds of ideological doubt sown in Nizan's mind, it is more appropriate to envisage 1934 as a necessary stage in Nizan's deepening awareness of social reality; the gradual abandonment, in other words, of a stylised and exaggerated picture of reality, and a progressive movement towards a recognition of the unpredictability and complexity of the social world.

The tense relationship that Nizan discovered in Soviet society between alienating metaphysical anguish and political struggle and social construction is clearly reflected in his writings of this phase. In this respect, it is too easy to interpret Nizan's discreet silence on Soviet society as implied criticism of the Soviet experiment. Although it is doubtless significant that the two texts on the Soviet Union written by Nizan, 'Le Tombeau de Timour' and 'Sindobod Toçikiston',[62] are centred on man's struggle for socialist construction against the forces of nature in Central Asia, far removed from the political intrigue of Moscow, their significance is to be located in a heightened awareness of metaphysical despair rather than in any fundamental disenchantment with the social and political advances of the Soviet experiment itself. The full significance of these texts emerges only when they are viewed in the context of Nizan's major work of the period, *Le Cheval de Troie*. The fine balance portrayed in this 'socialist realist' novel between political struggle and metaphysical anguish places 'Le Tombeau de Timour' and 'Sindobod Toçikiston' in perspective.

It is doubtless true that following his realisation in 1934 that even in post-revolutionary Soviet society men and women were ultimately not liberated from the anguish and fear of individual death and obliteration, Nizan was forced to adopt a more modest, less euphoric tone when praising Soviet achievements. However, it is important not to lose sight of the fact that this metaphysical disillusionment in no way diminished his belief in the moral justice of the Soviet cause. The Soviet Union remained in Nizan's eyes the practical expression of a moral crusade against class oppression, a revolutionary inspiration to the millions of oppressed people throughout the world. Indeed, international events conspired at this particular juncture to enhance the moral reputation of the USSR as the primary bulwark against oppression. The myth of metaphysical reconciliation within the bosom of post-revolutionary society was exploded in 1934. However, the myth of the moral integrity of the Soviet state more than compensated for its metaphysical shortcomings.

The growing threat of fascism after Hitler's accession to power in Germany in 1933 was to transform perceptions of the Soviet state not simply in Nizan's mind but in the minds of a whole generation of left-wing intellectuals. The openly aggressive posture of fascist Germany to the revolutionary communist state, its frequently proclaimed intention to exterminate what it perceived as the sickness of communism, inevitably mobilised support for the defence of threatened revolutionary ideals. Critical attention, in short, was diverted away from the economic, social, political or metaphysical shortcomings of the USSR. Inadequacies were glossed over and the focus of attention became the necessary defence of the revolutionary Soviet state, the guardian protector of peace, freedom and equality, currently threatened by a barbaric and expansionist fascist state. The Soviet Union was increasingly perceived as a moral and just counterforce to fascism. Nizan's metaphysical doubts, although heightened during his stay in the Soviet Union, were consequently relegated to secondary importance when considered in the light of the moral crusade against fascism.

This latter point cannot be overstated. It is unlikely that Nizan was entirely duped, for example, by the Stalinist purges and Moscow trials that were to occur from 1935. Yet whatever his inner revulsion may have been, Nizan remained silent for the cause of a greater Good, a greater ethic: the struggle against fascism. As long as the Soviet Union subscribed to this anti-fascist ethic, Nizan was willing to avert his gaze from the internal contradictions of the Soviet state itself.

With the rise of fascism came a change in the tactics of the Communist International and the French communist party. As early as December 1932, at a time when Nizan himself was still fully committed to a highly sectarian 'class against class' ideology, both

Thorez and Duclos were arguing a case for a more realistic popular front policy. With the removal of Barbé and Célor from the PCF leadership in August 1931, the days of sectarian politics were numbered. By February 1933 the PCF was appealing to socialist workers to form a united proletarian front. The events of February 1934 were simply the final jolt which forced the labour movement into a recognition of the need to abandon the sterility of sectarian politics and enter the phase of popular front co-operation.

It is important to contextualise Nizan's political and ideological development at this juncture. In February 1934 Nizan was in the Soviet Union. He consequently witnessed the February days, the potential civil war *at a distance*. *Le Cheval de Troie*, focusing as it does on the street confrontation between communism and fascism, is evidently a fictional distillation of these events viewed from the vantage-point of Moscow.

The formal adoption of the new popular front strategy in France took place in June and July 1934. Nizan found himself in a curiously paradoxical situation at this jucture. In many ways the archetypal Young Turk of the sectarian phase, Nizan was forced to reassess this strategy completely. It was no doubt easy for him to embrace the theme of a united front against the barbarism of fascism. Nizan was only too pleased to attack fascism with the same verve as he had until then been attacking the 'evils' of social democracy. It is ironic, however, that Nizan, who had previously denounced the liberal cultural policy of Barbusse, the PCF's own leading writer,[63] now found himself called upon to woo fellow-travelling bourgeois writers such as Gide[64] in order to gain maximum support for a popular front political and cultural policy suddenly in favour.

1934 was clearly a watershed in Nizan's development in a number of interconnected ways. The abandoning of unproductive sectarian politics and the embracing of a more realistic popular front strategy coincided with Nizan's own more realistic scrutiny of the Soviet state. Awareness of the social reality of the USSR, recognition that Soviet men and women experienced the same *angst* as those peoples living in pre-revolutionary societies disturbed Nizan but did not shake his faith in the ultimate justice and morality of the Soviet cause. The moral justice that Nizan attributed to the Soviet state was heightened by the rise of fascism on the international scene, by the need for a popular front anti-fascist movement. After 1934 the moral crusade was primarily anti-fascist. It became the defence of peace and culture from the war-mongering philistinism of fascism.

Henriette Nizan recalled in 1980 the events surrounding the assassination of Kirov in Moscow in December 1934.[65] Although Nizan was in Moscow at the very outset of the Stalinist purges, his gaze was focused less on the national than on the international scene. The true significance of Kirov's death doubtless eluded him. When Nizan returned to France in January 1935, he returned not disillusioned, chastened perhaps, but above all convinced of the necessity to become involved in the great moral crusade of the next few years, the struggle against fascism. Between 1935 and 1939, the last four years of Nizan's membership of the PCF, his thoughts were dominated by little else.

1935–9: Collaborative Complexity

Six months after returning from the Soviet Union, Nizan spoke at the International Congress for the Defence of Culture of the possibilities in the current socio-political climate of establishing a genuinely human society freed from class divisions and class oppression. His comments were brutally depressing:

> Our Soviet friends are alone in witnessing the dawn of a new beginning for man on their future horizon. Here it would be a bitter mockery to spread the word of an outdated and mythical humanism in a society where mutilation, subservience, degeneration and anguish have never held greater sway. Man is increasingly wretched, humiliated, alone and oppressed by those economic, political, legal and law enforcement powers which are the reality of what is called destiny. We can see hunger, destitution, torture; we are living in a state of war.[66]

Nizan's disappointment at the realisation that the new Soviet society was still very much in its infancy, and that a fully developed Soviet state, liberated from morbid thoughts of death, was still only a distant future possibility, merely served to heighten his anger at what he perceived as the limitless class oppression of French society: hunger, poverty, torture, war.

With hindsight, bearing in mind particularly the fatal events leading to Munich and the Second World War, Nizan's gloomy prognostication might appear to have a certain validity. From another perspective, however, his comments would appear to be anachronostic, reflecting far more the sectarian, persecuted mentality of 1928–32, than the popular front attitude of post-1934. The apparent paradox of Nizan's ideological/psychological mentality needs to be scrutinised at this juncture since it is clear that after 1935 his intellectual itinerary became far more complex, shaped as it was by countless pressures arising not only from a new party strategy but also from a deepening international political crisis.

When Nizan returned to France in January 1935 the political landscape had been transformed. Sectarian politics were a thing of the past. Following the events of February 1934 and the decision of the PCF in June 1934 to abandon the 'class against class' strategy, the popular front policy was gathering momentum. Communists and socialists alike were committed to a strategy of co-operation aimed at combating reactionary government policies at home and stifling the threat of international fascism abroad.

Nizan's political stance at this juncture was a curious mixture of uncompromising denunciation and sweet-talking collaboration. With the abandonment of sectarian politics and the adoption of the popular front strategy, he was forced to relinquish the tactics of undifferentiated confrontation and engage instead in a complex ideological process in which unequivocal condemnation of the agents of fascism was interspersed with sophisticated and complex support for a wide range of liberal fellow-travellers who only a short time previously would have been roundly condemned as class enemies. Nizan's overtly sectarian stance of the pre-1934 period was suddenly out of phase with the current political climate. An unpredictable quirk of history had forced him to take stock and change direction. It was not to be the last time.

Having turned his back on what he considered to be the sophistry, deception and compromise of bourgeois culture and bourgeois politics, in favour of the clarity and ideological certainty of what proved to be an unrealistic sectarian politics, force of circumstances compelled him after 1934 to engage in the compromising task of co-operative politics. Although, in the final analysis, Nizan retained a fundamentally manichean view of the world, and was consequently able, despite a growing recognition of the complex reality of political activity, to propose the clarity of an ultimate division into Good and Evil, anti-fascist and fascist, the urgent political need to enter into dialogue with liberal bourgeois organisations and liberal bourgeois writers and artists necessitated on occasions quite convoluted argumentation, justification and explanation which stand in stark contrast to the simplistic black and white denunciations of the period prior to 1934.[67]

Nevertheless, despite all the necessary caveats regarding Nizan's possible disenchantment with the reality of the Soviet experiment, and the difficulty he experienced in making the transition from sectarian to popular front tactics, *Nizan remained fully committed to communism and the PCF between 1935 and 1939.* Indeed, in many ways, the 'moral' dimension of the communist cause was enhanced after 1935 precisely because of the existence of a hostile, aggressive fascist bloc determined to crush the Soviet state. The deteriorating international political situation literally strengthened Nizan's commitment to the communist cause.

There undoubtedly existed in Nizan's mind a clearly articulated political ethic during this period, an ethic which divided the world between those forces defending peace, culture, oppressed nations, democratic rights and freedoms, and those forces advocating war, barbarism, the destruction of culture, the oppression of nation states and the suppression of democratic rights and freedoms. Before proceeding to an assessment of Nizan's psychological development between 1935 and 1939, it is consequently appropriate and instructive initially to trace out the underlying structure of this communist political ethic. Its constituent elements can be conveniently classified in three areas:

1. Defence of the revolutionary Soviet state;
2. Opposition to fascism in France;
3. Opposition to international fascism: collective security.

Defence of the revolutionary state
With hindsight, there is a tendency to overstate Nizan's implicit criticisms/disavowals of the Soviet Union during the 1930s. There is little evidence to support the view that Nizan was anything other than a faithful, orthodox party member; a Stalinist in short. His public pronouncements are unequivocal in this respect, and although it is clearly not possible to accept such public pronouncements as the definitive expression of a man's innermost beliefs and convictions, and although it is also evidently the case that to be published in *L'Humanité* and *Ce Soir* inevitably necessitates obedience to the party line, nonetheless the consistency and vigour with which Nizan presented an entirely positive view of developments within the Soviet Union are an instructive antidote to those critics desperately searching for evidence of Nizan's growing anti-Stalinism/anti-

communism during this period.

In 1936, for example, Nizan asserted in no uncertain manner:

> The USSR presents a picture of democratic development previously
> unknown in history, of a political system in which confrontation
> between parties is gradually ceasing as the classes from which
> they arise are being abolished.[68]

It is easy to dismiss a statement of this kind as self-deluding
communist rhetoric, the necessary slogans that a communist
journalist must include in any article destined for publication in
L'Humanité. Yet Nizan was quite explicit in his attempts to counter
the arguments of 'those who accuse communism of crushing men
and of withdrawing freedom'. The impending threat of fascism
simply made criticism of the USSR strategically unthinkable in
Nizan's eyes. Nizan sided unequivocally with Stalin, noting: 'In the
USSR only the myths of freedom are dying out, but true freedom has
come into being.'[69]

The depth of Nizan's commitment to the Soviet Union was
similarly visible a few months later when he described the great
steps made by the mass of the Soviet people in terms of cultural
development:

> When you have seen young workers in Moscow or Tashkent . . .
> speaking passionately of Gogol or Gorky, you realise that the
> Soviet people have gained admission to the high culture that was
> previously a privilege of the bourgeoisie. . . . The Bolsheviks
> have succeeded in encouraging men, who twenty years ago could
> not read, to take an interest in the most difficult works of the
> imagination.[70]

There is a sense of deep admiration for the Soviet people and Soviet
state here which cannot be denied, an admiration echoing personal
experience. The Soviet masses were in the process of acceding to a
cultural awareness that had been denied to his father. Here is an
expression not of metaphysical disillusionment but of profound
belief in the value of the Soviet socialist cause.

Nizan's systematic refusal to countenance hostile assessments of
the developing Soviet state was again illustrated in 1937 when he
was called upon to carry out the difficult task of responding to
André Gide's highly critical view of the Soviet Union articulated in
the latter's *Retour de l'URSS*.[71] Although this was an extremely

delicate operation for Nizan to perform, given that in 1934 he had carried out the rather complex act of ideological rehabilitation designed to demonstrate that Gide's intellectual itinerary was such as to lead him inevitably to a commitment to communism, he none the less succeeded in combining professional respect for Gide's qualities as a writer with penetrating criticism of what he considered to be Gide's superficial analysis and hasty dismissal of the Soviet state.[72] It is a highly instructive piece to the extent that it foregrounds not only Nizan's unequivocally realistic perception of the USSR, but also his own personal commitment to the revolutionary achievements of the Soviet people.

'Not everything is untrue, but almost everything is incorrectly interpreted through lack of genuine knowledge',[73] Nizan pointedly remarks. He accuses Gide of interpreting the Soviet experience from an excessively psychological, literary perspective with the result that genuine advances on the socio-economic front are obscured, on the one hand, by an unwarranted preoccupation with the psychology of the Soviet people, and on the other, by bourgeois prejudices regarding the stultifying 'conformism' of Soviet society.

The interesting aspect of this essay is not be found in Nizan's comments on Gide, however. It is of interest above all for the light that it sheds on Nizan's allegiance to the Soviet cause in 1937. Nizan is clearly dismissive of what he considers as the ill-informed and frankly false perceptions of the USSR based on liberal prejudices: 'I am not impressed by accounts of a "new" bourgeoisie. It is the old defending itself', he notes.[74] Although he was ready to accept the shortcomings of the Soviet state in its current phase of historical development – 'it is true that Soviet society is harsh and that many of its citizens are not philanthropists'[75] – the harshness of Soviet society, however, can in no sense invalidate in Nizan's eyes the justice of its struggle against the remaining vestiges of the capitalist mentality in the consciousness of the Soviet people.

Nizan's Stalinist mentality is clearly visible in this article where a 'conformist commitment' to the constructive material advances of a Stalinist Soviet state is preferred to the mystification of a liberal bourgeois democracy or the dilettantism of a Trotskyite permanent revolution. To label Nizan a Stalinist may appear unjustified and even reprehensible to those whose image of Nizan is circumscribed by the rebellious, iconoclastic picture projected by Sartre. Yet the simple truth of the matter is that Nizan was genuinely committed to the material construction and development taking place in the

USSR, a construction process masterminded by Stalin.

This allegiance to Stalinist construction was perhaps most forcefully articulated in 1938 in Nizan's critical review of Georges Friedmann's *De la Sainte Russie à l'URSS*.[76] It has been argued that this essay is vitiated by 'bad faith'.[77] Such an interpretation would appear to be based far more on wishful thinking than reality. It reads as a profession of orthodox Stalinism.

Unlike the essay on Gide, Nizan finds much that is positive in Friedmann's analysis, particularly its historical dimension, stressing as it does the abject poverty of the masses and the arbitrary and oppressive power of orthodox religion prior to 1917. Assessments of the current situation in the Soviet Union have meaning in Nizan's eyes only in the context of this material progress: 'Soviet achievements cannot be properly evaluated unless they are linked historically to the effort which produced them',[78] he stresses.

Nizan is nonetheless pointedly critical of what he perceives as Friedmann's presumptuousness in judging recent historical developments in the Soviet Union from a purely subjective perspective. He categorically rejects, for example, what he denotes as Friedmann's 'aesthetic' perception of the Moscow trials and purges. Friedmann is accused of focusing attention excessively on the structural inadequacies of the Soviet system which make such show trials necessary, rather than highlighting what Nizan considers to be the treacherous acts of the Trotskyites and Bukharinites conspiring to overthrow the Soviet state itself. Because, Nizan asserts, Friedmann is unable to perceive the necessity of the organic link between theory and practice, he is led not only to the purely academic conclusion that it is incorrect to speak of the 'philosophy' of either Lenin or Stalin, but also, and more significantly, to an inability to perceive the fundamentally different objectives pursued by Lenin and Trotsky. 'There is no longer any possible comparison to be made between the man who is actively organising the construction of socialism, and the man who is endeavouring to wreck it.'[79]

There is nothing tongue-in-cheek about these statements. Nizan is not simply mouthing the party line here. This is the expression of a man deeply committed to the practical development of the Soviet socialist state, dismissive of esoteric philosophical debates which fail to take into account the material conditions of the socialist experiment, and preoccupied above all with the need to defend an increasingly isolated Soviet Union from potentially damaging criticisms, however well intentioned they might be. The fact that

Friedmann's assessment of the USSR was historically more accurate than Nizan's is not at issue here. What it is important to establish at this juncture is Nizan's systematic refusal to countenance any form of public criticism of the internal running of the Soviet state between 1935 and 1939. Nizan chose not simply to suspend judgement, but to give public support to the Moscow version of events on the grounds that critical accounts of the Soviet state generally lacked both historical perspective and scientific rigour, and more importantly, that the defence of the Soviet Union in the torrid international political climate of the late 1930s was imperative. There is little evidence to suggest that between 1935 and 1939 Nizan's defence of the revolutionary Soviet state was anything other than unswerving and total.

Opposition to fascism in France

Between 1935 and 1939 Nizan's commitment to the anti-fascist lobby in France was resolute and unyielding. Although his energies were devoted primarily to the international dimension of the anti-fascist struggle, his uncompromising opposition to those individuals and institutions within France actively assisting the spread of the fascist menace can be graphically illustrated by two examples, the first from the year 1935, the second from the year 1939.

In 1935 Nizan turned his attention once again to the French educational system. Unlike the sectarian views articulated in *Les Chiens de garde* in which the abstract idealism of bourgeois philosophers was condemned as a mystification, Nizan's popular front interpretation was more realistic, more politicised.[80] With the rise of the fascist menace, the bourgeois educational system was no longer perceived as the site of idealistic mystification, but rather as the site of a political struggle; a political struggle in which the vast majority of the teaching profession, committed to the idea of cultural enlightenment, were refusing to be silenced, gagged by a bourgeois state progressively more dominated by fascist ideas at a time of deepening political crisis.

> There is a major offensive under way against the enemies of deception. The State, the bourgeois press are engaging in a general campaign against universities, because universities, true to their vocation, are continuing to carry out their traditional role of clarification and explanation.[81]

The description Nizan offers of a fascist-motivated plot against the teaching profession in France, with its resonances of policing, spying, informing, and so on, was as much coloured by Nizan's personal experience as a philosophy teacher in Bourg-en-Bresse in 1932–3, as it was informed by the experiences of the other cited teachers committed to the anti-fascist struggle and inevitably embroiled in professional persecution and legal prosecution. The conclusion that Nizan wishes to highlight is lucidly straightforward:

> The forces of fascism are taking up the fight against the anti-fascist educator. They are demanding that the State sanction this fight. The State is not defending its teachers: it is already at the beck and call of reaction and fascism, obediently acquiescing and taking sanctions. It is becoming an instrument of fascism.[82]

By July 1939, over four years later, Nizan's anti-fascist denunciations had become more acerbic, more bitter, more personalised, heightened by the increased tensions of a highly volatile international political situation. What had been perceived in 1935 as an implicit fascist disease had by 1939 reached epidemic proportions. In July 1939 Nizan publicly proclaimed that France had been betrayed by fascist infiltrators and fascist collaborators.[83] There is a curious sense in which the no-holds-barred style that Nizan adopted in this series of five articles, the last he ever wrote for *Ce Soir*, marked a return to the sectarian, aggressive, uncompromising Nizan of 1932. The fascist enemy within France had quite simply to be unmasked and eradicated.

The explosiveness of these articles by Nizan is doubtless explained as much by Nizan's anger at the reporting restrictions imposed by the Garde des Sceaux on *sub judice* matters affecting fascist infiltration in France, as it is by his visceral fear and hatred of what he considers to be the terrible consequences of the spread of fascism within his homeland. He is scathing in his attacks on those French politicians, journalists and writers who 'have collaborated in word and deed with the policies of Hitler', and who 'at critical moments have given support to the guiding principles of these policies: anti-semitism, anti-communism, anti-democracy, hegemonic mission of the Reich in Europe, national-socialist "pacifism"'.[84] Between 1935 and 1939 Nizan's opposition to the spread of fascism within the fabric of French society became progressively more hostile, more ferocious.

Opposition to international fascism: collective security
During the four years that Nizan was writing in his capacity as foreign-affairs correspondent for *L'Humanité* (1935–7) and *Ce Soir* (1937–9),[85] he ceaselessly and fearlessly articulated a coherent anti-fascist diplomatic strategy based on the principle of collective security. The fundamental themes of Nizan's argument did not vary. Only the style and tone with which he expressed them evolved in unison with the avatars of a progressively deepening international crisis.

'Fascism has no greater enemy than peace', noted Nizan in 1935.[86] The anti-fascist struggle was synonymous in Nizan's mind with the peace movement. Only a united peace front could halt the aggressive, war-mongering development of fascist nation states such as Germany and Italy. Time after time Nizan hammered out his basic message: the internal logic of fascism is rearmament leading to war; the only way to prevent the catastrophe of a world-wide conflict is the creation of a potent counterbalancing force expressly designed to curb the expansionist tendencies of fascist nation states; peace will be possible only if it is guaranteed by an effective network of alliances forged between civilised, peace-loving nations such as France, Great Britain and, above all, the USSR. Peace, in other words, depends solely on collective security.

When Nizan repeatedly asserted that peace was 'indivisible', his intention was to highlight the inadequacy of 'localising' disputes between nation states, of allowing one nation to use force against another with impunity. Nation states could only coexist peaceably if a strong collective security arrangement were respected by all. Collective security necessarily imposed obligations on all nation states, powerful and weak alike, to respect each other's separate identity and autonomy, and to sanction any member who failed to respect such obligations. It appeared to Nizan as the only realistic method of conducting human affairs in a civilised manner. To abandon collective security was to abandon peace, civilisation and democracy in favour of war, barbarism and fascism. In the final analysis, collective security was founded on what Nizan referred to as the Soviet formula of 'treaties accessible to everyone', not on the Hitlerian formula of 'treaties accessible to a few at the exclusion of everyone else'.[87] Nizan ceaselessly denounced all attempts to reduce international diplomacy to what he disparagingly termed 'private agreements between gang leaders'. 'This is a fascist policy', he remarked, 'only the collective effort of nation states can guarantee that such a policy is not imposed on a world-wide scale'.[88]

It is quite clear that between 1935 and 1939 Nizan formulated a coherent and realistic communist political strategy centred, on the one hand, on unfailing support for the Soviet socialist state, the site of cultural enlightenment and material freedom, and the guardian of international peace and security, and on the other, on unequivocal opposition to the fascist states of Germany and Italy, the site of cultural barbarism and material oppression, and the harbingers of international war and instability.

This was more than a political strategy, however. In Nizan's imagination it assumed the status of a moral crusade. Beyond the intricacies of international diplomacy, beyond the day-to-day rebuffal of fascism and defence of communist party policy, Nizan interpreted his political activity in a profoundly moral sense. The forces of fascist barbarism were threatening to engulf the civilised world. The ultimate defender of this civilised world was not, in Nizan's eyes, the democratically elected governments of France and Great Britain, but the developing Soviet socialist state. If everything else failed, Nizan was convinced that the Soviet Union could be depended upon to stand resolute against the rising tide of fascist oppression. This fervent conviction was the linchpin of Nizan's communist ethic between 1935 and 1939.

Political psychology, 1935–9
Although Nizan adhered to a clear set of communist principles between 1935 and 1939, his psychological state fluctuated in accordance with national and international political events. From a resolute and calm determination to highlight the inadequacies and internal contradictions of Hitler's Nazi Germany in 1935, Nizan progressed to an optimistic, almost euphoric state of mind throughout 1936, the product of the Popular Front experiences in both France and Spain. From the growing disillusionment of the Spanish experience in 1937, Nizan was led inexorably to incredulity and disbelief during the Munich crisis of September 1938, and ultimately to bewilderment and total despair following the Nazi–Soviet pact and the outbreak of the Second World War in 1939.

The trip to the Soviet Union in 1934 had deepened Nizan's grasp of reality. His recognition that the catch-phrases, myths and sectarian politics of the 1928–32 period bore little resemblance to the real world heightened his metaphysical *angst*, but in no sense diminished his commitment to the communist cause. On his return to France in 1935 Nizan's conviction that the Soviet state represented the ultimate international safeguard against fascist barbarism and oppression was strengthened by the growing success of the Popular Front movements in France and Spain. Despite the storm clouds gathering over Europe in Nazi Germany and fascist Italy, Nizan remained confident that the international political situation could be regulated on a peaceful basis by marshalling Republican, democratic forces in a united front determined to halt the fascist advance.

In 1935 Nizan was very much on the offensive. The Hitlerian regime, he asserted, was in a state of crisis.[89] The ebullience with which Nizan highlighted the disenchantment of Hitler's own petty bourgeois supporters confronted by impending economic ruin, the logical outcome of a Nazi political dictatorship, was tempered only by an awareness that such economic ruin might ultimately only be avoided by a massive rearmament programme and a policy of fascist colonial expansion that would seriously undermine international security. Although under no illusions concerning the brutal repression of the German communist party, Nizan was nonetheless optimistic enough at this stage not only to proclaim the tenacity of communist resistance to two years of fascist dictatorship, but also to assert the growing strength of the German masses, a potential opposition force to Nazi oppression.[90] In similar vein, Nizan extended the attack on fascism to the international sphere. Throughout the Italo-Abyssinian conflict of this period, Nizan forcefully argued the need for collective security,[91] on the one hand, by voicing his implacable opposition to the colonial ambitions of Mussolini, and on the other, by focusing attention on the highly dubious diplomatic manoeuvres of the British and French governments, the more reactionary elements of which were seeking to use the conflict as a 'pretext for a new imperialist arms race'.[92]

Nizan was quite explicit, for example, in his criticism of Pierre Laval. Laval was targeted as a 'saboteur of Franco-British co-operation',[93] and a potential 'traitor' of 'indivisible peace' enshrined in collective security.[94] 'When Laval starts praising collective security and multilateral treaties, it is time to be wary', Nizan laconically remarked,[95] dismissing out of hand Laval's professed support for the politics of peace as no more than 'carefully phrased remarks'.[96]

Although under no illusions, therefore, that reactionary French and British governments would act resolutely to counter the imminent fascist threat, Nizan remained confident at this stage that international security could be maintained. The Nazi state itself was fraught with internal contradictions, and in the last resort, the

Soviet Union could be relied upon not only to oppose fascist aggression, but also to thwart the potentially treacherous politics of reactionary French and British governments. Between June and December 1935, Nizan was cautiously optimistic that the diplomatic campaign for collective security, spearheaded by the Soviet Union, would ultimately triumph. This cautious optimism blossomed during 1936.

1936: the year of the Popular Front successes in France and Spain. For Nizan, it was above all else the year of the Spanish experience. The events in Spain became linked in Nizan's psyche to the global outcome on the international scene. Spain became a barometer of Republican hopes and aspirations. Spain was the battle-ground on which the moral crusade against fascism would be won or lost. 'Here, in the midst of this revolution, I am in tune with everything', he is alleged to have frequently asserted.[97] 'There were no barriers between Nizan and this revolution . . . he was filled with emotion by everything that he witnessed', a fellow journalist recalls.[98] Unquestionably, Spain in 1936 represented the pinnacle of Nizan's revolutionary and Republican aspirations.

As early as 4 January 1936 he was speaking of the political crisis in Spain, predicting a violent confrontation between Popular Front Republicanism and the fascism of Gil Roblès.[99] By 16 February, on the eve of the elections, Nizan described Spain as being at the 'crossroads of fascism and liberty'.[100] On 18 February, following the Popular Front electoral success, Nizan did not allow the euphoria that he undoubtedly experienced after 'the defeat of Spanish fascism' to blind him to the fact that the real struggle was about to begin. 'Sunday's victory is not a conclusion, it is a prelude.'[101] In retrospect these words have a prophetic ring about them. During the next few months a violent fascist backlash, an orchestrated campaign of civil disorder and terrorism culminating in armed insurrection, led Nizan to the conclusion that very firm Republican counter-measures were necessary.[102]

Nizan's exceptionally good grasp of the Spanish political situation was doubtless the product of numerous visits that he made to Spain during 1936. Between 1 and 15 June, following the electoral success of the Popular Front, he produced a long report on Spain for *La Correspondance internationale*, the French language version of the Communist International political weekly.[103] Similarly, between 27 July and 3 September, following the outbreak of the civil war, he was assigned to the Spanish front by *L'Humanité*.

Written in June 1936, 'Secrets de l'Espagne', Nizan's extended analysis of the Spanish situation for *La Correspondance internationale*, bears witness not only to his perceptiveness ('There is emerging on the Republican horizon a fascist bid for power the conditions for which are being prepared by the social unrest orchestrated by the right'[104]), but also to his enormous talent as a political reporter. In this text, as in others written by Nizan as a result of direct experience in Spain, coexist incisive social and political commentary, disturbing and explosive literary images and a sense of personal involvement, almost self-fulfilment. It is probably here that the greatness of Nizan's writing ability is most clearly exemplified, at the line where the political and the personal collide. Texts such as 'Secrets de l'Espagne', and 'Renaissance de l'Espagne'[105] illustrate the intimate relationship that exists in Nizan's mind between his activities as a political reporter and his activities as a political novelist.

This interconnection between the political and the literary was again visible in the reports that he sent from the Aragon front in August 1936, following the outbreak of the civil war. On 4 August, at the very moment that an important battle was raging near Somosierra north of Madrid, Nizan reported a conversation that he had had with President Azana which had left an indelible impression in his mind:

> The President pointed to the smoke rising from the distant peaks of the sierra. 'A forest fire started by the rebels', he said. 'Do you see that smoke? Over there our fate is being decided, *and yours as well*'.[106] (My italics)

Nizan was only too willing to share Azana's conviction that Republican Spain would ultimately be victorious, but as always the bottom line was collective security. The cause of Republican Spain was, in the final analysis, the cause of all democratic, anti-fascist countries. The prospects for world peace would be gauged by the support given to the democratically elected Popular Front government of Spain in its efforts to stave off the fascist threat. Hence, beneath the individual self-fulfilment and euphoria of the early stages of the Spanish Civil War, Nizan remained lucidly aware of political realities. In the emotionally charged pieces that he wrote from the war front, Nizan pointed up the inescapable fact that the future of France was being decided on the soil of Spain. An ardent sentiment of revolutionary romanticism tempered by a clear sense of political realism formed the texture of Nizan's thinking at this juncture.

It is not an overstatement to maintain, therefore, that throughout 1936 the struggle in Spain came to symbolise in Nizan's eyes, as in the eyes of countless intellectuals of the period, the ultimate stand against fascism. And for the most part Nizan was optimistic about the outcome. Initially elated by the electoral successes of the Popular Front in France and Spain, subsequently encouraged by the spirited defence of Republican Spain, and convinced at all times that the ultimate safeguard for international security was the presence of a strong revolutionary Soviet state, Nizan remained confident. Admittedly, he was disturbed by the news of the remilitarisation of the Rhineland in March, and dismayed above all by the non-interventionist policies adopted by France and Great Britain towards Spain during the latter part of the year, but despite these setbacks, Nizan's mood throughout 1936 was generally optimistic.

Between 1937 and 1939, however, the slow decline and eventual disintegration of Republican hopes in Spain mirrored a gradual process of disenchantment and growing despair in Nizan's own psyche. Towards the end of 1936 it had already become clear that the French blockade of Spain represented a serious blow to the Republican cause. In November Nizan correctly assessed the situation when he commented: 'At the present moment in time, the policies of the fascist government are being thwarted only by the diplomacy of the USSR and the heroic resistance of the Spanish people'.[107] During 1937, however, the credibility of this resistance to the fascist threat was progressively undermined in Nizan's eyes by a series of political problems confronting both the Soviet Union and Spain.

In January 1937, for example, *L'Humanité* devoted much space to an account of the Moscow trials.[108] Karl Radek, who, only five months earlier, had himself written in *L'Humanité* of the need to eradicate Trotskyite subversion and anti-Soviet activities,[109] was placed on trial together with his 'accomplices', accused of espionage, terrorism and collaboration with Hitler and Trotsky in an attempt to overthrow the Soviet state. Although Nizan himself was willing to accept the Moscow version of events, it is probable that the highly publicised nature of the trials, the seemingly endless ramifications of the anti-state activities exposed, did little to boost his confidence in the future development of the Soviet state itself.

As a Stalinist, Nizan was doubtless reassured that prompt action to deal with the anti-Soviet activities had been taken. Yet the very need for such public show-trials, apparently highlighting the fragility of the Soviet Union, its vulnerability to fascist and capitalist subversion, must inevitably have been a cause of concern and growing disquiet. Despite the panegyric on the Soviet state published in *L'Humanité* following the adoption of a new constitution in June 1936,[110] and despite the great international prestige enjoyed by the Soviet Union during 1937, consequent upon its material support for Republican Spain, Nizan could no longer take the future strength and stability of the USSR for granted. His reply to Gide's *Retour de l'URSS*, published in March 1937, was a clear signal of the need to defend an increasingly beleaguered Soviet state from damaging hostile criticism, whatever its source.

Above all else, however, 1937 was in Nizan's eyes, the year of the abandonment of Spain by France and Great Britain, the year when the Republican hopes, kindled during the exhilarating months of Popular Front unity in 1936, were dashed. In January 1937, Nizan asked rhetorically: 'Is it going to be argued now that it is preferable for Spain to be sacrified?'[111] In March he was forced to contemplate the spectacle of direct Italian fascist intervention in Spanish affairs,[112] and in April he responded with a feeling of impotent outrage at the pitiless bombing of Guernica, yet another example of brutal fascist inhumanity. Decidedly, Republican hopes for a successful outcome in Spain were on the wane.

The spectre of fascism began to haunt Nizan wherever he might be. In May, he was sent to England to cover the coronation of George VI. His natural instincts led him away from the pomp and ceremony of regal splendour to the poverty of London's East End. In Bethnal Green the spectacle was not one of royal celebration but of fascist confrontation. Although Nizan was entirely dismissive of the intellectual pretentiousness and inanity of Oswald Mosley, it is abundantly clear from his account of the incident that nowhere did Nizan underestimate the threat of fascism, even in the realm of kings and coronations.[113]

This growing feeling during the first half of 1937 that the forces of fascism were very much on the offensive and that the initiative was gradually slipping away from the Republican cause was abruptly and symbolically confirmed in July 1937. Only a few days after the conclusion of the Second International Congress of Writers for the Defence of Culture, held for the most part in Spain,[114] itself a highly symbolic act of political and cultural allegiance to the Republican cause, Nizan was deeply shocked to learn of the tragic and unforeseen death of Gerda Taro, a young female photographer working for *Ce Soir* at the battle front near Brunete.[115]

At this highly critical phase in the unfolding of the Spanish drama, the senseless death of this courageous young woman conjured up in Nizan's imagination the bitter tragedy of the Spanish cause itself. Once again death brutally shattered Nizan's existence. The hopes and expectations of the Popular Front experiences of France and Spain in 1936 were slowly being transformed into the despair and disillusionment of the non-interventionist policies of France and Great Britain in 1937. The solitary death of Gerda Taro in July 1937 came to symbolise in Nizan's mind this tragic development. In late July and early August, he was assigned the sombre task of accompanying the body of Gerda Taro in its journey back to France. This errand of death which took Nizan to Spain for the fourth time within fourteen months was symbolically appropriate. After August 1937 the international political setting and Nizan's individual emotional state were bathed in a progressively more sombre hue. Gerda Taro was dead. Republican Spain was dying.

From August 1937 until August 1939 the record is of deepening international crisis and disaster. The progressively more strident and bellicose demands of Nazi Germany were matched only by the progressively more acquiescent and neutralist responses of France and Great Britain. Nizan followed each stage with a gloomy sense of foreboding, yet convinced all the while that collective security still offered the only route to the preservation of peace. From the conference of Berchtesgaden in November 1937 to the Anschluss of Austria in March 1938, from the increasingly threatening noises over Czechoslovakia in March 1938 to the abdication of Munich in September 1938, from the last-ditch, desperate attempts to cobble together a tripartite agreement in May 1939 to the signing of the Nazi-Soviet pact in August 1939, there was a sense of deathly inevitability compared to which Nizan's repeated calls for collective security appear as no more than the efforts of a man crying in the wilderness.

August 1937 was doubtless an *emotional* turning-point in Nizan's development. September 1938 was the decisive *political* turning-point. The disaster of Munich was, in fact, so monumental in Nizan's eyes that he felt constrained to write an account of the whole affair in order the more effectively to understand it. *Chronique de septembre*, Nizan's last published work, is a detailed record of the diplomatic manoeuvring which culminated in the 'peace' agreement signed by Chamberlain, Daladier and Hitler in September 1938. Written with the scrupulous precision and meticulous care for detail of a professional journalist, it is clearly a text of a different order from Nizan's early sectarian writings.

The apparently objective, ideologically neutral tone of *Chronique de septembre* is deceptive, however. It is tempting, too tempting in fact, to read into this more ideologically restrained account a certain disillusionment with communism and communist party politics which prefigures in some way Nizan's break from the party a few months later. The style and tone of *Chronique de septembre* may differ, but ultimately the message is the same. As Olivier Todd notes in his preface to the 1978 edition, 'Even after leaving the PC five months later, Nizan does not become a liberal. He does not renege on Marxism-Leninism.'[116]

Beyond the labyrinthine complexity of the diplomatic manoeuvrings detailed in the *Chronique*, Nizan articulates three hypotheses to explain the events of September 1938: (a) the British and French governments, convinced that Hitler's threats of war were no mere bluff, simply capitulated; (b) the British and French governments exploited the political tension on the international scene in order to reap maximum dividends on the domestic front. Munich, in other words, was expressly orchestrated to destabilise public opinion at home, to terrify whole populations with the threat of war and coerce them to accept reactionary government measures in exchange for peace; (c) the British and French governments recoiled from inflicting the diplomatic humiliation on Hitler that would have resulted from resorting to the anti-fascist resistance offered by Washington and above all by Moscow. They preferred, in short, the fascist 'order' of Hitler to the communist 'revolution' of Moscow.[117] Nizan's preferences are clearly for the second and third hypotheses which interconnect. The subdued tone and diplomatic style of *Chronique de septembre* in no sense blunt the cutting edge of Nizan's communist analysis. Despite appearances, this is not the work of a budding liberal.

There was little, in fact, that was subdued in Nizan's contributions to *Ce Soir* after Munich. Munich became synonymous in Nizan's vocabulary with the abandonment of the principles of collective security, the deliberate mystification of nation states, appeasement, acquiescence and capitulation to fascist oppression and death. With the fall of Madrid in March 1939,[118] and the worsening situation in Poland,[119] Nizan's attitude became progressively more desperate, more frenetic.

In this context of impending war, Nizan began clutching at straws. Miraculously, during the early months of 1939, the much vaunted tripartite agreement between France, Great Britain and the USSR, the cornerstone of collective security and peace, seemed somehow to be within grasp. It is ironic, in retrospect, that Nizan's leading article announcing the seemingly miraculous news was published on 1 April 1939.[120]

By May Nizan felt confident enough to announce the imminent signing of the pact.[121] The stalling of negotiations and the eventual failure to sign any agreement, however, were attributed by Nizan to a complete lack of commitment on the part of the French and British governments. It is significant that in July 1939, at a time when Stalin was actively negotiating the Nazi-Soviet pact with Hitler,[122] Nizan was quoting Zhdanov to the effect that the finalising of the tripartite peace agreement was being held up solely by the delaying tactics of France and Great Britain.[123] Decidedly, Nizan's belief in the moral integrity of Soviet foreign policy was total.

By July 1939, the words 'betrayal' and 'treason' recurred as a leitmotiv in all his articles. The failure to sign the tripartite agreement was attributed uniquely to the duplicitous tactics of the governments of Britain and France,[124] and his final articles for *Ce Soir*, a series entitled 'La France trahie', provided Nizan with the opportunity to vent his anger on fascist spies, infiltrators and collaborators undermining the fabric of French society.[125]

July 1939: a decisive moment in Nizan's life, the 150th anniversary of the French Revolution. At this moment of Republican celebration, Nizan was preoccupied with the defence of the homeland. In an article almost certainly written on 14 July, he quotes Poincaré citing Demosthenes on the need to root out the 'enemy within'.[126] It is poignant, in retrospect, to consider that Nizan's final words as a French communist writer were centred on the theme of fascist betrayal and the defence of the homeland. By a curious twist of fate, it was precisely Nizan's implacable opposition to fascism and his deep commitment to Republican France that were ultimately to place him in contradiction with the imperialist war thesis advocated by the Communist International a few months later.

At the end of July, Nizan, en route to Corsica, by chance encountered Sartre and de Beauvoir in Marseille. It was the last time that they met. In her memoirs, de Beauvoir describes Nizan as 'feverishly exultant, triumphantly confident' that the signing of the tripartite pact was imminent.[127] This description, if accurate, would appear to reflect more a desire on Nizan's part to reassure his friends than a genuine assessment of current diplomatic realities. Merleau-Ponty, who met Nizan a few weeks later at Laurent Casanova's villa in Porto, recalls that Nizan seemed resigned to the inevitability of war, but still confident in the belief that a tripartite alliance between France, Great Britain and the USSR was a necessary and inevitable prerequisite to the defeat of fascism.[128]

The truth of the matter is that, despite Nizan's abiding suspicions of the motives of the French and British governments, the logic of the situation seemed to him to lead to only one solution: a common alliance with the USSR against fascism. By July-August 1939, with Republican Spain defeated,[129] Nizan was left with one solitary but unshakeable conviction. The sole bulwark against fascism remained the Soviet Union. Everything now depended on the resolution and strength of the revolutionary Soviet state to halt the advance of fascism.

3
Exit the Party

When Ribbentrop and Molotov signed the Nazi-Soviet pact of non-aggression on 23 August 1939,[1] they signed the death warrant of Paul Nizan. 'Dying, leaving the party, it's all the same', reflects Brunet sadly in 'Drôle d'amitié'.[2] Although Nizan died physically on 23 May 1940, there can be little doubt that he died for the first time, politically and to a large extent emotionally, that afternoon in late August 1939 when, standing on the harbour at Ajaccio, he read Aragon's editorial in *Ce Soir* and was confronted by the bitter reality of Nazi-Soviet collaboration.

(i) BREAKING AND DYING, 1939–40

Nizan,[3] like Péri,[4] like Thorez himself,[5] was devastated by the pact. For a communist militant who had devoted his life to the struggle against fascist barbarism and oppression, the revelation that the Soviet communist state had come to a private agreement with Hitler's Nazi Germany was a mortal body blow. The sheer monstrousness of such a reversal simply defied belief. Stalin, the architect of the revolutionary Soviet state, the instigator of unprecedented social reforms and freedoms, the defender of international peace and security, the supporter of Republican Spain, had struck a cynical deal with Hitler, had in one stroke abandoned the principles of collective security and defence of nation states, and had opted for the fascist diplomacy of 'bilateral agreements between gang leaders'. The world had simply been turned upside-down.

Nizan had never seriously considered the possibility of a Nazi-Soviet pact. It had never been on the agenda. As early as December 1935, he publicly recorded Nazi Germany's refusal to conclude any pact with the Soviet Union, arguing that such a pact would 'not remove the causes of the differences between the USSR and Germany', and that a pact of this kind 'would be the classic type of "dishonest" pact because it would be drawn up with the intention of being broken'.[6]

Nizan's willingness to envisage international diplomacy as an act of moral integrity rather than a process of tactical and strategic expediency was highlighted several years later in May 1939, at a moment when Stalin tightened his grip on foreign policy by replacing Litvinov with Molotov. 'It would be incorrect', noted Nizan, 'to think that this decision in any way heralds a spectacular reversal in the policy of the USSR . . . continuity is the essential characteristic of Soviet foreign policy, and nobody has outlined the principles of this policy more forcefully than M. Molotov'.[7]

Although Nizan was later to pour scorn on the moral self-righteousess and indignation of a non-communist majority in France venting its spleen on the treacherousness of the USSR,[8] and although he was also to recognise the Soviet Union's need to act expediently at a time of impending international disaster,[9] nonetheless something fundamental had clearly snapped in Nizan's psychology. After August 1939 Nizan was no longer willing to grant Stalin the benefit of the doubt. After August 1939 it was no longer possible to have complete faith in a nation state which collaborated for whatever reason with fascism, even if that state happened to be the Soviet Union itself.

Nizan did not react immediately, however. The publication of his letter of resignation from the party on 25 September 1939 came four weeks after the signing of the pact.[10] Between the announcement on 26 August of a government ban on L'Humanité and Ce Soir, and the anouncement of his own resignation on 25 September, he spent four weeks wrestling with his conscience and attempting to understand the full implications of what had happened.

Inevitably, the situation was complicated by the contradictory nature of the PCF's own political strategy, divided as it was between an allegiance on the one hand to a defence of the interests of Republican France, and on the other to a defence of the interests of the Soviet state. The evolution in party policy from the beginning of September, when, despite a ruthless government crackdown on its activities, it stressed the 'anti-fascist' nature of the war, and the beginning of October when, following pressure from the Communist International, it began to give prominence to the 'imperialist' nature of the struggle,[11] is of major significance when assessing Nizan's decision to resign. Nizan's war correspondence makes it clear that his resignation was motivated as much by a refusal to accept the moral integrity of the Soviet alliance with Hitler, as it was by a complete lack of faith in the French communist party leadership to think beyond blind and servile acquiescence to Moscow.

He was initially unimpressed by Aragon's editorials in *Ce Soir*. Aragon, the perennial survivor, was prompt to defend the actions of the Soviet Union from what he considered to be a snivelling chorus of criticism emanating from the partisans of Munich. In Aragon's eyes, the pact was a major step in the direction of peace, not only because it represented a curbing of fascist aggression towards the Soviet Union, but also since it was not in theory incompatible with the signing of a tripartite agreement between France, Great Britain and the USSR.[12] 'The tripartite pact is a marvellous supplement to a non-aggression pact between Germany and the Soviet Union. The non-aggression pact in no sense implies desertion on the part of the USSR',[13] noted Aragon quite categorically. In his public pronouncements at least, Aragon was convinced that the Nazi-Soviet pact did not invalidate the mutual assistance treaties in existence between France and Poland on the one hand, and France and the Soviet Union on the other. 'If France, through the obligations of her own treaties, were to give assistance to a state which was the victim of aggression (Poland, for example), THE USSR WILL OF NECESSITY ASSIST FRANCE'.[14]

Nizan was clearly justified in treating Aragon's analysis with the scepticism that it deserved. Stalin had no intention of honouring previously signed mutual assistance treaties. A secret protocol of the Nazi-Soviet pact, designating German and Soviet spheres of influence in Finland, Estonia, Lithuania, Latvia and Poland,[15] highlights in retrospect the casuistry of Aragon's analysis and the inevitability of Nizan's departure from the PCF.

On 17 September 1939 the Soviet Union invaded Poland. This event triggered Nizan's departure from the communist party. Nizan was sickened by the spectacle of a revolutionary communist state sinking to the depths of fascist barbarism. Everything that he had written during the previous four years on the overriding need to oppose fascism, on the need to defend nation states through the creation of a strong system of alliances based on collective security, and on the central role of the Soviet Union in promoting peace and stability, all was reduced to the level of absurdity by the Nazi-Soviet pact, the invasion of Poland and subsequently the war in Finland. At the very moment that he resigned, he remarked bitterly: 'The events in Poland are an unacceptable implementation of *realpolitik*.'[16] Later, in a more morbid vein, he confessed:'I suspected all along that there was little possibility that I would be forgiven for making known publicly that Stalin disgusted me, and that I could not stomach the Nazi-Soviet pact and the events in Finland.'[17]

His resignation was also motivated, however, by a highly critical view of the leadership of the French communist party. 'They behaved like imbeciles', he dismissively remarked on 30 September.[18] Three weeks later, at a time when the imperialist war thesis was very much in the ascendency, he was more specific:

> The French communists lacked the necessary cynicism and the capacity for political deception that would have been required to gain the maximum benefit from a dangerous diplomatic operation. Why did they not act boldly like the Russians?[19]

Beneath this apparent recognition of the necessity for an 'imaginative' politics of expediency, however, there remained a firm moral imperative. The imaginatively cynical Soviet political strategy had been devised, Nizan concluded, in order to defend the revolutionary-Soviet state and to defeat fascism in the long term. Fascism had to be temporarily embraced in order ultimately to be defeated. A similar, equally cynical and equally imaginative, French communist strategy would have entailed disconnecting French communist interests from those of the Soviet Union. Soviet communism would necessarily have been temporarily rejected in order to defend Republican France and ultimately to defeat fascism.

Views such as these highlight the fundamental mechanics of Nizan's political psychology: a willingness to accept expedient political tactics provided that a justifiable link could be established between the tactics themselves and the long term 'moral' strategy; a consequent unwillingness to accept expedient political tactics relayed unthinkingly by leading party officials whose only concern was the efficient management of the current party line.

When Nizan berates orthodox French Stalinists for their inability to differentiate between loyalty and blind adherence to bureaucracy,[20] he not only specifically highlights his deep commitment to Republican France, but more generally he signals in no uncertain terms that his continued membership of the communist party depended on the continuing ability of the party itself to demonstrate its genuine commitment to the moral struggle against oppression of whatever kind. Once the party aligned itself with the ranks of the oppressors, either through cynical design (Stalin), or through incompetence (the PCF leadership), it was time to leave.

Nizan left the party on 25 September 1939. He spent the last five months of his life writing his fourth novel, *La Soirée à Somosierra*, and reflecting on the outcome of his departure from the party, only vaguely aware of the incipient communist campaign to blacken his name.

He died during the afternoon of Wednesday, 23 May 1940 in the Château de Cocove in Recques sur Hem. He died in a pool of blood, shot in the head by a stray bullet fired by a nameless German soldier. 'The important thing is to know what it is that you are dying for', noted Nizan in 1935.[21] In his own eyes at least, he died fighting the cause of Republican France.

(ii) COMMUNIST RENEGADE, 1940-60

Breaking from the party was a terrrible experience for Nizan. His war correspondence testifies to the fact. Although convinced in his own mind that his decision to resign was correct, his confidence was slowly undermined by a growing awareness that the party itself was about to respond violently to what it considered to be a cowardly act of betrayal.

Nizan could have been under no illusions as to the fate of those who were perceived as traitors to the party. The vicious campaigns conducted during the 1930s against Doriot, Trotsky, Radek and Bukharin would have left him in no doubt on that score. During the eight short months that he lived following his resignation, he was plagued by a sense of foreboding that the future would hold a similar fate for himself. On 10 December 1939 he remarked ominously that André Chamson had informed him that 'a storm was brewing in Aragon's mind'.[22] By 5 February 1940, in the grip of a persecution complex, he was voicing fears that his resignation from the party would be publicly perceived as an act of treachery that had finally laid bare his 'inner soul'.[23]

Nizan sensed that the *manner* of his resignation was unlikely to charm any of his erstwhile Stalinist comrades. He had neither remained discreetly silent, nor had he made any attempt to explain in public the reasons for his resignation. He had, however, chosen to publicise his act of departure, and this public disavowal, coinciding as it did with a ferocious government anti-communist crackdown, was inevitably interpreted as a treacherous stab in the back that could not pass unavenged.

Vengeance was swift and brutal. In March 1940, two months prior to Nizan's death, Thorez launched a vitriolic attack on what he contemptuously designated as 'the handful of wretched deserters, . . . cowards and weaklings, spies and *agents-provocateurs*', who 'had abandoned the position of the working class for that of the imperialists and planned to turn (the) fight for peace by the side of the Soviet Union into a policy of supporting the imperialist war mongering of the French bourgeoisie'.[24]

Branded a 'police spy' by Thorez, Nizan was pilloried on two counts: first, for spreading the pernicious doctrine of "National Communism", that is, communism in word and nationalism in deed';[25] secondly, for enacting in the reality of his life the treachery and cowardice portrayed in the fiction of his literature. Thorez noted:

> Nizan has been satisfied to play in real life the wretched part of Pluvinage, the police spy he brings into his latest novel. This cowardly and servile Nizan-Pluvinage was ready to lick the dust to deceive the intended victims of his spying. He has earned special laurels in the salons where cynicism and shamelessness are marks of distinction.[26]

Six years later, Henri Lefebvre's willing corroboration of Thorez's accusations sparked off what has become known as the 'Nizan Case'. In a highly polemical piece Lefebvre reworks the link made by Thorez between Nizan's act of betrayal in September 1939 and the theme of betrayal in his literature.[27] Nizan, Lefebvre argues, was obsessed, tormented by the act of betrayal. His treacherous relations with his friends and comrades are both confirmed and explained by the treacherous interpersonal relations that form the substance of his three major texts, *Antoine Bloyé*, *Le Cheval de Troie* and *La Conspiration*.[28]

The efforts made at that time by Sartre, Camus, Merleau-Ponty *et alia* to rehabilitate Nizan achieved no more than to illustrate the impossibility of reasoned dialogue with the French communist party at moments of extreme ideological polarisation. In the Cold War climate of postwar France, the Nizan Case became a pretext for a political slanging match. Despite a conspicuous absence of the merest shred of evidence that Nizan had 'betrayed' the PCF in any sense other than resigning from the party itself, it was objectively impossible for a communist in postwar France to view Nizan in terms other than those of betrayal and treachery. Not only had he resigned at a particularly sensitive historical moment, it was also a political fact of life that the Cold War situation literally demanded that no concessions be made to anyone venturing to attack the party; and the attempt to rehabilitate the 'police spy' Nizan was undoubtedly perceived as an attack on the party.[29]

The demands of Cold War politics prompted Aragon to go one step further and fabricate a fictional representation of Nizan's treachery which had in the first instance itself been fabricated from Nizan's own fictional productions. There has perhaps been no more striking an example of the word preceding the deed. In 1949, at the height of the Cold War, almost exactly ten years after the events themselves, the storm that had been brewing in Aragon's mind since 1940 finally burst, with the publication of *Les Communistes*. The treacherous Nizan-Pluvinage police spy invented by Thorez in 1940, was transformed in 1949 into the cowardly Nizan-Orfilat communist renegade. Patrice Orfilat, a fearful, whimpering wretch bearing a grudge against Thorez whom, he assumes, had prevented him from being nominated as a PCF candidate for the 1936 elections, petrified at the thought of war and his own death, attempts to find a job in the Foreign Affairs Ministry, and is ultimately disdainfully rebuffed by an orthodox party member unperturbed by the Nazi–Soviet pact.[30]

This rather petty, predictably prosaic fiction is ultimately as vindictively misrepresentative of Nizan as the fictional account of Nizan's existence in Simone Téry's *Beaux enfants qui n'hesitez pas*, published in 1957, is fatuously misrepresentative,[31] Téry's fictional transposition of Nizan in the character of Pierre Dumont merely submerges the reality of Nizan's life beneath a flood of naïve communist rhetoric.

It is a curious fact that the Nizan Case was ultimately dominated more by fiction than by fact. The original accusations levelled by Thorez were based on a fictitious analogy between Nizan himself and the fictional character Pluvinage. The crux of Lefebvre's analysis in 1946 was the interconnection between the reality of Nizan's 'betrayal' of the party in 1939 and the fictional theme of betrayal in his novels. Aragon's description of the activities and thoughts of the Orfilat-Nizan character in *Les Communistes* is as fictionally far-fetched as Téry's account of the Dumont-Nizan character in *Beaux enfants qui n'hésitez pas*. The political and the literary are as inextricably merged in Nizan's posthumous existence as they were in his lived existence.

Although it is undoubtedly true that Sartre *et alia* achieved a moral victory in 1947 by highlighting the purely imaginary and hence illusory nature of the accusations made against Nizan, and although Sartre's own final fictional account of Nizan, narrated emotionally in 'Drôle d'amitié', is a powerful antidote to the negative and hostile account in Aragon's *Les Communistes*, nonetheless, from the moment of his death in 1940 until the moment of republication of *Aden Arabie* in 1960, Nizan remained an unwanted communist renegade. Initially vilified, he was subsequently forgotten. Between 1940 and 1960, virtually nobody read anything that he had written.[32] There was simply no place for a communist renegade in the Cold War political climate of postwar France. The ghost of Stalin had to be exorcised before Nizan could be rehabilitated.

(iii) DISSIDENT COMMUNIST, 1960–80

Nizan occupied a privileged position in Sartre's life both intellectually and emotionally. In 1975 Sartre conceded that the *only* person who had even marginally influenced him intellectually had been Nizan.[33] The previous year, in a conversation with Simone de Beauvoir, he confessed that throughout his life his only true friendships had been with a number of women and with Nizan.[34]

The depth of Sartre's feelings for Nizan can be measured by the frequency with which Nizan recurs in Sartre's autobiographical and fictional writings. Apart from the preface to *Aden Arabie*, both his autobiography, *Les Mots*, and autobiographical fiction, 'La Semence et le scaphandre',[35] centre on the Sartre-Nizan relationship. If one adds to this not only the fictionalised account of Nizan's existence in *Les Chemins de la liberté* and 'Drôle d'amitié' in the guise of Brunet and Schneider/Vicarios, but also the dramatised account of Nizan's existence in *Les Mains sales* in the guise of Hugo and Hoederer, it is clear that Nizan played a highly significant role in Sartre's life, and that his memory lingered long after Nizan's death in 1940.

The publication of the preface to *Aden Arabie* in 1960 signalled Nizan's return from the wilderness to which he had been consigned by Cold War politics. Overnight a highly suspect communist renegade was transformed into an eternally youthful dissident communist, a beacon of hope for a generation of young men and women rebelling against the anarchronistic irrelevance of an outmoded educational system and the serial alienation of a post-industrial society.

Nizan's rehabilitation in 1960 had been made possible by a gradual evolution in the political and ideological climate in France, itself reflected in Sartre's own intellectual itinerary. As Ory astutely remarks, Sartre's preface is as much an expression of remorse that he had failed to rehabilitate Nizan successfully in 1947, as it is a eulogy of the dynamic Nizan-Sartre relationship in the early 1920s.[36]

And yet the possibilities for rehabilitation between 1940 and 1960 had been virtually non-existent. Not only had dialogue with the French communist party on this highly sensitive issue rapidly degenerated into counter-productive name calling, but also Sartre himself had been gradually moving progressively closer during the late 1940s and early 1950s to the politics of the PCF. The logic of such a development was that previous allegiances to Nizan were necessarily passed over in silence.

'Drôle d'amitié' was published in *Les Temps modernes* in November and December 1949. Between October 1949, when Sartre resigned from the Rassemblement Démocratique Révolutionnaire, on the grounds that the RDR was an abstract political movement out of touch with the social reality of postwar France, and July 1952, the date of publication in *Les Temps modernes* of 'Les Communistes et la paix',[37] Sartre was drawn irreversibly, under the pressure of national and international events, towards close collaboration with the French communist party.[38] For a period of four years in the early to mid 1950s, Sartre was consequently closely associated with the PCF. Such collaboration included participation in the campaign to free Henri Martin imprisoned for alleged subversive, anti-colonial activities,[39] the publication of a series of enthusiastic reports on the Soviet Union following a visit to the USSR in 1954, twenty years exactly after Nizan had made his own pilgrimage to the mecca of communism,[40] and the production of a pro-communist play *Nekrassov*.[41] Given the Cold War political climate of the time and Sartre's ideological need to be closely associated with the PCF, it is hardly surprising that the campaign to set the record straight on Nizan was given a low priority.

It needed the shock waves of the Hungarian uprising in 1956 to transform the situation. The publication in January 1957 of a triple number of *Les Temps modernes*, in which Sartre not only condemned Soviet intervention in Hugary, but also located the source of Soviet repression as those elements of the Soviet leadership which continued to resist destalinisation,[42] marked a sudden, bitter disenchantment with the Soviet experiment and the PCF. Between 1957 and 1960

Sartre's thoughts were dominated, on the one hand, by Soviet intransigence and seeming inability to destalinise, and on the other, by the burgeoning of new revolutionary movements in the Third World.

When the political and moral credibility of the Soviet system collapsed in 1956, something that had been slumbering in the depths of Sartre's consciousness was suddenly reawakened. The long muted voice of Nizan, unfashionable for almost twenty years, began speaking again with an urgency and topicality that simply could not be ignored. Nizan's despair in 1939 at the Nazi-Soviet pact and the Soviet invasion of Poland echoed Sartre's despair in 1956 at the Soviet repression in Hungary. Force of historical circumstances had dramatically reunited two friends temporarily disunited as a consequence of Cold War expediency.

After 1956, with the Soviet cause politically and morally bankrupt, there came a gradual softening of the brutal Stalinist line of the immediate postwar years. Henri Lefebvre, for example, formerly a bitter opponent of both Sartre and Nizan, recanted in 1959, offering a more accommodating analysis of Nizan in particular, and Sartrean existentialism in general.[43] Gradually, revolutionary aspirations that had been dashed by the Soviet intervention in Hungary were rekindled in the anti-colonial struggles of the Third World.

By a curious twist of fate, Sartre's preface to *Aden Arabie*, Nizan's account of his own journey to a third world colonial country in 1926–7, a journey which Sartre pinpoints as the moment when their student friendship began to end,[44] was written at the height of a momentous third-world revolutionary struggle. *Aden Arabie*, almost a 'pre-communist' text in terms of Nizan's own ideological evolution, became the pretext for Sartre's own 'post-communist' radicalisation.

Speaking in 1975 of his relationship with Nizan, Sartre noted that what had ultimately come between them after Nizan's return from Aden, was Nizan's Marxism. 'I felt threatened by Marxism because it was the doctrine of a friend, and because it cut across our friendship', noted Sartre.[45] Between 1927, the date of Nizan's entry in the PCF, and 1960, the date of republication of *Aden Arabie*, lies the record of two intellectual itineraries within Marxism. For Nizan, the journey ended in 1939 with the signing of the Nazi-Soviet pact and the invasion of Poland. For Sartre, the journey came to a halt in 1956 when Soviet tanks rolled into Budapest.

It is almost as if both men had to be chastened by the bitter lessons of Marxism in practice before there could be a return to the unproblematical friendship prior to the advent of Marxism in their lives. Here lies the origin of the Sartrean myth of Nizan. By 1960 Sartre had progressed to a radical 'post-communist' phase in his thinking, a phase which coincided exactly with Nizan's 'pre-communist' phase in Aden. Sartre ultimately chose to ignore the constructive Marxist elements in Nizan's life and work which, from the vantage point of 1960, were perceived as no more than a Stalinist mystification and selected instead as the model for a post-Stalinist epoch, the uncompromising rebellion of a young intellectual of the 1920s venting his spleen on the iniquities of bourgeois oppression at home and colonial oppression abroad.

Sartre's choice of *Aden Arabie* was consequently not arbitrary. Although originally asked to preface *Les Chiens de garde*, his preference for *Aden Arabie* is explained by his ideological position in 1960. It is explained as much by *Aden Arabie's* colonial, third-world dimension, as it is by its lyrically explosive and liberatingly destructive style which undoubtedly held more appeal for Sartre in 1960 than the more prosaic, communist militant style of *Les Chiens de garde*, with its undertones of Stalinist party dogma. It is highly significant that the two texts which Sartre chooses for the most part to ignore are *Les Chiens de garde* and *Le Cheval de Troie*, the two texts where Nizan's communist party allegiances are most clearly visible.

The events of May 1968 inflated still further the Sartrean myth of Nizan the youthful iconoclast. Reproduced in the heady atmosphere of the May events, Nizan's work at last coincided with its socio-political environment. Above all, the belligerent youthfulness of his writings struck a chord in the hearts of student militants. Nothing illustrates more dramatically the extent to which Nizan's work fired the imagination than the spectacle of Sartre himself publicly criticising traditional 'institutionalised' intellectuals for their lack of imagination,[46] publicly insulting Raymond Aron for his failure to take note of the significance of the May events,[47] and extolling by implication Nizan the youthful iconoclast, an exemplary dissident intellectual in tune with the spirit of the times.

Beyond the immediate cultural spectacle of the May events, however, a more fundamental question was being asked concerning the political strategy of the French communist party. Rejected contemptuously by Sartre in 1968 as an integral part of the conservative forces of reaction,[48] the PCF has subsequently entered a period of possibly irreversible decline during the 1970s and 1980s. The consequence of this progressive decline in popularity has been not only a sustained attack on what are perceived as the inadequacies of communist ideology and the Soviet system itself in the 1980s (and there is no more iconoclastic an exponent of this form of criticism than Nizan's own grandson, Emmanuel Todd),[49] but more specifically, a tendency to overplay the critically dissident aspects of Nizan's life and work, and to pass over in silence the more constructive, orthodox communist slant of his writings.[50]

Between 1960 and 1980, in short, Nizan has come to symbolise almost exclusively in the public consciousness the impossibility of sustaining credibility as an intellectual within the confines of the French communist party. The pre-communist Nizan and the post-communist Sartre have, in other words, become fused in the public imagination as an example of the impossibility of the communist intellectual, the communist writer, the communist novelist.

Sartre died in 1980. One year after his death, Simone de Beauvoir noted: 'His death separates us. My death will not reunite us; that's the way it is';[51] poignant words that Sartre himself could have written after the death of Nizan in 1940. And yet, separated by Aden, separated by Marxism, separated by death, they remain forever reunited in the preface and text of *Aden Arabie*.

4

Autopsy

'I find peace of mind acceptable only in winners and in those losers who have exhausted every means at their disposal, and who have peace of mind *despite being losers*', noted Nizan in October 1939, one month after his resignation from the party.[1] Nizan's refusal to be a loser remained with him to the end. Yet in 1939 he could not have envisaged the full irony of the destiny that history had reserved for him.

Committed initially in 1916 to an abstract, defensive project of avoiding the humiliating fate of his father by succeeding within the alienating structure of a bourgeois educational system, Nizan reinvented his life in 1927, joined the PCF and conceived a plan to become a winner by fighting the cause of all those losers in the world, victims like his father of an oppressive social system. Between 1927 and 1938 he appeared to have found the route to success. In December 1938, despite impending disaster on the international political front, Nizan, the celebrated winner of the Prix Interallié, remained confident of future literary success. In 1938 Nizan was unquestionably a winner, in his own eyes and in the eyes of his peers.

In 1939 history intervened and in the space of a few months the work of a lifetime was in ruins. His name blackened, his writings neglected, for two decades Nizan was allotted the role of loser. The fate of the son seemed in retrospect to have been predestined in the fate of the father. 1960: another unpredictable quirk of history, Sartre's preface to *Aden Arabie*, and Nizan returned from the grave. 1968: the May events and Nizan was reborn. The loser finally, definitively became a winner.

This tale of success and failure, of winners and losers, is too often interpreted as signifying the impossibility of constructive critical allegiance to the communist party. In Nizan's case such an interpretation is entirely false. In 1937, in his reply to Gide's *Retour de l'URSS*, Nizan clarified the nature of his allegiance to the communist party by differentiating between opportunistic conformism and genuine, principled membership:

69

Conformism must not be confused with commitment. . . . A true
conformist is a man who in word and deed conforms to the values
of a society that he rejects. He consequently lives a lie. Commitment is an affirmation of man. The values that he advocates are
identical with his life.[2]

The truth of the matter is consequently quite simple. Nizan was not
a conformist. He was a genuinely committed party member. He
belonged to the French communist party because the values of that
party, as he perceived them, coincided with his own beliefs. When
he finally reached the conclusion that the party itself had abandoned
those beliefs, he left. The conformists, on the other hand, remained.
This obstinate refusal to be a conformist explains not only the difficulties of integration that Nizan experienced within the party, but
also – and this needs stressing – underlines the extent to which he
succeeded in retaining intellectual autonomy and integrity within
the party itself.

It is undoubtedly necessary to identify the reasons why Nizan
failed to become as fully integrated within the structure of the party
as Politzer, Cogniot or Aragon, for example. Cohen-Solal's identifi-
cation of three strategies, expertise, orthodoxy and prestige, enabling
these three prominent communists to carve out a particular niche for
themselves within the party structure, cannot be faulted.[3] However,
Nizan's failure to do likewise is not simply an illustration of the
structural inflexibility of the PCF in its dealings with petty bourgeois
intellectuals such as Nizan himself. It is also a demonstration of the
possibility of retaining intellectual integrity *within* the party. Nizan's
writings are not those of a man incapacitated by the restrictions of
party dogma. They are those of a man working imaginatively within
the framework of an ideological system with which he is in entire
agreement.

In a similar vein, Emmanuel Todd is also undoubtedly correct in
his assertion that the history of the French communist party, unlike
that of its Italian counterpart, is the record of the progressive
elimination of the petty bourgeoisie from the leadership, with a
consequent loss of political autonomy and control to Moscow. 'The
venerable Stalinist institution rejects and pushes aside authentic
and ambitious Leninists who are not allowed to carve out a career in
the PCF because of their bourgeois origins.'[4]

Although this is certainly borne out by the example of Nizan
himself who experienced a degree of mistrust from within the ranks

of the PCF as a consequence of his petty bourgeois class origins and schooling, ultimately this is of secondary importance compared to Nizan's overriding reason for being in the communist party in the first place. The communist party in Nizan's eyes was not simply a refuge from oppression. It was the site of a counter-culture, an alternative society to which he fully subscribed. Above all else, Nizan's commitment to the PCF was underwritten by a profound belief in the natural justice of the communist cause. Personal ambitions, the structural inadequacies of the PCF leadership, even the possible shortcomings of the Soviet experiment itself, were all of secondary importance to what may be most accurately described as a 'communist ethic'.

It was precisely the moral, ethical dimension of communism which initially made it impossible for Nizan not to join the party and work within its ranks. It was this same moral, ethical dimension which finally, after September 1939, made it impossible for Nizan to remain working within the ranks of that same party.

From the beginning to the end of his life, Nizan was dominated by a manichean belief that the world could ultimately be divided into Good and Evil. Until September 1939 Nizan remained convinced that alone, the communist party and the Soviet Union coincided with the forces of Good. With the signing of the Nazi-Soviet pact, the Soviet invasion of Poland, and the unthinking acquiescence of the PCF leadership to Moscow throughout the entire series of events, Good and Evil suddenly became ill-defined concepts. Nizan stuck to his principles, but after 1939 he became a political refugee. His only sanctuary would be death.

'Ethics, politics, nothing is simple any more', noted Sartre in 1959.[5] Almost a decade earlier, he had reached the conclusion that an ethic was in the final analysis 'inevitable', but that in the current historical climate it was 'impossible'.[6] A decade or so previously, Nizan had been taught the same bitter lesson. In September 1939 he discovered to his cost that a communist ethic, although in the long term doubtless 'inevitable', was at that historical moment 'impossible'.

Part Two
Paul Nizan:
Communist Novelist

Literature does not generate literature; ideologies do not create ideologies; superstructures do not generate superstructures except as an inert and passive inheritance: they are not generated by 'parthenogenesis', but by the intervention of the 'male' element, history, that is to say new social relations.

Gramsci

Introduction

There are three published novels by Paul Nizan. Critical evaluation of these three novels ranges from the polemically hostile to the genuinely sympathetic.[1]

For the most part, however, there is a tendency to examine the texts as autonomous products, isolating them in the process from their political, ideological and historical moments of production and reproduction. Attention is consequently focused primarily on the manner in which a given novel succeeds or fails in conforming to an abstract, archetypal model of the genre, and only lip service is paid to the manner in which politics, ideology and history are mediated in the texts themselves.

The thrust of the ensuing analysis will be the attempt to disclose the process of mediation whereby the political and ideological history of a given period is produced and reproduced in three consecutive texts. Personal preferences for this or that novel, although clearly visible in the analysis, will be of a purely anecdotal significance. It goes without saying that I consider Nizan's trilogy of novels to be an exemplary piece of writing worthy of serious critical attention. This subjective appreciation of the work of Nizan is merely the starting point of analysis, however. The questions to be resolved centre crucially on the relationship between political history, communist ideology and literary form. Before examining the novels in detail, it is necessary initially to assess the political and cultural climate in which the three novels were originally produced. It would seem appropriate, therefore, to begin by reviewing not only the cultural politics of the period, with specific reference to Nizan's cultural production, but also the dominant left-wing literary theory of the time, socialist realism, with special reference to Nizan's ideas on revolutionary literature.

5

Cultural Politics

Barthes has differentiated between a postwar period during which the cultural influence of the French writer/intellectual has gradually diminished, and an interwar period during which 'great writers . . . such as Gide, Claudel, Valéry, Malraux . . . were at the centre of intense activity, exerting enormous cultural influence'.[1] The political and ideological ferment of the interwar period, when the ideological and cultural were fused, created the historical conditions in which intellectuals, writers and artists were no longer distanced from the social process and were to play a significant role in national and international events.

The turbulent nature of the cultural politics of the period should not, however, divert attention away from two significant points regarding the political and cultural evolution of the French communist party at this time. First, it is important to recognise that political and cultural developments in France, although closely interconnected, did not always coincide historically one with another. Secondly, it is necessary to bear in mind that the cultural policy of the PCF in this interwar phase was influenced as much by French national cultural traditions, as by the revolutionary cultural experiments of the Soviet Union. Nizan's own political and cultural practice is a testimony to both points.

(i) INTELLECTUALS, POLITICS AND CULTURE, 1927–39

Nizan's membership of the PCF between 1927 and 1939 straddled two markedly different periods of French communist history, political, ideological and cultural. For six years following the adoption in November 1927 by the PCF Central Committee of the 'class against class' tactic, the party followed an increasingly doctrinaire, Bolshevik course. In the wake of the events of February 1934, however, with the threat of fascism looming large on the international horizon, the party was by contrast to revert to a more flexible, collaborative political strategy.

The initial phase was characterised above all by an uncompromisingly sectarian political mentality and the growing isolation of the party within the French national political community. Between 1927 and 1934 the PCF became less a political group with a mass following, more an extremist ideological sect, an ideal target for repression and persecution by reactionary governments.

The subsequent phase between 1934 and 1939 signalled the return of the party from the political wilderness of sectarian isolationism. The adoption of a co-operative strategy in 1934 rapidly brought the PCF back into the mainstream of French party politics, capturing as it did the popular imagination of the French nation. This highly successful phase in communist party history was brought to a sudden end by Stalin's rigorous application of *realpolitik* in September 1939.

In many respects, the date of Nizan's entry to the PCF in 1927–8 marks a watershed in the cultural policy of the party itself. By 1927–8 many of the first generation of intellectuals had already left, disillusioned by increasingly sectarian politics and rigorously disciplined organisational structures. There remained only one major intellectual/cultural figure of international standing: Henri Barbusse. Given the party's increasingly isolated situation, given its general lack of prestigious cultural figures, it is not surprising that by 1928 Barbusse had come to enjoy a particularly favoured position within the ranks of the PCF itself.[2]

In 1927–8, however, the party was rejuvenated by an influx of new blood from a second generation of young intellectuals, on the one hand the Surrealists – Breton, Aragon, Eluard, Péret and Unik – and on the other, the Marxist 'Philosophies' group comprising Politzer, Lefebvre, Nizan, Morhange and Guterman.

In 1927 and 1928, therefore, were planted the seeds of a cultural conflict between a first generation of intellectuals who had, like Barbusse, joined the party as a reaction to the sickening personal experiences of the First World War and who were above all else humanist and pacifist, and a younger second generation of Surrealists and Marxists who were more in tune with the sectarian Bolshevism advocated by Moscow.

The history of the development of PCF cultural policy between 1927 and 1934 is consequently the history of a series of tactical skirmishes between these two factions, one humanist and pacifist, the other revolutionary and Bolshevik, between which the party leadership necessarily had to adjudicate.

The contradictory nature of the party leadership's stance on cultural matters between 1928 and 1934 was most strikingly illustrated by Barbusse's editorial control of the journal *Monde*. Ostensibly set up in 1928 with the aim of promoting the development of French proletarian literature and propagating the sectarian cultural views of RAPP (the Association of Soviet Proletarian Writers), *Monde* became in the hands of Barbusse the site of cultural collaboration between communists and non-communists alike. Although in 1927 Barbusse had attended the First Congress of Proletarian Writers held in Moscow, and although he had appeared to voice support for the new policy of subordinating the literary process to the construction of socialism, his actual writing practice was completely out of step with the doctrinaire ideas of RAPP.

The editorial policy that he pursued in *Monde* was ultimately no doubt as much a product of his natural inclination for popular front co-operative politics, as it was a consequence of his scepticism regarding the possibilities for the development of proletarian literature in interwar capitalist France dominated by a hegemonic bourgeois cultural tradition. Be that as it may, the discrepancy between the editorial objectives of *Monde* and its editorial practice was so great as to cause embarassment in official communist circles, and to provoke open hostility from Young Turks such as Breton, Aragon and Nizan himself.[3] Matters came to a head at the International Congress of Proletarian Writers held at Kharkov in November 1930. The Kharkov congress, attended by Aragon and Sadoul, was the occasion for public condemnation of the 'right-wing deviationist' editorial policy pursued by Barbusse in *Monde*. Aragon was not reluctant to join in the chorus of voices repudiating Barbusse.

What is most interesting in this entire episode is the discretion with which the PCF leadership handled the Kharkov condemnation of Barbusse. The resolution of the Kharkov congress unequivocally rejecting the Barbusse line was, in fact, not published in *L'Humanité* until October–November 1931, one year after the congress itself.[4] At a time when the party leadership was dominated by the sectarian views of Barbé and Célor, such reticence cannot simply be explained by a sense of personal solidarity on the part of Thorez, and especially Vaillant-Couturier, for Barbusse. It indicates rather a degree of hesitation in the leadership of the party as to the correct cultural policy to be pursued.

It is, of course, possible to explain the relatively confused state of party cultural policy at this time as the inevitable consequence of the leadership's lack of interest in cultural matters. More pressing political problems would doubtless have necessitated the relegation of such matters to a secondary role. Yet in Thorez's case, for example, his natural preference for the practical realities of daily politics rather than the abstract myths of sectarian rhetoric would almost certainly have sown doubts in his own mind regarding the viability of the implantation of Soviet cultural policies within a French context. Despite the heresy of Barbusse's cultural strategy between 1928 and 1934, it is possible that the strategy itself did not appear to lack credibility in the minds of certain members of the PCF leadership.

The removal of Barbé and Célor from the leadership in August 1931, and the growing stature of Thorez within the party, conspired to create a situation in which a final decision on cultural policy was left in abeyance. It is as if between 1927 and 1934 a party unequivocally committed to a sectarian strategy on the political front nevertheless consciously chose to hedge its bets on the cultural front. Although publicly subscribing to the sectarian theses of Kharkov, the party continued to countenance the dissemination of a heretical collaborative policy within the pages of Barbusse's *Monde*. Only with the change of party strategy in 1934 was it possible to speak of a genuine coincidence between PCF political and cultural policy.

This gradual evolution towards a coherent and unified PCF political and cultural strategy is most effectively displayed through close scrutiny of the various political and cultural events involving both communist and fellow-travelling intellectuals which took place between 1930 and 1937. Table 5.1 records the significant events chronologically.

The 1930 Kharkov congress, at which artistic subjectivism and individualism were denounced in favour of collective cultural production and the fostering of proletarian literature, represents the high point of RAPP domination of cultural policy. The effect of the congress on Aragon was apparently profound.[5] Yet the dominance of this sectarian cultural line was to prove short-lived. In April 1932 RAPP was disbanded, and although in the Soviet Union the ensuing liberalising effect was only temporary, lasting until 1935–6 when rigid cultural controls were reintroduced under the watchful eye of Zhdanov, in France, by contrast, 1932 was to mark the beginning of a prolonged period not only of cultural liberalisation within the PCF but also of political co-operation between communists and fellow-travelling sympathisers.

TABLE 5.1 Cultural politics, 1930–7

Date	Venue	Event
Nov 1930	Kharkov	International Proletarian Writers' Congress
Apr 1932	——	Dissolution of RAPP (Association of Soviet Proletarian Writers)
Aug 1932	Amsterdam	International Congress against War and Imperialism
Dec 1932	——	Formation of AEAR (Association of Revolutionary Writers and Artists)
Jun 1933	Paris (Salle Pleyel)	European Anti-Fascist Congress
Aug 1934	Moscow	Soviet Writers' Congress
Jun 1935	Paris	First International Congress of Writers for the Defence of Culture
Jul 1937	Valencia, Madrid, Barcelona, Paris	Second International Congress of Writers for the Defence of Culture

The extent to which cultural developments were paving the way for political developments can be gauged by the success of the Amsterdam International Congress against War and Imperialism organised by Barbusse and Rolland in August 1932. This event, together with the Anti-Fascist Congress held at the Salle Pleyel in Paris in June 1933, was not merely a major personal triumph for Barbusse in his struggle for co-operative politics. The success of the Amsterdam-Pleyel Movement also sent a clear signal to equivocating party political leaders that a unified front to combat the growing threat of fascism was now a matter of urgency. In this sense a *cultural* popular front was undoubtedly in existence prior to the formation of a *political* popular front, and doubtless was instrumental in fostering the global popular front mentality.

Thorez was not slow to recognise the signficance of these developments. Not only was he supportive of the 1932 Amsterdam congress, he was also quick to seize the initiative and promote the founding in December 1932 of the AEAR, the Association of Revolutionary Writers and Artists, in which Nizan was to play a prominent role. By 1934, following the February events and the signing in July of the popular front agreement, the route was clear for rapid development of co-operative communist cultural politics.

The history of communist cultural politics after 1934 is the history of a series of collaborative enterprises involving communist intellectuals and a wide range of fellow-travellers. In August 1934 the Soviet Writers' Congress held in Moscow provided a unique forum at which communists and non-communists could discuss positive measures to promote an anti-fascist cultural front. Constructive dialogue between the communists – Nizan, Aragon and Pozner – and the non-communists – Malraux, Gide and Bloch – was the order of the day.

The two International Congresses of Writers for the Defence of Culture, the first held in Paris in July 1935, the second held in Valencia, Madrid, Barcelona and Paris in July 1937 at the height of the Spanish Civil War, were simply the prolongation of collaborative cultural politics initiated at the Amsterdam Congress of 1932.

The extent to which the PCF was committed to popular front cultural politics can be appreciated both by the amount of time and energy that it devoted to the anti-fascist congresses, peace movements and revolutionary cultural associations of the period, and by its willingness to engage in the policy of *la main tendue* ('the outstretched hand') in its relations with sympathisers of any persuasion, ideological or religious, willing to collaborate in its struggle against capitalist warmongering, imperialism, fascism and oppression.

Overall, the exuberant, outward-looking image of the PCF during the popular front phase contrasted markedly with its defensive, inward-looking image prior to 1934. Although the sectarian image of the party between 1928 and 1934 clearly exercised a deep fascination over intellectuals such as Aragon and Nizan, who were filled with hatred and revulsion for the oppressive structures and reactionary governments of a bourgeois French state, its appeal was necessarily limited. The party's popular front image, by contrast, captured the imagination of countless intellectuals wishing to be involved in a broad cultural movement committed to the struggle against fascism.

From a purely cultural perspective, it is clear that developments in France were by no means a faithful reflection of cultural developments in the Soviet Union. The sectarian theses of Kharkov, although implemented by young communist intellectuals such as Aragon and Nizan, were nonetheless rejected by older party members such as Barbusse. Equally, the post-1934 popular front phase was a generally liberal phase of cultural development in French communist circles, unlike not only the RAPP experiment and the subsequent Zhdanovite policies in the Soviet Union, but also the Cold War communist cultural politics of post-1945 France.

All Nizan's major work was produced between 1927 and 1939, a historical moment of intense activity in the political and cultural spheres, when the French communist party progressed from sectarian isolationism to popular front collaboration. It would consequently seem appropriate to examine the extent of Nizan's personal involvement in cultural politics between 1927 and 1939, and to assess the nature of his wide-ranging cultural production within the context of the highly charged political and cultural atmosphere of this specific historical moment.

(ii) NIZAN'S CULTURAL PRODUCTION, 1927–39

Nobody in 1935 is capable of writing the sequel to the books of 1933. We are living at a time when everyone is forced to adopt a political position: one day it will become clear that 6 February 1934 marked a dividing point in literature as well as in politics.[6]

Nizan was convinced that February 1934 was a watershed not only in terms of cultural politics, but also in terms of cultural production. When he entered the party in 1927, his radical, iconoclastic temperament made it relatively easy for him to align his own cultural views with those of a sectarian political group. In 1934, during his visit to the Soviet Union, he was confronted by the urgent need to change tack and embrace a popular front collaborative approach. The evolution of Nizan's cultural politics and cultural production after 1934 is consequently the progressive attempt to redirect his originally sectarian cultural views along more accommodating lines.

Different political phases of development require different cultural responses. In 1930, at the height of the sectarian Barbé-Célor leadership, Nizan declared in a tone that was reminiscent of the cultural theses of Kharkov: 'Do not recommend the latest bourgeois treasures to the workers: if they take your advice, the confusion and failures of the bourgeoisie will become their confusion and their failures. . . . If a worker grows to like Picasso, he will be more easily corrupted than if he were to like Gozzoli.'[7]

By 1936, with the popular front, anti-fascist line now dominant, Nizan shifted the emphasis from sectarian revolutionary purity to a broad-based defence of culture from the tyranny of fascism:

> Berlin is burning the books that it fears. Moscow is re-editing and
> distributing the books of Dostoievsky. The bonfires of Berlin and
> the libraries of Moscow symbolise two worlds in opposition. The
> first is the world of terror and death; the second is referred to by
> Hitlerites from Germany and elsewhere as the world of barbarians.[8]

In purely practical terms, Nizan was fully involved in the cultural
politics of the period. This involvement testifies to a gradual shift of
emphasis from the sectarian to the collaborative. In 1931, in the
name of sectarian orthodoxy, Nizan challenged the heretical Barbusse, sought to wrest the editorial control of *Monde* from the hands
of this unrepentant 'right-wing deviationist', and came away the
loser. Two years later, in the aftermath of the Amsterdam Congress,
he was appointed secretary with Aragon of *Commune*, the monthly
publication of the AEAR, the Association of Revolutionary Writers
and Artists. Nizan's entry to the AEAR and his initial involvement
in *Commune*, coinciding as it did with Hitler's accession to power,
doubtless marked the beginning of a gradual transition to popular
front politics.

Following the change of party line in 1934, which occurred during
his stay in the Soviet Union, Nizan was entrusted with the task of
liaising with fellow-travelling intellectuals such as Malraux, Gide and
Bloch, who were attending the Soviet Writers Congress of that year.
One year later in July 1935, he delivered a major speech at the First
International Congress of Writers for the Defence of Culture,[9] and
also played a significant role in orchestrating the behind-the-scenes
collaboration between communist and non-communist contributors
to the congress itself. This liaison role included the very specific task
of entering into contact with the catholic community within the
framework of the PCF's 'outstretched hand' policy. In July 1936,
Nizan in the company of Vaillant Couturier and two catholic speakers,
Jacques Madaule and Louis Martin-Chauffier, participated in a
debate entitled 'Christianism and Communism', and in March 1937,
Nizan spelt out the nature and limits of possible co-operation between
catholics and communists in a review of *Catholicisme et communisme*
by the catholic writer Robert Honnert.[10] Finally, in July 1937, at the
height of the Spanish Civil War, Nizan attended the Second International Congress of Writers for the Defence of Culture held in the
beleaguered and bombarded city of Madrid.

Globally, therefore, Nizan's practical involvement in the cultural politics of the period faithfully reflected the developing cultural policy of the PCF. As a loyal party member, Nizan was prepared to follow a cultural itinerary which began in sectarian isolationism and ended in popular front co-operation. An early hostility to capitalist oppression and a refusal to contemplate co-operation with social democratic reformers was transformed in the space of a few years into a wide-ranging crusade against fascism in which geniune sympathisers of whatever creed were welcome participants. Nizan's extensive cultural production embracing fiction, drama, film, documentary, journalism, editing and translation work, reflects a similar development from the sectarian to the collaborative.

His early work, produced between 1930 and 1933, bears the stamp of sectarianism. Both *Aden Arabie* (1931) and *Les Chiens de garde* (1932), are manifestly products of the period. The three programmatic essays, 'Notes-programme sur la philosophie' (1930), an aggressive rejection of self-deluding, complacent idealist philosophy, 'Littérature révolutionnaire en France' (1932), an uncompromising literary manifesto combining a denunciation of capitalism, fascism and social democratic treachery with a rallying call for revolutionary literature committed to the cause of the proletariat, and 'Les Conséquences du refus' (1930), a withering attack on imperialist warmongering and bourgeois oppression culminating in a proclamation of faith in the French communist party and the revolutionary Soviet state, all three bear the imprint of an unequivocally sectarian frame of mind.

By contrast, his later work, produced between 1935 and 1939 bears the stamp of popular front co-operation. *Les Acharniens* (1937), *Visages de la France* (1937), and *Chronique de septembre* (1939), for example, are all products of this period. The programmatic essays 'L'Ennemi public numéro 1' (1935), a sustained defence of all those members of the French teaching profession persecuted by an oppressive bourgeois state for their involvement in the anti-fascist struggle,[11] and 'Sur l'humanisme' (1935), a declaration of faith in the humanist values shared only by those involved in the struggle against fascism, both bear the imprint of a co-operative, popular front frame of mind.

Each facet of Nizan's cultural production evidently needs to be contextualised *precisely*. Nizan's communist novels are no exception. Each of his three published novels, produced within a specific ideological and cultural context, can be consecutively designated as sectarian (*Antoine Bloyé*), transitional (*Le Cheval de Troie*), and popular frontist (*La Conspiration*), 1934 functioning as the line of demarcation.

Although in 1927 Nizan had remarked that 'neither in imaginary nor in real existence are there absolute beginnings or endings',[12] by 1935 he recognised the fact that political events in the real world occasionally ruptured the flow of history, realigned social and cultural practices, and necessitated a completely fresh start in the imaginary world of the novel. It is consequently vital, when assessing Nizan's communist novels, to bear in mind the importance that Nizan himself attached to the transition date of 1934. This significance is visible not only at the ideological and cultural level, but also at the economic and political level.

Nizan's membership of the PCF and his active life as a novelist between 1927 and 1940 coincided precisely with a period described by Lucien Goldmann as a moment of deep structural crisis in early twentieth-century capitalism.[13] In 1929, two years after Nizan's entry to the party, the Wall Street Crash was to signal the seriousness of the impending economic disaster.

In France, however, there seemed initially to be little concern in government circles at the economic recession abroad. The economic prosperity of the 1920s, and the docility of an increasingly impoverished labour movement, systematically ignored by successive governments since the end of the First World War, had created an all-pervading illusion of economic prosperity and political stability. Only in 1931, when the crisis became widespread, did alarm bells start to ring. In 1929 thoughts of economic stagnation and decline were simply pushed aside. Attention was focused instead on a witch-hunt of an isolated French communist party articulating working class demands but marginalised by dead-end sectarian politics. The arrest and imprisonment of Paul Vaillant-Couturier, for example, from July to September 1929 was symptomatic of the largely irrelevant policies of a reactionary government refusing to confront the reality of socio-economic developments.

By 1933, however, with unemployment rising and no solutions visible, public disapproval began to manifest itself in meetings, demonstrations, even strikes. The Amsterdam-Pleyel Movement of this period was just one sign among many of growing public discontent which was to lead eventually to the events of February 1934.

1934 is consequently a point of historical transition not only ideologically and culturally, but above all, politically and economically.

After 1934, against a background of economic recession and political polarisation, the social grievances of the French working class became clearly visible and could no longer be conveniently swept under the carpet.

Nizan's communist novels, produced within this global historical framework, may consequently be contextualised in the following manner:

(a) *Antoine Bloyé*, written between 1931 and 1933, was produced at a moment of sectarian cultural politics, a moment when the French communist party was just beginning to emerge from political isolationism, a moment when the French working class was just beginning to reassert itself.

(b) *Le Cheval de Troie*, written in 1934 and 1935, was produced at a moment of transition from sectarian to co-operative cultural politics, a moment when the Popular Front was born.

(c) *La Conspiration*, written in 1937 and 1938, was produced at a moment of co-operative cultural politics when the consequences of the Popular Front experiences in both France and Spain were to the fore.

The political, ideological and cultural context in which each novel was produced will be at the forefront of the textual analysis in Chapter 7. Before engaging in textual analysis, however, it is appropriate to examine the fundamental left-wing literary movement of the interwar period, socialist realism, and to assess the extent to which Nizan's ideas on revolutionary literature were influenced by socialist realist theory and practice.

6

Interwar Socialist Realism

Socialist realism has a bad press in the West. Even Marxist critics are generally dismissive. Eagleton, for example, describes socialist realism as 'one of the most devastating assaults on artistic culture ever witnessed in modern history', and refers to its principal Soviet advocate, Zhdanov, as 'Stalin's cultural thug'.[1] However, like all else, hostile value-judgements such as these assume significance only when placed within a clearly articulated historical context. The extremism of the antagonistic, Western, post-Stalinist critic is mirrored in the extremism of the sycophantic Stalinist party apparatchik. To make sense of these conflicting assessments of socialist realism, each phase of its development must be assessed with reference to the specific set of social determinants which shaped its emergence. This general methodological point needs to be made forcefully at the outset since assessments of socialist realism tend to be somewhat peremptory and superficial through lack of a clearly articulated *historical* and *theoretical* view of the subject itself. There is a recurrent failure not only to ground the subject fully in its historical context, but also to propose an adequate theoretical model by means of which to assess socialist realist literature. The result is a predictably idealistic criticism which at one level contents itself with rapid reference to formalistic definitions, and at another assesses the products of socialist realism with imprecise criteria culled generally from a liberal bourgeois critical tradition.

The starting point for any analysis must consequently be historical contextualisation of the national and international specificity of socialist realism, and elucidation of the criteria which are being used to assess the movement itself. The objective of this part of my analysis is therefore to provide a historical and theoretical overview of socialist realism with specific reference to the situation in interwar France, in order to establish a conceptual framework within which to place the work of Paul Nizan.

A preliminary statement on the historical development of French socialist realism is immediately appropriate to the extent that it reveals the very different nature of socialist realism in its different

87

historical manifestations, and as a consequence highlights the inadequacy of sweeping and inevitably facile value-judgements.

The political and cultural climate between 1927 and 1939 has already been discussed. What needs to be stressed at this juncture is the fact that this historical moment, the focus of attention in this book, centred as it is on the literary production of an interwar French communist writer, marks only the *first phase* of development of French socialist realism, a phase characterised in the international sphere by an objective alliance after 1934 between Western liberalism and Soviet communism designed to counter the threat of fascism, and characterised in the French national context by practical collaboration between the PCF and bourgeois liberal parties. The relative cultural 'liberalism' arising from this situation will be analysed more fully later.

This first phase (1934–9) is to be contrasted with a subsequent postwar phase (1945–56), corresponding almost exactly with the lifespan of the French Fourth Republic and characterised in contrast by the bitter and polarised struggle of the Cold War period, a moment of relentless anti-communism in the Western world, a moment of uncompromising Zhdanovism in the Soviet sphere, when the cultural production of the French communist party was envisaged exclusively as a legitimate and necessary line of defence against an increasingly hostile capitalist onslaught. This second phase (1945–56) must in turn be contrasted with the post-1956, post-Stalinist phase during which the credibility of the Zhdanov line was slowly but irreversibly undermined,[2] and the centre of gravity of Marxist cultural activity shifted away from orthodox socialist realism to a variety of experiments involving linkages between revolutionary politics and formalist experimentation at the level of imaginative writing, and between Marxist theory and innovations in the human sciences at the level of critical analysis.[3]

Eagleton's unqualified rejection of socialist realism evidently needs to be understood as a manifestation of post-Stalinist, liberal developments in Western Marxist theory. Retrospectively, socialist realism is being condemned on three counts: first, artistically, since the imposition of party dogma in the artistic field is viewed as creatively debilitating; secondly, theoretically, since the subordination of cultural theory and practice to current political expediency is viewed as methodologically crude and inadequate; thirdly, politically, since the exploitation of cultural activity to serve reprehensible Stalinist strategic objectives is viewed as morally unacceptable.

It is not within the scope of this book to offer a full account of the development of socialist realism in France,[4] yet the point that needs to emerge clearly at this stage is that contemporary hostile assessments are themselves a product of a post-Stalinist epoch reacting violently against the crude excesses of Cold War politics and cultural policy. Clearly, to contextualise ideological responses historically is not to neutralise the ideological responses themselves, but it is to take a significant step towards understanding more fully the issues involved.

The objectives in this section, therefore, are twofold: first, to present the initial phase of socialist realism (1934–9) as a product of a given historical experience and attempt in the process to elucidate the undoubted attraction that Soviet communism and socialist realism exerted on many French intellectuals of the time; secondly, to review the criticisms of socialist realism made both by supporters and opponents of the movement, not in order to *resolve* the highly problematical issues at stake, but in order rather to *highlight* the nexus of problems and difficulties associated with socialist realism and, very specifically, to draw up an agenda, both political and formal, for discussion when analysing Nizan's communist novels.

(i) PARTY ORTHODOXY AND DISSENTING VOICES

In 1935 Louis Aragon proudly proclaimed to the world that his encounter with communism and the revolutionary society of the Soviet Union had transformed him into an entirely new man, had rejuvenated him, re-educated him, and in the process cured him of the social disease of his bourgeois class origins.[5] He described this radical conversion as a movement from the darkness and despair of capitalism and surrealism to the light and hope of communism and socialist realism. The tone of Aragon's remarks needs to be noted. His words constitute a fervent expression of faith in a new creed, a new political and social system, a new kind of literature which together have a rejuvenating and energising capacity that stands in marked contrast to the corruption and dissolution of a decaying, moribund capitalist society.

Viewed from the perspective of the late-1980's, when archaic ideological attitudes and inflexible organisational structures have at one level unquestionably arrested the originally dynamic social development of the Soviet experiment, and at another level appear to have condemned the PCF to a peripheral status, if not imminent extinction, this seems strange. Yet in the 1930s the Soviet experiment, in the eyes of Western intellectuals, had a monopoly on health, vitality, youth and hope for the future. Admittedly, it needs to be borne in mind that Aragon's statements are doubtless slightly exaggerated expressions of feeling written for delivery as conference speeches.[6] Despite this caveat, however, the frequency with which images of health, construction and 'the growth of the new man'[7] in the Soviet Union are contrasted with images of sickness, decay and decline in the capitalist West is itself a telling statement on the intellectual climate of the time.

It is consequently essential in any preliminary comments on socialist realism to highlight the great hope and cause for optimism which the Soviet experiment symbolised to many Western intellectuals between 1927 and 1939. This point cannot be overstated in any attempt to understand the subjective mood of the interwar French left-wing writer. At home, the sombre and all-too-present reality of capitalism sinking deeper and deeper into crisis; on the horizon, the gleaming and distant image of communism constructing a new world, a new man, a new life. At home, oppression, degeneracy, the sickness of capitalism and its attendant cultural products; on the horizon, liberation, vitality, the health of communism and its attendant cultural processes.

This 'subjective' attraction of the Soviet experiment is nonetheless not based on a purely aesthetic stance. When Aragon asserts that he has become 'an entirely new man', he is not simply engaging in literary rhetoric, but referring quite explicitly to social and political events which have had a profound effect on his life-style. The implication is that he has not only been deeply disgusted by the political and social oppression in capitalist and colonial France,[8] but has also been fatally attracted to the entirely new set of social relations apparently emerging in the post-revolutionary situation in the Soviet Union.

It is doubtless this new set of social relations which constituted the main attraction of the Soviet experiment in the 1930s for intellectuals such as Aragon and Nizan. Unlike the capitalist social relations of interwar France in which the writer/intellectual was set apart from his/her real and potential reading public, a distant and alienated 'specialist', the new social relations of Soviet society appeared to provide the writer/intellectual with a pivotal role in social construction. 'Intellectuals are brothers on an equal footing with peasants and workers', notes Aragon. 'They have an established position. They speak with conviction. . . . They are the builders of socialism.'[9]

This subjective impression among left-wing intellectuals such as Aragon and Nizan that the Soviet experiment would in some way resolve the contradictions of the writer/intellectual ensnared in the alienating social relations of capitalism is a key factor in explaining its attractiveness for dissident French writers in the 1930s. The distinct possibility of comradeship, equality of status between intellectuals and manual workers in the construction of socialism undoubtedly seduced both Aragon and Nizan. Whether such equality materialised in practice, particularly in the French context, is entirely another matter. What is important to highlight at this juncture is the attraction that such a possibility held out for the intellectual workers of the time.

Compared to the extensive debate on socialist realism that took place in the Soviet Union in 1934, Aragon's sympathetic eulogising in 1935 was substantively limited. It amounted to a general statement of belief in socialist realism rather than a systematic attempt to offer a coherent theory relevant to the French context.[10] Detailed analysis is ignored in favour of a sustained defence of 'realism' in literature: 'I call for a return to reality', Aragon repeats six times in as many pages.[11] Predictably, it is precisely this expression of a 'return to reality' that Nizan himself takes up when assessing Aragon's text.[12] Both writers were concerned with the polemical task of contrasting a revolutionary view of literature as the revelation of reality with a reactionary view of literature as the masking of reality. The problematical task of theorising socialist realist practice was ignored by both.

Ironically, it may very well be that the potency of socialist realism is to be located precisely in this global strategy of revelation and disclosure rather than in any attempt to arrive at narrow prescriptive theories. Georg Lukács, doubtless the most sophisticated advocate of socialist realism, makes this point quite forcefully in his analysis of contemporary realism written in the aftermath of the Twentieth Congress of the Soviet Communist Party in 1956. Lukács is insistent that '*any* accurate account of reality', any form of realism, is ultimately a positive contribution to the progressive development of history. Only oppressive, reactionary and mystifying régimes, argues Lukács, aim at suppressing realism.[13] His assertion that postwar socialist realism has much to learn from the bourgeois tradition of critical realism marks paradoxically a return to the spirit of the intellectual climate in France in the 1930s when a general belief in the coincidence between the movement of history, socialism and realism led to a fruitful collaboration between the socialist realist writers of the French communist party, such as Aragon and Nizan, and sympathetic fellow-travellers such as Bloch, Malraux and Gide.

In order to gain a deeper insight into the emergence of socialist realism in interwar France, it is clearly necessary to examine the significance of the 1934 Soviet Writers' Congress during which the new literary ideology was officially consecrated.[14] 1934, as had already been emphasised, is a significant date for a number of reasons. First, because it marks the date on which Moscow officially adopted a policy of collaboration between national communist parties and bourgeois political parties in an effort to halt the rise of fascism. Secondly, because it marks the moment in French history when, following the 'February days', ideological positions crystallised around the themes of a fascist seizure of state versus a unified left-wing defence of democracy. Thirdly, because it marks the moment at which, following the initiative of the Amsterdam-Pleyel movement of 1932–3, cultural activity began to be officially organised around socio-political themes in Western democracies such as France. The Soviet Writers' Congress is consequently a symbol of the global politico-cultural developments of the time, a moment when cultural production was publicly recognised as a powerful weapon to combat an increasingly dangerous fascist threat.Interestingly, it has been argued that within the Soviet Union itself the key date in terms of the development of socialist realism was not 1934 but 1936, the moment at which Stalin finally acceded to full power, the moment of the Stalinist 'purges', the moment when the 'nationalist' theses of Zhdanov came to the fore, coinciding with Stalin's own preferred thesis of 'socialism in one country'.[15]

The progressively more inward-looking and doctrinaire views of Zhdanov which came to pre-eminence within the Soviet Union from 1936 onwards paradoxically encouraged in France the development of a communist 'national' literature not overtly preoccupied with Soviet orthodoxy. By a curious twist of fate, the prevailing socio-political conditions of the time were to give rise to a situation in which the French communist writer in the 1930s enjoyed relative freedom to give full artistic expression to the dominant themes of anti-fascism and anti-capitalism within a specifically French cultural context. This situation was fostered, on the one hand, by the lack of interest on the part of Moscow to export an increasingly nationalistic and doctrinaire literary theory designed primarily for strategic domestic purposes, and on the other, by the enormous interest on the part of Moscow to recruit as many prestigious fellow-travelling intellectuals to the ranks of the anti-fascist lobby as possible.[16] From the French perspective, therefore, 1934 marks a major turning-point.

Although, as has been argued already, the significance of the 1934 Congress is to be located in its general guiding principles rather than in specific theories, it is nonetheless worthwhile examining briefly the substance of the 1934 debate not only because it sets out the agenda for a detailed discussion of socialist realism, but also because Nizan's second novel, *Le Cheval de Troie*, was produced, for the most part in the Soviet Union during 1934 in the shadow of the Congress itself.

The key-note speeches at the Congress were delivered by Zhdanov, Gorky, Radek, Bukharin and Stetsky.[17] The speeches themselves vary in tone, subject-matter and substance. Zhdanov's contribution was predictably tendentious and hectoring. With hindsight, it is clear that Zhdanov's doctrinaire views were to become progressively dominant and reach their greatest influence during the Cold War period. However, it would be a false interpretation of the Congress to perceive it as totally dominated by the ideas of Zhdanov.[18] The ideological extremism of Zhdanov, echoed in the contributions of both Radek and Stetsky, was in fact quite explicitly challenged by Bukharin. This challenge needs to be noted at this juncture since the difference of emphasis between Zhdanov, Radek and Stetsky on the one hand, and Bukharin on the other, reflects a fundamental tension in Nizan's own literary theory and practice.

The issue at stake is the relationship between literature and ideology. In the eyes of Zhdanov and Radek, literature is to be judged above all by its ideological 'correctness', by the extent, in other words, to which it reveals the world in accordance with ideologically sound Marxist-Leninist principles. The formal or aesthetic qualities of literature are consequently subordinated to ideological ends and the writer is called upon exclusively to produce literature which mobilises the masses in the spirit of socialism. Whatever such a literature might lack in technical sophistication will, it is alleged, be more than compensated for by ideological exuberance.

For Bukharin, by contrast, to adopt such a view is to fail to grasp the full complexities of the process of literary production. Above all, it is to fail to distinguish between the *'ideological source* of content' and the 'artistic transformation of content'. It is to fail in other words, to understand that literature cannot simply be reduced to ideology, that literature has its own specificity, and that it consequently 'reflects' the social process in a highly complex and mediated form.[19]

This more sophisticated view of literary production is clearly at odds with the vulgar Marxist criticism of Zhdanov, Radek and Stetsky. Zhdanov, in particular, evidently did not share Bukharin's view that in 1934 the time was past when literary criticism should be a 'battering ram which smashed the enemy'.[20] For Zhdanov and company the socio-political climate was ripe for battering and smashing the ideological enemies of the Soviet Union with every available cultural and artistic weapon.

The contrast at the Congress between a vulgar and a relatively sophisticated aesthetic as exemplified in the difference of emphasis between Zhdanov and Bukharin is interesting to the degree that it has reverberations in the work of Nizan. As will be seen in the next section, Nizan's fundamentally manichean view of the world leads him to be fatally attracted to the hard-line sectarian views of Radek and Zhdanov at the theoretical level. There are many examples of polemical statements made by Nizan which deliberately simplify the process of literary production by stressing its unmediated ideological function. Nizan is always willing to oblige with the battering ram technique, if required. Yet, at the same time, in his literary practice, as will become apparent in the assessment of Nizan's novels, the more sophisticated, mediated aesthetic of Bukharin is more fully representative of Nizan's work. Nizan's novels are not faithful mirrors of ideological correctness, but rather refracted and distorted artistic representations of a complex socio-political context. They are, in short, a fusion of ideology and aesthetics in a constantly evolving revolutionary synthesis.

The preference for ideology over aesthetics, however, was a marked characteristic of the contributions of Zhdanov and Radek at the 1934 Congress, and it is clear, if only from the wording of the resolutions adopted,[21] that this approach generally carried the day. Zhdanov, for example, gave prominence to the ideological task of promoting socialist construction within Soviet society, a task that required the writer to transform him/herself into an 'engineer of the human soul', by infusing his/her writings with a spirit of 'revolutionary romanticism' originating in the teachings of Lenin and Stalin, and by adopting an explicitly 'tendentious', anti-bourgeois, anti-fascist stance.[22]

Radek was equally polemical and uncompromising,[23] although he broadened the debate to include the international scene. 'Since literature is a reflection of social life', he argued, 'the standard by which it should be gauged is precisely the attitude which it takes to such great facts of historical development as the war, the October Revolution and fascism.'[24] Choosing quite deliberately to envisage literature as a 'cog and a screw' in an ideological crusade against the combined forces of capitalism, colonialism and fascism, Radek reviewed and assessed foreign literatures in terms of their responses to the major historical events of the early twentieth century. Bourgeois literature was unequivocally condemned on three counts: first, for its failure to voice opposition to the First World War, a failure in other words to disclose the true reality of the war as an imperialist struggle; secondly, for its refusal to offer an accurate depiction of the Soviet revolution, a failure explained as the cowardly refusal of the bourgeois writer to disclose the deepening crisis of capitalism after 1929, a crisis highlighted by the success of the five year plan in the Soviet Union; finally, for its refusal to face up to the growing threat of fascism.[25]

When Radek divided world literature into three camps, 'the literature of decaying capitalism, inevitably evolving towards fascism, the new proletarian literature, and the literature of the wavering elements',[26] he merely underlined the extent to which cultural activity in the 1930s had become subordinated to ideological objectives. Radek's exhortation to the 'wavering elements' of bourgeois literature to join the ranks of the proletarian cause and combat the fascist threat was couched in political and ideological terms. Aragon's response to this exhortation, as has already been noted, was similarly formulated in ethical, emotional and political terms as a conversion to ideological health. Clearly the aesthetic and technical problems of literary production had been conveniently neglected and subsumed within a strategically advantageous ideological reference system.

Consequently, despite the efforts of Bukharin to argue a case for an 'integral science of literature' which would include a recognition of formal specificity within a socio-political and ideological context, the general thrust of the Congress was towards obliterating formal aspects and locating the debate at a purely ideological level. The result of this preponderance of the ideological in the literary debate was that discussion tended to centre exclusively on recurrent programmatic themes – positive heroes, revolutionary romanticism, partisanship, tendentiousness, and so on – in which were sown the seeds of a sterile, bureaucratic and immobile aesthetic theory unable to adapt to changing socio-political conditions, capable only of mouthing the current party line.

This general theoretical problem of the complex relationship between literature, ideology and history, is articulated in Georg Lukács's work on literary realism. Lukács's more sophisticated Marxist view of the dialectical interaction between the ideological source of literary content and the artistic transformation of this ideological source during the process of literary production echoes the general views on cultural activity outlined by Bukharin at the 1934 Congress. It is worthwhile briefly examining Lukács's ideas on socialist realism at this juncture since they not only provide a constructive critical alternative to the mindless ideological stance adopted by Zhdanov, Radek and Stetsky, but also broaden the global conceptual framework within which to examine Nizan's communist novels.[27]

In 1965, Lukács retrospectively described his critical essays as the 'two-front' struggle which constituted 'an indictment of the impoverishment in artistic content and in fictional representation both in Western avant-garde movements and what is customarily called socialist realism'.[28] There was nothing new in Lukacs's total opposition to what he contemptuously referred to as the decadent and sick art of modernism. His criticisms were aimed at portraying an excessive modernist preoccupation with formal innovation as the artistic accompaniment to a fundamentally misguided and despairing ideological stance, itself the product of the solitary and consequently socially blind existence of the contemporary bourgeois writer.[29] Lukács's rejection of Joyce, for example, is hardly less categorical than Radek's critical assassination of the luckless Irish novelist in 1934.

What was new, and what is of interest in this context, was his fundamental critical reappraisal of socialist realism. By starting from the premise that the historical moment had arrived to sweep away not only the nihilistic, *angst*-ridden literature of modernism but also the crass simplicity of Stalinist socialist realism, Lukács envisaged the possibility of a beneficial mutual interaction between bourgeois critical realism and a rejuvenated socialist realism. Paradoxically, Lukács's comments at the theoretical level mark a return to the collaborative possibilities that were available at a practical level in

France during the 1930s. 'Today, critical and socialist realism are at one in their struggle against reactionary forces in politics and art', he notes.[30]

Underlying all Lukács's comments on the nature of literary realism, whether bourgeois or socialist, is the necessary transposition on to the literary plane of the rich complexity of existence in its progressive and dynamic historical movement. What is inadmissible in Lukács's eyes is any impoverishment of this historical complexity. He is critical not only of what he views as the aesthetic escapism of modernism, but also of the crude and facile schematisation of Stalinist socialist realism. It goes without saying that Lukács's approach is itself problematical. Based as it is on 'literary standards' culled from the nineteenth-century realist tradition, it does not envisage the possibility of 'reflecting' the complexity of the historical process in anything other than relatively conventional and traditional formal terms. The possibility that a new, revolutionary technique might be required to portray the multi-faceted processes of historical change is implicitly denied in Lukács's system. Nonetheless, the significance of Lukács's theory is that even in a post-Stalinist epoch it presents socialist realism as rich in possibilities.

These rich possibilities, as ever, are founded on the material existence of socialism, the guiding ideological perspective of the socialist realist writer. Significantly, for Lukács, it is precisely the material situation of the writer in relation to socialism that sets the socialist realist apart from the bourgeois critical realist. Whereas the authentic socialist realist writer, by virtue of his/her ideological position, is able to 'describe the forces working towards socialism *from the inside*',[31] the critical realist, although potentially capable in Lukacs's terms of 'grasping the new realities of the old order and of the old consciousness in their actual novelty and not as elements of disintegration of decay',[32] cannot ultimately accede to a socialist revelation of the world, trammelled as he/she is by vestiges of bourgeois ideology.

This is evidently a fascinating line of enquiry with which to approach Nizan's communist novels. Nizan's class status, as has already been pointed out, is ambiguous. His cultural education was a process of bourgeois ideological indoctrination, yet his adult allegiance to socialism remained constant even after his departure from the PCF. The extent to which Nizan depicts in his novels the forces working towards socialism *from the inside* is consequently an intriguing problem which can only be resolved by detailed analysis of the texts within the context of their specific moments of production and reproduction.

To dwell on the *potential* of socialist realism as a revolutionary literary theory is an instructive experience since it is all too easy to dismiss it out of hand as a crude and dogmatic Stalinist aberration. Nonetheless, hostility to socialist realism runs deep and it would seem appropriate and productive at this stage to examine briefly the more critical views of the practice of Stalinist socialist realism articulated quite dramatically by Georg Lukács himself, in order to draw up another set of criteria by which to assess Nizan's communist novels.

The main thrust of Lukács's criticism is that the rich potentiality of socialist realism degenerated for the most part into what he terms the 'anaemia of socialist naturalism' because its practitioners deliberately chose to substitute the profundity of Marx's original dialectical understanding of reality for the banality and facility of Stalinist 'economic subjectivism', the inevitable consequence of the Stalinist personality cult. Throughout Lukács's analysis there occurs as a leitmotiv this underlying contrast between a correct understanding of objective reality synonymous with an authentic Marxist tradition and consequently synonymous with successful socialist realism, and a superficial and subjective view of reality synonymous with the Stalinist corruption of authentic Marxism, and consequently synonymous with socialist naturalism.

More specifically, Lukács shows himself to be extremely hostile to a number of key concepts on the socialist realist agenda precisely because they are symptomatic of an excessively subjectivist and false, because partial, view of reality. The propagandist view of literature, literature as illustration, tendentiousness, are denounced on the grounds that the desire to illustrate one particular ideological viewpoint at the expense of all else, has disastrous consequences at the artistic level since such an approach is at odds with any attempt to display the inherent contradictions and complexities within a given historical situation; indeed, the case is quite the reverse: it actually masks such contradictions. Revolutionary romanticism is severely censured by Lukács for the same reason. The arbitrary introduction into the cultural sphere of what Lukács describes as a 'schematic optimism' simplifies and hence falsifies the contradictory reality of the concrete historical situation. By the same token, positive heroes are also regarded with scepticism by Lukács. Far from being typical in the Lukácsian sense of synthesising the decisive problems of a particular epoch, they degenerate to the level of the 'topical', a fictional means of supplying appropriate, ideologically correct solutions to current political problems.[33] Globally, Lukács's retrospective indictment of the glaring inadequacies of Stalinist socialist realism is conducted in the name of a return to genuine realism. It amounts, in short, to a rejection of the unmediated, dogmatic view of literature as preached by Stalin, Zhdanov, Radek and Stetsky in 1934, the implication of which is that the task of literature is primarily to serve immediate propagandist ends, and the adoption of a more sensitive cultural perspective which distances literature from ideology, grants greater specificity to literary production, and in the process provides a richer, more complex and refracted view of social reality.

It is ironic that this dual aspiration, on the one hand, to give back autonomy to the socialist writer to produce works which balance the twin exigencies of socialist ideology and literary form, and on the other, to generate *as a consequence* a fuller, richer, more complex depiction of reality, marks, in fact, a return to the spirit of Nizan's understanding of socialist realism in France in the 1930s.

Lukács's adumbration of the problems facing the socialist realist writer, his examination of three tendencies within realism – bourgeois critical realism, socialist realism as a theoretical potentiality, and socialist realism as a Stalinist corruption (socialist naturalism) – set the agenda for an analysis of Nizan's work. Before examining the practice of Nizan's creative writing in detail, however, it is appropriate to elucidate the general theoretical approach informing this practice, the manner, in short, in which Nizan responded to the general debate on socialist realism when formulating his own highly individual theory of revolutionary literature.

(ii) NIZAN'S REVOLUTIONARY LITERATURE

All literature is propaganda. Bourgeois propaganda is idealist. It masks its true intentions, it conceals the objectives that it secretly pursues: these objectives cannot be disclosed. Revolutionary propaganda is aware that it is propaganda. It publicises its objectives frankly and honestly. These views will shock bourgeois critics who proclaim that propaganda does not have any artistic value, and that it is self-evident that Art should be impartial. This crude critical ploy is derisory. These lackeys of bourgeois criticism can yap in vain. For us art is what makes propaganda effective.[34]

With these words Nizan set out in 1932 his fundamental views on literary production. They are particularly sectarian, uncompromising and seemingly unsophisticated; all good Stalinist stuff. The world is divided into two camps, two classes. Literature is viewed primarily as an ideological process, either implicit or explicit, depending on its reactionary or revolutionary objectives. Art becomes a 'cog and a screw' in the process of mobilising the masses in the spirit of socialism.

And yet, Nizan's cultural theory is deceptively simplistic. It needs to be borne in mind initially that the ideas expressed in this statement of 1932 reflect the sectarian cultural views prevalent in communist circles following the 1930 Kharkov RAPP Congress, and prior to the 1934 Soviet Writers' Congress.

Equally, as will become apparent in the ensuing analysis, Nizan's willingness to link literature and propaganda does not originate in a philistine effort to destroy culture but, on the contrary, in an attempt to show that literature, ideology and politics are intimately interconnected, and that the task of the revolutionary writer is to seek out artistically convincing ways of fusing revolutionary ideology within the matrix of literature. The mere fact that Nizan, in an important article on Chamson published in 1935, chose to give prominence to the contribution of Bukharin at the 1934 Congress is symptomatic of the fact that an acceptance of the ideological function of literature does not signal in Nizan's eyes the complete abandonment of art to the demands of ideology.[35] The specificity of literature, as Bukharin resolutely argued at the 1934 Congress, must be retained if the ideological effect of literature is itself not to be rendered impotent.

There can be little doubt that Nizan was profoundly affected by the 1934 Soviet Writers' Congress. It clearly represented for him a literary turning-point since it not only swept aside all mystifying attempts to separate the literary activity from the contemporary socio-political context, but also injected a coherent set of political arguments squarely into the literary debate: anti-fascism, anti-colonialism, anti-capitalism, arguments that were beginning to find much grass-roots and intellectual support in France.

It would be totally incorrect, however, to view Nizan's literary production at this time as a passive reflection of the Soviet socialist realism outlined in the 1934 Congress. The development of Nizan's literary and cultural outlook was the result of something far more complex: the fusion of a highly idiosyncratic metaphysical view of the world, a wide-ranging and sophisticated cultural education, and a radical social and political viewpoint. It is significant, for example, that Nizan does not refer to his literature as 'socialist realist', but rather as 'revolutionary'. This difference in description is not merely a stylistic quibble. It is a visible sign of Nizan's recognition that abstract literary theories can at most act as general guidelines for the creative writer, and that the cultural specificity of the French national context cannot be obliterated beneath a hegemonic Soviet model.

Ironically, Nizan's first published novel, *Antoine Bloyé*, was the first French text to be officially consecrated with the title 'socialist realist',[36] yet unlike Aragon who explicitly aligned his literature in the camp of socialist realism, Nizan was more equivocal about his work. Although his praise of socialist realism as a theory, Soviet socialist realist writers, and Aragon's 'socialist realist' novels was quite genuine,[37] Nizan was convinced in his own mind that his task as a writer was to produce 'revolutionary' literature. Such a literature doubtless resembled Soviet socialist realism in its general principles, but was nevertheless different in the final analysis because framed within a specifically French cultural context. Nizan evidently judged 'socialist realism' to be the appropriate literary theory for post-revolutionary Soviet society, and 'revolutionary literature' to be the appropriate literary theory for pre-revolutionary French society.

To understand the full significance of Nizan's communist novels, it is consequently necessary to elucidate the precise nature of Nizan's theory of revolutionary literature. The global 'problematic' would appear to be located at three levels: (a) cultural, (b) meta-physical/political, (c) technical.

Cultural Divisions

Cultural activity for Nizan is a manifestation of class conflict. There is no room for obfuscation in Nizan's system. Cultural products reflect in a mediated form the aspirations and interests of specific classes. However complex and sophisticated the process of mediation, however differentiated and fluctuating the reality of class stratification, Nizan is ultimately unequivocal on this particular point. All culture is inevitably affiliated to one of two fundamental classes: bourgeoisie or proletariat.

Nizan's literary and political activities are in many ways best understood as a contribution to what he would doubtless have designated as a 'cultural revolution'. In a review of Jean-Richard Bloch's essay, *Naissance d'une culture*, Nizan refers to the issue of the 'legacy of cultures and the invention of a new culture' as the major problem confronting the contemporary writer, intellectual, artist.[38] Nizan signals his agreement with Bloch that bourgeois humanist and individualist culture, optimistic, progressive and outward-looking in its origins, degenerated during the latter part of the nineteenth century into a solitary, self-preoccupied and defensively reactionary activity. The early part of the twentieth century is consequently perceived as an opportune moment for what Nizan describes as a 'renaissance of both man and culture'.[39]

In truly Sartrean terms, Nizan concludes that for the contemporary revolutionary writer the central dilemma is located in the problematical relationship between writer and reading public. Given that revolutionary literature is designed to give pre-eminence to the construction of a new culture, a new man, a new reading public, drawn primarily from the working class, there arises an obvious clash of interests between the revolutionary writer and the bourgeois reading public. This clash of interests, this conflict of class expectations is the bedrock of Nizan's literary theories and results in a series of clearly articulated cultural divisions.

Nizan's theory of revolutionary literature is based on a rejection of what he globally designates as 'classicism'. Classical periods of literature are judged severely since they represent a moment of complacent self-satisfaction in which the movement of history is artificially suspended, in which social formations and institutions appear to have a permanent position in a fixed, hierarchical structure. The illusion of permanence and stability fostered during classical periods frequently leads the writer/intellectual astray, tempting him/her to engage in narcissistic and uncritical self-contemplation rather than engaging in social and political debate.

For Nizan the originality of the contemporary period, however, is that history has violently entered the arena and fractured the classical mould. The non-reflective, naturally ordained existence of the classical period has been ruptured. Classicism is now forced to defend itself against the onslaught of a disruptive non-classical culture with the result that the contemporary cultural sphere has polarised into two competing ideological positions which, for the sake of clarity, have been tabulated in Table 6.1.

The cultural divisions displayed in Table 6.1 are presented by Nizan in class terms. Those writers collaborating with the bourgeoisie,

TABLE 6.1   Classical and new culture

Classical culture	New culture
bourgeoisie	proletariat
idealism	Marxism
myth	reality
resistance	movement
irresponsibility	responsibility
deception	disclosure
symbolism	realism
polite literature	disquieting literature

intent on defending a 'classical' position, produce an *irresponsible* literature of *resistance* to change which in a variety of forms seeks to mask the reality of existence. Classical literature is systematically castigated by Nizan as a process of *deception* centred on *myth-making*, *idealism* and *symbolism*, and designed to defend the oppressive practices of a dying class. In contrast, those writers allied with the working class, committed to a 'non-classical' position, produce a *responsible* literature of *movement* which in a variety of forms seeks to foreground the reality of existence. Progressive literature is consistently upheld by Nizan as a process of *disclosure* centred on *reality*, *Marxism* and *realism*, and designed to advocate the justifiable demands of an aspiring class.

Classical literature is a *polite literature* luxuriating in endless prevarication and self-indulgence. Non-classical literature is an unpleasant, *disquieting literature* which refuses to allow the sophisms of bourgeois complacency to go unchallenged.

This theoretical division into two cultures is graphically illustrated by Nizan in his practical criticism of other writers. The polite, complacent literature of fully integrated bourgeois writers such as Andre' Maurois,[40] Jacques de Lacretelle[41] and Julien Green[42] is unceremoniously attacked, as is the work of Jean Giono classified by Nizan as a naïve form of utopian escapism in the face of modern industrial society.[43] Equally, Nizan is extremely hostile to the sentimental, colonial and populist literature produced by the bourgeoisie for the mystification of the proletariat.[44] In particular, P. Souvestre and M. Allain are virulently denounced for producing pernicious detective stories in which the fight against crime is insidiously transformed in the reader's mind into the struggle against the revolution.[45]

In contrast, the disquieting literature of more dissident bourgeois intellectuals/writers such as André Malraux,[46] Louis Aragon[47] and Elsa Triolet[48] is unreservedly praised, and a sympathetic account is given of the cultural activity of working-class writers such as Georgette Guéguen-Dreyfus,[49] Eugène Dabit[50] and André Philippe.[51] Equally, Nizan is favourably impressed by the violent and erotic literature of Erskine Caldwell[52] and John Steinbeck,[53] and the realistically descriptive power of Charles Dickens.[54]

The example of Dickens is instructive. Nizan notes:

> Perhaps if you are squeamish, you cannot appreciate this world where the good guys are ruthlessly divided from the bad guys, this world of Good and Evil, this Dickensian liking for the triumph of the good guys. I am fond of this manichean world. The world is like that.[55]

This preference for an explicitly manichean vision of the world which Nizan retained throughout his life is symptomatic of the fundamental divisions which permeate all his thinking on cultural activity. In Nizan's eyes the world was essentially divided into Good and Evil: those working for the forces of Good who produced revolutionary, disquieting literature; those working for the forces of Evil who produced reactionary, politely complacent literature. Although occasionally Nizan's assessment of a writer fluctuated over a period of time (Gide, Giono, Mauriac),[56] although on occasions Nizan was simultaneously attracted and repelled by individual writers (Mauriac, Drieu la Rochelle, Céline),[57] the bottom line was always a clear differentiation between a progressive and a reactionary attitude to culture. Indeed, as has already been highlighted in the previous discussion of cultural politics, the opposition between progressive and reactionary forces became so marked with the rise of fascism that it was less a question of reactionary versus progressive culture, than a struggle for the very existence of culture itself. The issue became a naked choice between the destruction or the defence of culture, and the intellectual/writer was called upon to defend culture against the barbaric and destructive philistinism of fascism. In cultural matters in the 1930s, as in all else, there was a choice to be made between Good and Evil. The world was like that.

Metaphysical and Political Perspectives

'Revolutionary literature is the modern form of tragedy',[58] wrote Nizan in 1936. The originality of Nizan's entire literary output resides in this particular assertion since it brings together the two dominant strands that coexist tensely in Nizan's intellectual and emotional outlook: (i) a brooding sense of anguish and desperation stemming from the gross injustices and inequalities in the world, and (ii) an explosive, irrepressible determination to enter into the struggle and combat the forces of oppression in order to gain access to a better life. The political response is the necessary and inevitable accompaniment to the metaphysical dilemma. A world of unequal chances dominated by the values and institutions of a hated class is a world in decomposition, a world of death. Escape into the world of the living is possible only by means of the purifying process of politics, the struggle, class conflict, designed to transform a dead world into a world of the living.

This intimate connection between the metaphysics of death and the politics of life is precisely what Nizan has in mind when he refers to revolutionary literature as 'the modern form of tragedy'. The world is tragic because men and women are compelled to struggle against the oppressive, deathly forces of their social condition in order to accede to the world of the living. The only difference between ancient Greek tragedy and modern revolutionary tragedy is that in the former the struggle was against a distant, unknowable, divine power, whereas in the latter the struggle is against an all-too-present social order manufacturing poverty, disease, unemployment and war.

The task of the revolutionary writer is therefore complex. He/she must not only offer an accurate description of the death-like oppressiveness of the capitalist world as it is developing in the first half of the twentieth century, but must also depict accurately and without facile romanticism or glib sentimentality, the angry and determined political struggle of men and women refusing to acquiesce to the oppressive forces of capitalist society. Such a picture is of necessity tragic, and this 'tragic' dialectical interaction between the objective social forces crushing men and women in their everyday lives, and the dynamic subjective response of those same men and women refusing to be crushed, has as its counterpart a 'tragic' dialectical interaction between revolutionary writer and oppressed reading public.

The novelist must not be a party to the bad habits of the reader. What appears to me to be essential both for the reader and for the novelist who together constitute a couple – and a couple always comprises two accomplices – is to guide complicity along a most exacting path. The real function of the reader is to be committed to learning how to live, and consequently to consider the novel, and literature in general, not as entertainment, but as a *means of raising consciousness*.[59]   [My italics]

Nizan was evidently committed to the idea of literature as a high moral adventure played out between reader and writer. Facile complicity with the reader is rejected in favour of a quite rigorous and demanding process of consciousness-raising, in which the legitimate social demands of an oppressed readership catalyse the revolutionary writer into becoming a stern and uncompromising task-master goading the reader into political action.

At one level, Nizan accepts that contemporary readers are easily misled, seduced by their baser instincts, and would readily turn their gaze away from the bitter reality of the socio-political situation, preferring instead to read the escapist, polite literature manufactured by the bourgeoisie for their mystification. 'Readers generally have very bad habits', Nizan remarks.[60] And yet, and this is crucial, Nizan does not equate a tendency towards evasion and self-indulgence with intellectual inadequacy or critical deficiency. 'Nobody is as simple-minded as edifying literature assumes', he asserts.[61]

This is the context within which the 'tragic' dialectical interaction between writer and reader takes place. The target of the revolutionary writer's attentions is a reading public readily and willingly collaborating in its own mystifications, yet retaining at heart a desire for cultural enlightenment and refusing adamantly to be patronised or taken in by glib and misguided preaching. This interaction between writer and reader is legitimately described as tragic insofar as literature becomes the site in which the reader is confronted by the tragedy of his/her social condition. The sophisms and mystifications of an oppressive class are dispelled, social injustices and inequalities are exposed, and an appeal to enter directly into the tragic political struggle is implicitly issued.

It is in this sense that Nizan's revolutionary literature demands a great deal from the reader. The stakes are not simply two alternative *literary* styles, one escapist, one realist, but rather two alternative *life* styles in which the death and oppression of one class are contrasted with the life and liberation of another. Literature for Nizan is a mirror reflecting an alternative way of living. More broadly, culture is a truly *critical* activity designed to awaken forcibly a self-indulgent and unreflective, though fundamentally astute, contemporary reader and drive him/her into the struggle for a better life.

Technical Problems

As a revolutionary writer Nizan was confronted by what he perceived as a series of particularly acute technical problems which had their origin in the specific historical situation of post-First World War France. Unlike the realist novelists of the nineteenth century, writers such as Balzac, Stendhal, Flaubert and Zola, who were called upon to depict individuals and social groups operating within a relatively stable, homogeneous society, the contemporary realist writer was required to portray a society in a state of turbulence, transformation and fundamental realignment. Between 1820 and 1870 there occurred a rare moment of historical calm, Nizan argues, during which French economic, social and political structures stabilised. Only towards the end of the Second Empire, when the increasing pace of modern capitalism accelerated the decline of the old economic infrastructure, did the serene and apparently permanent reality of the bourgeois political and social order begin to show signs of crumbling. The writer's task in such a historical context was relatively unproblematical.

In sharp contrast, the turmoil and violent historical changes occurring in post-1914 France constituted a major problem as well as a major opportunity for the revolutionary writer. The opportunity is self-evident. Moments of structural crisis in a nation state are harbingers of revolution and inevitably give rise to the necessary social and political climate for the production of revolutionary literature. The problem is less obvious but deep-rooted, and can perhaps be most clearly formulated in the following question: Given the turbulent and unstable historical context of post-1914 France, is it possible to produce novels which are technically and artistically successful, politically effective, and accurately reflect contemporary social reality? Nizan himself expressed it more simply: 'The major problems consist in infusing art with the spirit of revolution without destroying art in the process.'[62]

When Nizan highlights the technically advantageous position of the writer who portrays a society of *stability*, and at the same time stresses the desirability and the necessity for the contemporary writer to engage fully in a portrayal of the political *instability* of post-1914 French society in its turbulent actuality, he locates with unerring precision the revolutionary writer's primary dilemma. This dilemma is given prominence in the distinction that Nizan draws between 'balance-sheet novels' ('*romans-bilan*'), which take stock of a finalised historical period, and 'problem-centred novels' ('*romans-problème*') which focus on contemporary issues.

From the perspective of the 1930s, the historical period prior to 1914 is 'closed', its actuality and unpredictability are no more. The secrets of the period, hidden and unknowable at the time, have been revealed in the historical conclusion of 1914. To write a novel in the 1930s depicting French society prior to 1914 is consequently to write a 'balance-sheet novel'. In Nizan's eyes this is to play safe.[63]

The revolutionary writer, by contrast, is a risk-taker. He/she must opt to write 'problem novels', novels which focus attention on the fluctuating, open-ended development of contemporary post-1914 French society and attempt to probe the secrets of historical development in its unfolding. The highly problematical nature of such an option finds its clearest expression in the dilemma of characterisation, type-casting in the novel. 'Since 1914', notes Nizan, 'the whole of life is in the public domain . . . nobody can escape from the world any longer. Private life is no longer possible.'[64] This sudden explosion of the public into the private domain after 1914, the inevitable result of profound structural changes in French society set in motion in the late nineteenth century, not only exploded the myth of an unchanging, clearly delineated set of social actors operating in a stable social environment, but also undermined the credibility of any attempt to separate the social from the psychological in the portrayal of individual characters.

Whereas the relative cohesion and stability of French economic, social and political structures between 1820 and 1870 produced a clearly recognisable type of French bourgeois representative of a specific class, the natural hero of the literary adventures of the period, no clearly discernible types existed after 1914. The situation had become so fluid, social mobility had become so pronounced, class stratification so complex and ramified, that no natural successor to the pre-1870 bourgeois 'type' had emerged. 'Social types rise up and die within the space of a few years, or a few months', declared Nizan.[65]

The conclusion that Nizan draws from this is the need to displace the focus of attention in the novel away from an outdated preoccupation with individual psychology and to direct the reader's attention to the complex interaction between the public and the private spheres, to focus in short on the tragic destiny that links the individual to his social group and his social environment.[66] Special attention, in other words, was to be paid to the political and social dimension of human existence.

A further consequence of the displacement of the centre of gravity of the novel is a loss of complicity between author and fictional characters. In his critical review of *La Conspiration* in 1938, Sartre described this lack of empathy between Nizan and the characters portrayed in his novel as a fundamental failing symptomatic of the impossibility of reconciling communist ideology with the artistic demands of the novel. Nizan, in short, was accused by Sartre of treating his characters as mere ciphers of a particular class.[67]

The preceding analysis illustrates the extent to which such a proposition is misguided. It does no more than demonstrate the fact that Sartre was assessing Nizan's revolutionary novels via his own specifically existentialist vision of the novelist's task. In 1938 Sartre, who by his own admission was still mystified to the core by bourgeois idealist presuppositions, would have had little sympathy for theories linking the technical structure of the novel to the historical reality of contemporary French society. Nizan's refusal to empathise fully with his fictional characters was consequently envisaged not as part of a global stategy to adapt the novel to the demands of contemporary social experience, but rather as the ideological inability of a communist novelist to engage in a complicity judged by Sartre to be a fundamental aspect of the novelist's art.

However, it should be clear that Nizan's refusal of complicity with his fictional characters is the result of a quite deliberate choice of narrative technique. Authorial complicity with fictional characters undoubtedly implicates the reader more directly in subjective experience, but frequently at the expense of a global critical understanding of the socio-political problems in which the characters themselves are enmeshed. Critical distance between author and characters, by contrast, creates a climate of greater objectivity and encourages the reader to analyse the political and social consequences of the characters' actions. Nizan's ironic, chiding tone must ultimately be understood as a facet of a global strategy to compel the reader to greater self-awareness.

It is in fact the reading contract, the explicit relationship between writer and reader that is at the heart of the technical problems experienced by Nizan as a revolutionary novelist. The style, tone and content of Nizan's literature are ultimately explained as much by his understanding of the complex links between reader, writer and text as they are by his commitment to the ideological function of literature itself.

Nizan's itinerary as a revolutionary writer is the record of a ceaseless interrogation on the problematical link between the ideological objective of literature as the site of political consciousness-raising in the here and now, and the aesthetic objective of literature as the site of universal and lasting values.[68] It might appear that these two objectives are mutually incompatible, and simply betray a naïve confusion in Nizan's mind between the ideological and the aesthetic. Yet Nizan is insistent that ideology and aesthetics are not necessarily mutually exclusive provided that the problem of their unification is viewed dialectically: that is to say, provided that literature is not perceived as a static object but the site of a dialectical process involving writer and reader in a moral and political adventure.

The reader's consciousness, in short, is the arena in which aesthetic and ideological success or failure is ultimately determined. Success of the literary process becomes a measure of the balance achieved between artistic techniques and ideological functions. If the balance is upset, the work inevitably degenerates into either aesthetic mystification or ideological propaganda. If the balance is maintained, the result is a revolutionary literature in which aesthetics mobilises ideology and ideology motivates aesthetics. And throughout the arbiter of success or failure is the reader:

> The quality of a work of art, that is to say the maximum level of effectiveness of a work of art, resides in the precision of the means employed to achieve the most profound results, to release the hidden resources locked away in the depths of the reader's psyche. Since the maximum level of effectiveness is linked to the maximum level of revelation, the reader will adhere to the work of art to the degree that he gains in awareness what he loses in complacency.[69]

The more effective the narrative technique, the more effective the ideological result. In Nizan's system, ideology does not stand in confrontation to aesthetics. A sophisticated and complex narrative technique is the necessary accompaniment to ideological success. A skilful narrative technique, in other words, is the only means of releasing the hidden capabilities locked away in the inner recesses of the reader's consciousness. A crude or facile narrative technique will inevitably fail to achieve the desired ideological objective.

In 1932 Nizan proclaimed that 'all literature was propaganda'. Maybe so, but there is good and bad, effective and ineffective propaganda, and, as Nizan himself was acutely aware, the technical problems associated with injecting ideology and politics into literature were so enormous that only the most adroit, the most cunning of revolutionary writers would be successful in creating an effective balance between ideological effect and aesthetic technique. 'The trick', notes Nizan 'consists in inviting the reader to reach conclusions that have not been explicitly stated. Another name for this trick is art.'[70]

Nizan's general conception of revolutionary literature is consequently far less dogmatic, crude and sectarian than his more polemical statements would seem to imply. At the heart of the entire enterprise is a dual ambition; on the one hand, to deliver literary production from the irresponsibility of an idealistic aestheticism by injecting a clearly articulated communist viewpoint into the literary process; on the other, to ensure both the effectiveness of the ideological viewpoint itself and the universal quality of the work produced, by maintaining a fine balance between ideological ends and artistic means.

Two names recur as a leitmotiv throughout Nizan's critical writings: *Lenin* and *Dostoievsky*. These two figures, one political, one literary, symbolise the two fundamental strands in Nizan's emotional and intellectual outlook, and together represent a politico-literary ideal to which Nizan ceaselessly aspires as a communist novelist. The great novelist, in Nizan's eyes, should be an 'anti-Dostoievsky',[71] that is to say, a writer who can at one level emulate Dostoievsky's ability to transpose on to the literary plane the anguish and despair of men and women struggling alone and unaided in the midst of a tragic social situation, and yet who can at another level go beyond Dostoievsky, offer a coherent explanation of the specific historical situation in which men and women are trapped, and focus attention at the same time on the political means of combating the injustices of their social condition.

Lenin provides Nizan with the political solutions absent in the work of Dostoievsky. The great revolutionary writer must retain the sophisticated *literary* qualities of Dostoievsky, whilst acceding to the clear-sighted *political* qualities of Lenin. The literary production of

the revolutionary novelist must in other words be underwritten by
the historical awareness of the political revolutionary:

> The novelist should possess qualities that are similar to those of a
> great statesman. A great politician is a man who does not interpret
> the world in which he intends to act on the basis of appearances.
> . . . he is a man who is capable at all times of making sense of the
> various motive forces which combine to produce historical events,
> and which when analysed provide a perspective on the future.
> The greatest example of such a statesman was undoubtedly
> Lenin. The greatest novelist will be the person who is capable of
> basing the description of events on as comprehensive a knowledge
> as possible of their constituent parts.[72]

Marxism, in short, constitutes the intellectual, moral and aesthetic
guidelines of revolutionary literature. Nizan's ambitions as a novelist
are to be located squarely within this frame of reference. Whether or
not these ambitions are achieved must now be assessed through a
detailed examination of Nizan's communist novels.

7

Nizan's Communist Novels

Nizan was convinced that the novel in the contemporary period was as significant a genre as tragedy had been in the classical period.[1] For Nizan an authentic modern writer was, of necessity, primarily a novelist. Nizan himself was actively engaged in writing novels from 1931 to 1932, when he began the production of *Antoine Bloyé*, until his death in 1940, when he was involved in the drafting of *La Soirée à Somosierra*. His novels, unlike other aspects of his literary production, span the full period of his adult writing career and constitute a global critical mirror in which are reflected, distorted, concealed and exaggerated the social, political and metaphysical problems of this particular historical period.

The novels are also the privileged site in Nizan's work where politics and metaphysics collide, where an uneasy balance is maintained between metaphysical *angst* and political construction. Unlike his exclusively militant writings in which the principal concern is to foreground the political and the social (the sectarian polemics of *Les Chiens de garde* at one extreme, the discreet implications of *Chronique de septembre* at the other), his novels accomplish a disturbing fusion between metaphysical disorientation and political action. It is precisely this fusion which constitutes the originality of Paul Nizan.

The novel is in many ways a problematical form for the communist writer. Synonymous for the most part with the hegemonic culture of the bourgeoisie, the novel is not a form easily adapted to the demands of a revolutionary communist ideology explicitly contesting the assumptions of the class by which the form itself was fashioned. Nizan is not unaware of the problem, but chooses to minimise its significance, stressing instead the critical, revelatory and educative aspects of the novel form. He is resolutely determined to counter the allegation that communism and the novel are incompatible, maintaining that the structural integrity of the novel is in no sense impaired by the introduction of ideology:

> My status as a communist and my status as a novelist are not irreconcilable. . . . Communism, like all profound experiences,

113

serves the novelist precisely because the novel is a means of raising consciousness and communism is an experiential method of consciousness-raising.[2]

Nizan makes no apologies for the presence of communism in the novel. Communism is not simply compatible with the novel. In Nizan's theory of the revolutionary novel it is elevated to the status of necessary pre-condition of authentic writing practices. There can be little doubt that Nizan was ideologically committed to the view that a writer's allegiance to communism enabled him/her to grasp the true significance of political developments *from the inside*, that is to say, from the perspective of the proletariat. By contrast, a writer whose allegiances ultimately lie with the bourgeoisie would necessarily understand political developments *from the outside*, that is to say from the perspective of an oppressive class.

For Nizan the moral strength afforded the writer by revolutionary ideology eliminates the need for self-justification within the ethos of his work, eliminates the need to apologise for failing to conform not only to the conventions of bourgeois political structures, but also to the conventions of bourgeois literary structures. The moral righteousness of communist ideology, in short, transforms apologetic social reformism into legitimate revolutionary demands, injects passion into writing and redesignates the novel as the site of political and moral regeneration.[3]

Technical disturbances arising from the interaction between communism and the novel form are consequently in Nizan's eyes merely the logical outcome of the communist writer's refusal to acquiesce to what are perceived as the oppressive structures of bourgeois politics, ethics and culture. To confront and openly subvert the privileged literary form of an oppressive class is to voice the legitimate grievances of the proletariat within the cultural homeland of the bourgeoisie. The formal disruption is itself the visible manifestation of the political demand.

It is precisely this formal disturbance in the texture of Nizan's fiction that constitutes the very essence of his project as a communist novelist. Lodged at the heart of Nizan's fictional enterprise are two competing discourses struggling in narrative combat. In his novels Nizan speaks with a forked tongue; he uses two different languages, two different voices within each narrative site, one political and historical, the other literary and metaphysical:

Language 1: Communist discourse – Historical authority
LENIN

Language 2: Existential discourse – Metaphysical *angst*
DOSTOIEVSKY

At one level Nizan's novels proclaim certainty, truth, authority. This is the voice of communism relaying to the reader unfaltering ideological orthodoxy, pushing the reader constantly towards greater political, social and historical awareness. It is the voice of Nizan speaking the language of Lenin.

At another level, Nizan's novels betray uncertainty, disorientation, doubt. This is the voice of existentialism transmitting to the reader a sense of metaphysical alienation and despair arising from the contemplation of death. It is the voice of Nizan speaking the language of Dostoievsky.

From a strictly communist perspective, the secondary existential discourse could be dismissed as 'petty bourgeois' and 'alienated' since it overflows the boundaries of orthodox communist ideology and points to an alternative vision. However, to classify this secondary discourse in a pejorative sense is to remain blind to the dynamic configuration of Nizan's narrative technique.

The object of the following analysis is not to carry out a Stalinist witch-hunt of the text in order to pillory a deviant, existential, petty-bourgeois discourse ensconced illegitimately at the centre of Nizan's literary production. The object is rather to demonstrate that the success of Nizan's writing technique is ultimately dependent on the interaction of two different but, in the final analysis, mutually dependent discourses.

These two discourses are at times indistinguishably fused, at times distinctly separate. Separate or fused, they contradict and complement each other simultaneously. The precise disposition, organisation and arrangement of these two discourses constitutes the basic fabric of Nizan's fictional technique. Irrespective of the content of each novel, whether it is a tale of apprenticeship (*Antoine Bloyé* and *La Conspiration*), or of confrontation (*Le Cheval de Troie*), the formal articulation of the content is achieved by means of two competing discourses. Nizan's global project as a novelist can therefore be defined above all else as the evolution of two interactive discourses.

What needs to be stressed at this point is that this evolution is rooted in a very specific historical moment of production. The formal and technical development of Nizan's novels reflects in a mediated form the changing historical circumstances in which each text was produced. In each novel the specific configuration of the two discourses, authoritative communist on the one hand, disorientating existential on the other, is the product of two overriding influences: first, the economic, political, ideological and cultural forces that together produced each particular text; secondly, and this is but a superstructural reflection of the first point, Nizan's divided ambitions as a novelist, attempting at one level to exploit bourgeois culture in order to disseminate communist ideology effectively (the communist project), and at another level to create a cultural product of value beyond its immediate moment of production (the bourgeois project).

Each of the three published novels will accordingly be analysed in three consecutive phases. In the first phase attention will be focused on historical and political problems encoded in an authoritative communist discourse. In the second phase attention will be focused on personal and metaphysical problems encoded in a disorientating existential discourse. Finally, in the third phase attention will be focused on the interaction between ideology and form; that is to say, on the textual intercourse between two discourses.

(i) *ANTOINE BLOYÉ*, 1933: DEATH OF THE FATHER

Nizan's first novel, *Antoine Bloyé*, was greeted initially with scepticism in orthodox communist circles. In December 1933 the novel was judged to be lacking in ideological clarity. At one level, Nizan was reprimanded for confusing the reader, particularly in the concluding stages of the novel, with an excess of petty-bourgeois metaphysics. The themes of illness, remorse, personal degeneration and death were dismissed as the signs of an outmoded naturalism. The punishment of the enemies and the traitors of the working class, it was alleged, was the sole right of the working class and could not be left to the processes of natural degeneration. At another level, Nizan was accused of a form of deviant populism. Excessive attention, so the criticism ran, had been paid to the activities of an amorphous, disorganised working-class movement, with the result that the revolutionary potential of the working class embodied in party or trade union organisations had been misrepresented. The undeniable literary qualities of the novel did not compensate for these ideological shortcomings.[4]

A few months later, Aragon reached very different conclusions. In Aragon's eyes the ideological dimension of *Antoine Bloyé* was decisive. The stylistic originality of the novel, although remarkable in itself, was judged ultimately to be of secondary importance. Above and beyond all else, the visible presence of communist ideology, Aragon insisted, released *Antoine Bloyé* from the limitations of naturalism and projected the novel into the sphere of socialist realism.[5]

Nizan's own comments tend, by contrast, to be more elusive, more enigmatic, granting equal weight to the twin themes of existential *angst* and ideological instruction: 'Death and the bourgeoisie are the principal themes of this book', he notes laconically.[6] It is consequently immediately apparent that the central problematic in Nizan's first novel is the tension between ideology and metaphysics as reflected in the configuration of communist and existential discourses within the text itself.

Antoine Bloyé was published in the autumn of 1933.[7] Although its moment of production was restricted to the years 1931–3, the time sequence in the novel itself covers the historical period 1864–1929, corresponding with the life-span of Antoine Bloyé, the central character. The novel is therefore a retrospective account of the 1864–1929 period *viewed from the vantage point of 1931–3*. As such, it constitutes a prime example of a 'balance-sheet' novel, a settling of accounts with a closed historical period.

The authority invested in the ideological judgements within the text arises from the superior (because later) historical position of the narrator in relation to the period under scrutiny. Unlike the central character struggling in the movement of history in its unfolding, the communist narrator, distanced from the events themselves, coolly and relentlessly exposes the myths and illusions of the period with the hindsight of history. It is significant, for example, that the last five chapters of the novel (XVIII–XXII), dealing with events occurring between 1914 and 1929, focus almost exclusively on Antoine's decline and death. Given Nizan's view that 1914 represents the moment of closure of this particular historical period, it is not surprising that in the concluding chapters of the novel the historical environment is virtually ignored and an anguished, existential discourse comes to the forefront. The construction of the novel merely corroborates Nizan's awareness of the difficulty of formulating accurate historical judgements in the on-going and open-ended situation of the contemporary period.

History

Antoine Bloyé is a negative exemplary narrative which seeks to
highlight the hollowness and sterility of a fragmented petty-bourgeois existence compared to the authenticity of working-class solidarity. The narrative itself is divided into three distinct parts, and
plots the working life of the central character, Antoine Bloyé, an
employee of the French railway system during the late nineteenth
and early twentieth centuries. Initially, origins, schooling and early
work experience are analysed (1864–90: section I); subsequently,
Antoine's betrayal of his working-class origins and progressive
integration in the petty bourgeoisie are analysed (1890–1914: section
II); and finally, Antoine's demotion, decline and death are recorded
(1914–29: section III).

The ideological significance of *Antoine Bloyé* emerges from two
different conflictual relationships encoded in the text. At one
level, there is a clearly visible opposition between a historical
and an existential perspective. At another level, however, there
is also a tension within the historical analysis itself, a tension generated by the dynamic relationship betwen the lived experiences of a
father in one historical period (1864–1929), and the compassionate/
judgemental narrative of a son/communist novelist written from the
perspective of 1931–3. This tension between two historical periods,
revealing itself in the narrative as an opposition between the uncon-
scious, non-reflective life style of a father, Antoine Bloyé, and the
critical, politically aware conscience of a son (Pierre Bloyé)/commun-
ist narrator (Paul Nizan), constitutes the historical centre of this
text.

This historical tension is linked to the autobiographical nature of
the novel. Nizan himself made no attempt to conceal its manifestly
autobiographical status: '*Antoine Bloyé* is the story of a man whom I
knew very well: my father.'[8] This autobiographical slant not only
adds a further dimension to an understanding of the novel as a
'balance sheet'. *Antoine Bloyé* is as much a settling of accounts with
Nizan's own pre-communist personality shaped by the destiny of
his own father who died in 1929, as it is a settling of accounts with a
closed historical period. The autobiographical source of the novel
also goes some way to explaining the method of presentation of
Antoine's character which at a personal level reflects a tension
between a father and a son, and at a historical level reflects a tension
between two different epochs.

Nizan's narrative is both an indictment of the illusions of the French petty bourgeoisie in a phase of rapid capitalist industrial expansion, and an attempt to understand precisely *who* his father was, an attempt to explain the reasons underlying the failure of his father's life. Towards the end of the novel, the narrator records: 'What Antoine needed at that time was to find someone capable of proving to him that his past was worthy of being admired, that it contained elements worthy of gratitude and friendship.'[9] The personal implication of the narrator in the story could not be more clearly signalled.

Antoine Bloyé is ultimately Nizan's testimony to his father. It is the book that Antoine himself was incapable of writing, a book written by a son to avenge a father. 'My son will avenge me' notes Antoine sadly, impotently.[10] *Antoine Bloyé* not only clarifies the meaning of Antoine's life and in the process immortalises it in a negative exemplary narrative. It also gestures towards excusing him, presenting him throughout as a pathetic, historically unaware, exploited and manipulated individual. It is this 'pathetic' quality in Antoine Bloyé's character which undoubtedly elicits the sympathy of the reader and at the same time has significant implications at the historical level.

Throughout the entire novel Antoine Bloyé never accedes to a full understanding of his predicament. Occasionally the spark of an intuition flashes across his consciousness, but for the most part his mind is a blank screen filtering out information which would lead to any profound political and social awareness. The lucid, pitiless voice of the communist narrator stands in sharp contrast to the amorphous, non-reflective consciousness of the central protagonist. Antoine's failure to analyse his actions in anything other than a purely technical sense is explained primarily by the tempo of his life dictated by an excessive work load that leaves no time for leisure, for reflection, for self-scrutiny:

Amidst the din of the machines, in his narrow sphere of activity, Antoine had no time to go through human motions other than the motions of his work. Like so many men his life was ruled by demands and decisions connected with his work; he was absorbed by his profession. . . . For fourteen or fifteen years no man could have been less conscious of himself and of his own life, less informed about the world than Antoine Bloyé. He was alive no doubt; who is not alive? All you need is a well-fed body to go through the motions of life. He moved and acted, but the springs of his life and the driving force of his actions were not within himself . . . his strength was being spent on the grindstone of alien work; he was not putting it to his own account. He was not using it to further his own human development, he was using it up for the profit of the people who paid him, the anonymous shareholders and their abstract interests. Such is the ill-fortune of many men.[11]

The pathos of Antoine's predicament is clearly articulated in this passage. The relentless, time-consuming nature of his work literally asphyxiates the self-reflective side of his personality. He becomes 'a man without a vocabulary'.[12] He does not think, he simply works. In this image Nizan evokes the plight not merely of one individual, but of an entire class. Disorganised, fragmented, rendered politically docile by the exigencies of late nineteenth-century capitalist industrialisation, the working class seemed totally dehumanised by the work process.

The non-reflective consciousness of the father contrasts not only with the penetrating critical gaze of the communist narrator, but also with the smouldering rebellion of the son. In the opening chapter of the novel, Pierre Bloyé, confronted by the corpse of his father, instinctively alienated by the rituals and incantations of an absurd funeral ceremony, despairing at his mother's willing acquiescence to the arid conventions of petty-bourgeois existence, asks himself the fundamental question: 'What sort of a man was my father?'[13] The answer is subsequently given by the communist narrator.

The dynamics of the novel are consequently far more complex than appearances would suggest. *Antoine Bloyé* is not simply the story of the life of a father recounted and explained by a communist narrator for the edification of a son. It is the story of the failures of one generation written for the enlightenment of a subsequent generation. This instructive dissonance between a non-reflective, depoliticised father recruited into the ranks of the petty bourgeoisie in the late nineteenth century, and an increasingly critical and politicised son rebelling against the alienation of petty-bourgeois existence in the early twentieth century captures precisely the ideological climate of the period leading to the events of February 1934. The entire narrative needs to be interpreted in the light of this historical tension. Aragon described *Antoine Bloyé* as a sustained analysis of the point of fracture between two classes.[14] This fracturing process is clearly visible in the value-laden communist discourse which ceaselessly highlights the moral and political degeneration associated with Antoine's abandonment and betrayal of the working class.

The value system informing this communist discourse is quite explicit. To enter the world of the bourgeoisie is to enter a world of death, an artificial world of polite ceremonies in which existence is kept at arm's length, a world of solitary individuals obsessed by careerist ambitions, a world of self-delusion in which disparaging assessments of the workers function as a reassuring screen masking a fearful hatred of an oppressed class which might one day disrupt the privileged existence of the bourgeoisie, a world of political and historical deception in which the social hierarchies of the late nineteenth century were perceived as naturally ordained and immutable; a world, in short, devoid of humanity, devoid of authentic human relations, devoid of a genuinely human social and political project.

The systematic denigration of the dead and oppressive existence of the bourgeoisie has as its counterpart an implicit affirmation of working-class values; implicit because for the most part Antoine is deprived of the experience of working-class solidarity, his knowledge of it is restricted to fleeting intuitions. At the moment of a strike in 1910:

> He was alone; the strikers were carrying away with them the secret of power. These unimportant men were carrying far away from him the strength, the friendship and the hope that he was denied. On that evening, Antoine came to understand that he was a solitary man.[15]

Towards the end of his life:

> All his life Antoine had vaguely realised that the real union, the union that defied loneliness, that even now was sweeping away the dust of bourgeois life, was the union of workers.[16]

The function of the communist discourse throughout the narrative is to prevent the reader's attention from straying from the all-encompassing value-judgement that to collaborate with the bourgeoisie is to sign one's own death warrant. The cruel destiny of Antoine Bloyé was to be duped into abandoning the class of his origins and to finish his life in the isolation and despair of a deathly bourgeois existence.

This moral judgement is corroborated by a lucid historical assessment which plots the progressive alienation of the central character in time and space. Born in Brittany at the onset of a period of rapid capitalist industrialisation, Antoine is progressively lured away from his rural origins by the bright lights of big city mechanisation. By the age of fifteen he is caught up in the feverish excitement of unprecedented growth and expansion in the town of St Nazaire. 'In all corners of France machines began to suck in the youth from the countryside.'[17]

Antoine's graduation in 1880 to the École Nationale d'Arts et Métiers in Angers is presented by the narrative voice of history as a trap, a management plot, a method of rapidly producing a technically qualified and subservient labour force required by an accelerating capitalist industrial machine, a method of transforming working-class ambitions to escape poverty into a betrayal of the working class itself:

> Everything at that time encouraged the working-class youth, the ambitious sons of artisans and minor officials, to enter into the plot of those in command. Antoine had been caught up in it like the others, and he was completely ignorant of the underlying forces of this great undertaking. He did not know that along with many other adolescents of his age he was one of the pawns of the huge game that the principal rulers of the French bourgeoisie were beginning to play. He had simply been told that he could escape the poverty and uncertainty of a worker's life, and these promises had coincided far too closely with the temptations that his city offered for him to refuse to listen. He knew nothing. Far from him, even before he was born, in offices, at shareholders' meetings, in parliaments, in learned bodies, factory owners had for the past thirty years been voicing their demands. Industry required new human material.[18]

This passage graphically illustrates the historical dissonance between the mystified consciousness of the central protagonist and the demystifying voice of the communist narrator. In the 1880s Antoine had been duped into becoming a pawn in a vast capitalist conspiracy. The function of the communist discourse in the text is to disclose the nature of the conspiracy and to highlight the lessons to be learned by the working class in the 1930s.

This process of revelation, disclosure, demystification is an integral part of the entire narrative but is doubtless most prominent at moments of significant professional and personal development in Antoine's life. The accelerating pace of capitalist industrialisation in the late nineteenth century has already been highlighted. This process of capitalist acceleration is the underlying historical explanation of Antoine's progressive abandonment of his working-class origins.

The second significant moment recorded in the novel is 1914, the moment of closure of this particular historical period, the moment when the First World War is unleashed, a moment of renewed acceleration in capitalist production, the moment of Antoine's professional downfall. It is noticeable, however, that this second major phase of historical development is not presented in a specifically communist perspective. The narrator focuses primarily on superstructural perceptions of events: the bourgeois illusion that peace could not be disturbed, the workers' illusion that socialism would prevent the war, and the stridently nationalist reaction once war had been declared.

Deeper, structural reasons are hinted at but they are never fully articulated. The description, for example, of Antoine's awareness of the significance of increased activity on the railways points tantalisingly to the wider, international ramifications of the impending conflict:

On the railways, there was already a certain hurried activity, a certain noise of preparation perceptible to a man as familiar as he was with his company's working environment. Instructions began to pour down from the main office. He was well aware that the war was completely assembled, like a mighty machine. To set it in motion all that was needed was to push the button.[19]

However, the underlying economic causes of the war are not disclosed. There is no attempt to analyse the development of capitalism in the early twentieth century and present the war as an imperialist struggle. This is a surprising omission, in many ways, given the fact that the language of Lenin could have been used to great effect at this stage in the narrative. Paradoxically, it is Jaurès, not Lenin, who is visibly present in the account of the events culminating in the outbreak of the war.[20] This omission of the imperialist war thesis and the emphasis on the nationalist dimension of the conflict prefigures in a strange and uncanny way Nizan's personal experiences during 1939 and 1940.

It would consequently appear that there is a marked attenuation of a specifically communist interpretation of events in the latter stages of the novel. A communist discourse, which is potent initially in section I when analysing the process of capitalist industrialisation in late nineteenth-century France, and subsequently in section II when undermining the pretensions and illusions of bourgeois existence ultimately loses its authoritarian grip in the third and final section of the novel in which the themes of existence and death are foregrounded. There are two possible explanations of this weakening of communist discourse in the final section of the novel, one historical, one thematic.

First, there is clearly a problem of historical perspective concerning the narration of events after 1914. For a communist narrator situated historically in 1931–3, the precise contours of the post-1914 period are far from clear. Errors of historical judgement when assessing the contemporary period are most effectively avoided by adopting the simple expedient of focusing on individual rather than historical developments. Secondly, the thematic structure of the novel itself needs to be borne in mind. In the final section of the novel the narrator is attempting to exploit the personal dissolution and death of the central protagonist in order to project a negative exemplary political morality. It is consequently technically advantageous to narrow the focus of the narrative to an individual dimension. A wider historical frame of reference might easily have disrupted the moral and political teleology of the narrative itself. This marked attenuation of communist discourse in the third section of the novel must now be examined in more detail through an analysis of the existential discourse in the text.

Existence

Existential discourse is encoded in the narrative in three central themes: sexuality, dreams and death. Although existential and communist discourses merge generally throughout *Antoine Bloyé*, it is possible to locate areas of the narrative where existential themes dominate and the voice of history is consequently silenced, or at least muted.

Descriptions of love and sexuality are not uniform. At times, description is ultimately subordinated to a global communist thesis which categorises sexuality in class terms. On occasions, however, the narrator's voice becomes bitterly poignant and the communist thesis is forgotten.

The opposition between a stereotypical, restrictive bourgeois existence and an unpredictable, spontaneous working-class existence is given a sexual dimension in the analysis of women and male-female relationships. The narrator carefully exploits the differences between Antoine's relationship with Marcelle, a working-class widow from Paris, and his relationship with Anne, his future wife, in order to highlight the gulf separating two social classes, one vibrant and living, the other constricted and dead. The prudish, repressed, virginal, middle-class sexuality of Anne is contrasted unfavourably with the wild, sensual, adventurous, working-class sexuality of Marcelle:

> Anne Bloyé belonged to an entirely different emotional world from Marcelle. Antoine vaguely wondered whether the passionate kingdom of women without a future and without reservations was not a greater prize for a man than the virginal sweetness, the chaste conspiracies of bourgeois virtues. To have resolved this dilemma would have required a degree of good sense that some-one like Antoine Bloyé had not yet had the time to acquire, which he would acquire too late, which he would perhaps never acquire.[21]

Occasionally, however, the narrative slips gear and a different tone emerges, both bitter and poignant. The specific case of Antoine Bloyé is momentarily forgotten and a more anguished discourse predomi-nates. Men and women are perceived as fundamentally estranged, alienated and set at a distance from each other by the conventions of work and the conventions of marriage. Work and marriage literally mutilate relationships between the sexes, prevent men and women from committing themselves to a deep and sustained mutual explora-tion of their global personalities:

> Neither men nor women love. Love is a task that requires too much patience, too much companionship, too many common goals, too much friendship. They have fabricated the passionate myths of love at first sight to serve the interests of their cowardly illusions, to excuse their indifference through ill luck. . . . Woman's world, man's world, a deep gulf divides them, as it divides the world of blacks from the world of whites. A man and his wife do not seek to

bridge this gulf: such a venture over the unknown frightens them.
. . . Married couples do not think of their partner as a creature
who is difficult to decipher, worthy perhaps of living a human
life, capable of living. They are not going to explore the mysteries
that enshroud existence.[22]

This anguished appeal to revolutionise the patterns of intercourse
between men and women overflows the boundaries of orthodox
communist discourse. Although the global narrative context of this
passage ultimately points to the fact that truly authentic relations are
possible only between men and women who are no longer crippled
by the oppressive social forces of modern capitalist society, nonetheless a more generalised metaphysical tone predominates here.
The narrative at this juncture implies more a yearning to escape
from the oppression of capitalism than a commitment to take up
arms against it. This escapist undercurrent manifests itself vividly in
those segments of the narrative recording the liberation of individual
human potential in the inner psychic experiences of dreams:

In the midst of the solitary idleness of the night, all the things that
day forbids emerge from obscurity, desires condemned by the
tribunals of good daytime citizens, by their strictures, by their
virtues. Shame, discipline, suppressed desires, lack of leisure
crush those obscure parts of a human being where truest needs
may perhaps be hidden. For as long as men are not complete and
free, sure on their feet and the earth that supports them, they will
dream at night. They will satisfy all their hungers, their real
hungers – for there are in the world all those men who do not eat
or drink their fill, wretched men with their thirst for vengeance –
they will score victories over their daytime oppressors, they will
conquer willing women.[23]

Although the dream sequence itself is presented as a sublimated
social revenge, a method of compensating for injustices endured in
the social sphere, and as such illustrates perfectly the structural
dynamics of Nizan's fictional technique in which the metaphysical
and the social merge, nonetheless here too there is a sense of
escapism and liberation which transcends orthodox communist
discourse.

Likewise the theme of death, a nakedly existential theme, the
leitmotiv of Nizan's entire literary production, although never

entirely detached from the social sphere, captures on occasions moments of existential anguish that deviate significantly from communist orthodoxy. Death is presented not only as a symbol of the ghostly, dried-up existence of the bourgeoisie, but more generally as a cancerous presence corroding and destroying the lives of all mankind.

The novel begins and ends in death. The opening chapter narrates Antoine's funeral, the final chapter narrates his moment of dying. The progressive intensification of the presence of death in the narrative is itself ideologically motivated. Apart from the opening chapter dealing explicitly with Antoine's funeral, the death theme is not to the forefront in section I. Given that this section is centred on Antoine's education and early working experience, a period of his life when he had not yet compromised himself in the deathly existence of the bourgeoisie, this relative absence tacitly confirms the global ideological thesis of the novel.

It is significant that the death theme reappears violently in the first chapter of section III at the moment of a railway accident in which two men die. The revelation of the death of these two railway employees is consequently located in the narrative immediately after Antoine's marriage to Anne and his integration in the bourgeoisie. The accident itself forces him to an awareness of his objective complicity in the death of the two men, and his betrayal of the working class. The deathly sickness of bourgeois existence is highlighted in the following chapter with an extended account of the birth and death of their first child, Marie-Antoinette. At this moment death becomes a mortifying presence at the heart of the narrative, and from the second chapter of section III the text literally overflows in death.

It is consequently no exaggeration to maintain not only that death permeates the entire narrative of *Antoine Bloyé*, on occasions obliterating everything else, but also that death is presented for the most part as a product of the inadequacies of a specific political and social environment. However preoccupied the text becomes in its final stages with the existential theme of death, the narrative itself remains contextualised by the wider political and social thesis articulated in other parts of the novel.

It is also undeniably the case, however, that in the latter stages of the novel there is a constant slippage between a discourse which links the existential theme of the death of an individual human being to the communist theme of the death of a social class, and a discourse which focuses predominately on a more general feeling of existential anguish arising from thoughts of personal death. The following extract, which could have been written almost word for word by Sartre, is a classic example of existential discourse embedded in the narrative of *Antoine Bloyé*:

> My life was given to me without my having bargained for it; it is added to the lives of others as one stone is added to a pile of stones. I might as well admit it, my life neither helps nor hinders anyone. Why should I not think of my own death? My life is empty and deserves nothing but death. . . . I am surplus to requirements, I am superfluous, I serve no purpose. I have already ceased to exist.[24]

Although the narrative context ultimately prevents such nakedly existential intrusions from undermining the credibility of the global political thesis of the novel, their mere presence signals a tension between its communist and existential discourses. It is this tension that must now be scrutinised through an assessment of ideology and form.

Ideology and Form

The visibility of the communist discourse in the narrative prompted criticisms in some quarters that *Antoine Bloyé* was excessively 'abstract'. The novel, it was alleged, contained a surfeit of ideas that were insufficiently integrated within the ethos of the fictional system itself. Whatever the value of this criticism, and quite clearly assessments of the degree of successful integration of ideology in fiction are themselves ideologically motivated, the criticism does focus attention on a fundamental problem: the nature of the configuration of ideological discourses within a given fictional system.

Antoine Bloyé is the textual site of a process of entanglement between two discourses. Although it is possible to disentangle the fabric of the narrative in such a manner as to pinpoint segments which illustrate the specificity of each of the discourses in their uniqueness, generally the textual pattern is not one of separation but one of fusion. The internal dynamics of the text are such that a potentially deviant existential discourse is in the final analysis inevitably rehabilitated within the orthodox ideological parameters of a communist novel. Even in the concluding stages of the narrative, when existential problems reach their climax, this process of textual rehabilitation is visibly operative:

> This deep anguish that had haunted him for years was probably not linked to bodily illness. It was fear. In a region deeper even than the blood system of the body where the symptoms of diseases are formed, he harboured a sickness that was even more serious than arteriosclerosis. It was no longer bodily death that he feared, but the shapeless image of his entire life, that defeated image of himself, that headless being that walked in the ashes of time with hurrying steps, aimlessly and in disorder. He was decapitated; no one had noticed that he had the whole time been living without a head. How polite people are. No one had ever called to his attention the fact that he had no head. It was too late. The whole time he had been living his own death.[25]

What appears initially as abstract metaphysical anxiety engendered by old age and the imminence of death is progressively transformed into a fearful realisation of the social causes of the anxiety itself. Antoine's metaphysical anguish is ultimately explained as a product of the mutilated existence that he has led in the deathly world of the bourgeoisie. Time after time, existential anguish and disorientation can be seen to function in the text as no more than an alienated stage in a purifying process of political and social education, both for the central protagonist and for the reader.

It is consequently incorrect to envisage existential discourse as a subversive threat to a dominant communist ideology. Although it is undoubtedly a deviant discourse, the deviationism itself contributes to the ultimate truth of the final ideological objective. In the same way that the personal, existential alienation of Paul Nizan was explained and resolved in the ideology and organisation of the communist party, so the narrative, existential alienation of *Antoine Bloyé* is explained and resolved in the ideology and organisation of the communist novel.

This is not the end of the story, however. Despite the ultimate compatibility between existential and communist discourses within the narrative, the ideological thesis of *Antoine Bloyé* is nonetheless blunted by other formal characteristics which need clarifying.

There is a definite temptation when reading *Antoine Bloyé* to interpret the novel not solely as an indictment of the social existence of a particular class, but also as a bitter lament on the failure of a man to achieve fulfilment in life. It is possible, in other words, to read the novel as a generalised statement on the human condition. The deeply metaphysical tone of the concluding part of the novel, stressing as it does existential despair in the face of death, can conceivably be viewed as supporting this latter interpretation. The fact that the metaphysical weight of the novel is located in the strategically important concluding chapters where the reader's critical judgements tend to be finalised, is in itself a quite decisive factor. Beyond this anguished, metaphysical conclusion, however, there are other formal characteristics which also conspire to give prominence to a more generalised, existential reading of the text. First, the relationship established in the course of the narrative between the reader and the central character has a decisive influence on critical responses to the novel. The pathetic quality of Antoine's life, the extent to which he is presented as a mere pawn in a wider social conspiracy, has already been pinpointed. There is little doubt that, confronted by such a sorry tale of failure, the reader instinctively sympathises with the plight of the luckless hero. The fact that the communist narrator, ruthless in his exposure of the political and social environment which created the conditions for the failure of Antoine's life, nonetheless displays compassion when analysing the central character's individual responsibility in the whole affair, tends ultimately to elicit the reader's sympathy. The inevitable consequence of this empathetic relationship between reader and central character is a marked displacement of attention on the reader's part away from those elements in the text which are directing him/her towards greater awareness of the underlying causes of social oppression, and towards those elements which are eliciting compassion and sympathy for the central character himself. This fascination with the personal inadequacies of the central character as opposed to the social inadequacies of the class to which he has given allegiance, substantially dilutes the ideological effect of the novel.

Secondly, the presence within the narrative of two very powerful, if hackneyed, images reinforces the generalised, existential interpretation of the novel at the expense of political interpretations. These two images which recur over and over again in *Antoine Bloyé*, and which project a generalised concept of man with as much insistency as the authoritarian voice of communist orthodoxy projects a particularised view, ultimately subvert the historical and political aspects of the novel.

The first of these images is the stereotypical expression of the ceaseless passage of time, not of specific, historical time, but of time in general; the fleeting journey of man, the relentless flow of existence, the dwindling sands of life. The entire novel is suffused in this cliché-ridden but extremely potent image which distances the reader from historical awareness, and draws him/her into a brooding preoccupation with the ceaseless passage of time. Antoine Bloyé becomes a symbol of the ephemeral quality of human existence so rapidly consumed by the passing years.

To use the imagery of the novel itself, man's existence is comparable to Antoine's journeys on so many speeding trains. The destination is reached too soon, there has been little possibility on the journey for significant thoughts, plans or projects, and the meaning of the entire event in retrospect is unclear. This image of the unstoppable passage of time hypnotises the reader, diverts his/her attention from the particulars of historical events and holds him/her fascinated by the spectacle of mortal man speeding to his death.

The second of these images is equally hackneyed: the image of nature. At one point in the narrative, the development of Antoine's existence is compared to a passage across mountains, plains and valleys, his progress being measured against the progress of the sun in the heavens. The very banality of such images reassures the reader. This is familiar territory. Natural settings linked to human endeavours, despite and perhaps because of their poignancy, are ultimately reassuring. The frequency with which natural images recur in the narrative in association not only with Antoine's personal development, but also with the historical development of the period creates paradoxically a naturalising effect in this communist novel. The processes of nature, cyclical and repetitive, compete with the dynamic forces of history. By a strange quirk of fate, descriptions which are designed to demystify the reader, to project the reader to a greater political and social awareness, achieve quite often the reverse effect. Rather than foregrounding the social significance of a life and a period, the significance itself is often blurred by a surfeit of naturalising images.

Lodged at the heart of this communist novel is a set of recurring images, images of time and images of nature, which by their frequency, familiarity and poetic intensity cast a naturalising shroud over a potentially demystifying historical discourse. The ideological effect of this novel rests ultimately on the capacity of the historical discourse to counter the naturalising propensity of these images.

Thirdly and finally, a significant absence in the novel militates against an exclusively communist interpretation. The French communist party does not figure in *Antoine Bloyé*. Given that the PCF did not come into being until 1920, a mere nine years before the death of Antoine himself, this absence is not surprising. To have introduced the PCF arbitrarily into a novel at a late stage would doubtless have been entirely inappropriate, bearing in mind Antoine Bloyé's political mystification and social integration in the petty bourgeoisie. Nonetheless, this absence of the party needs to be registered. Not only are the technically difficult problems associated with the integration of the party in the narrative itself not confronted, but also the scope for non-communist interpretations of the novel is widened. Rightly or wrongly, with the party absent, it is possible to give more credence to interpretations that present the novel as a bitter lament on the human condition rather than a sustained attack on the mortifying life-style of a particular class.

It is not inappropriate overall, therefore, to speak of this novel as a process of entrapment of the communist ideological thesis by a series of naturalising bourgeois formal devices. This process of entrapment within the novel doubtless reflects on a social scale the entrapment of the working class within the structures of bourgeois society during the period to which the narrative fiction alludes.

There is a sad and haunting quality about *Antoine Bloyé*. The particular fusion that Nizan accomplishes in this novel between social oppression and metaphysical *angst* lingers in the mind. The bitterness and poignancy of the description of a life wasted, unfulfilled, broken, allied to an unequivocal indictment of the perceived causes of such dissolution, the deathly oppression and duplicity of bourgeois society, all this constitutes a theme and a melody that affect communist and non-communist readers alike. Reproduced in a contemporary context, this negative exemplary tale of an ordinary man whose life was stolen away from him by political and social forces over which he had little control, finds echoes in the minds of millions of ordinary people trapped in the serial relations of a modern capitalist society. In *Antoine Bloyé* Nizan created a ghostly figure that will continue to haunt the consciousness of the contemporary reader.

(ii) *LE CHEVAL DE TROIE*, 1935: DYING FOR THE PARTY

The socialist realist pedigree of Nizan's second novel, *Le Cheval de*

Troie, has done little to enhance its reputation. Perceptions of this novel not only as a 'classic example of Zhdanovite socialist realism',[26] but also as a 'particularly "pure" version of the structure of confrontation in the *roman à thèse*',[27] are doubtless reassuring to critics seeking to restrict the novel within established ideological and technical boundaries, but are ultimately an impoverishment of the problematical textual specificity of the novel itself.

This lack-lustre critical performance is compounded by the significant omission of *Le Cheval de Troie* from Sartre's otherwise globally positive assessments of Nizan's work. Sartre is, in fact, curiously tight-lipped regarding this particular novel. His eloquence when speaking of other aspects of Nizan's literary production stands in marked contrast to a decided unwillingness even to mention *Le Cheval de Troie*, an unwillingness that can only be interpreted as tacit criticism. Such reticence could be explained in political or technical terms, given Sartre's opposition to socialist realist literature.[28] More likely, however, is a purely personal explanation. Despite Nizan's protestations to the contrary, Sartre remained convinced that the character of Lange, an abstract, solitary individual obsessed by thoughts of death and ultimately aligning himself with fascism, was based on himself.[29] The discretion with which Sartre treats *Le Cheval de Troie* is consequently more probably motivated by personal than by ideological or literary reasons.

Ultimately, however, hostile, condescending and even discreetly critical value-judgements merely function as an ideological screen, an obstacle impeding understanding. In order to assess the legitimacy of categorising *Le Cheval de Troie* as an unproblematical exemplification of Zhdanovite socialist realism, it is necessary to probe the specific ideological and formal structure of this novel by focusing on the relationship between its historical moment of production and the configuration of its two dominant discourses.

Le Cheval de Troie was published in 1935. It was written partly in the Soviet Union in 1934 in the aftermath of the Soviet Writers' Congress, and partly in France in 1935 amidst growing popular front optimism engendered initially by the events of February 1934. Its moment of production therefore coincides with a highly significant transition phase politically, ideologically and culturally. *Le Cheval de Troie* is in this sense a unique text since it reflects in mediated form Nizan's attempts not merely to formulate a technical response to the exigencies of socialist realist doctrine as articulated in the 1934 Congress, but also to formulate a political and ideological response to the transformed historical climate that was to culminate in the governments of the Popular Front.

It is important to stress the transitional nature of this moment of production. Since the ideological objective of the novel is to pinpoint the year 1934 as a historical watershed, a moment when political consciousness was transformed, there are of necessity two perspectives encoded in the narrative: a past perspective of communist party isolationism and working-class docility and defeatism prior to the events of 1934, and a future perspective of popular front co-operation and working-class social awareness and militancy subsequent to the events of 1934. Although the novel is divided into two distinct parts corresponding in terms of the narration of events with a past perspective of despair and a future perspective of hope, the text overall testifies to a sustained tension between a sectarian and a popular front ideological stance, a tension reflecting this transitional moment between two phases in the political development of the French communist party.

Despite a residual sectarianism manifesting itself in this narrative ideological tension, *Le Cheval de Troie* unquestionably constitutes a radical departure from Nizan's previous writing practice, and graphically illustrates his conviction that 'Nobody in 1935 is capable of writing the sequel to the books of 1933'.[30] There are major differences politically, historically and technically between *Antoine Bloyé* published in 1933, and *Le Cheval de Troie* published in 1935.

The political development could not be more visibly apparent. The lessons of the negative exemplary narrative, *Antoine Bloyé*, recording the story of a father alienated in the deathly existence of the petty bourgeoisie, have been learnt and put into practice by his son, Pierre Bloyé, a militant communist party member who is elevated to the status of narrator in *Le Cheval de Troie*. The centre of gravity has consequently shifted decisively from the analysis of petty-bourgeois alienation to the description of communist party militancy. A negative tale of apprenticeship within an oppressive class has been transformed into a positive tale of confrontation with the same oppressive class.

It is the change in historical perspective, however, which is the most profound development and which has the most far-reaching consequences for the tone, structure and content of the novel itself. Unlike *Antoine Bloyé*, a 'balance-sheet' novel aimed at drawing up an account of a closed historical period, *Le Cheval de Troie* is manifestly 'problem-centred'; that is to say, set in the confusing flux of contemporary events at a moment when the full implications of the events themselves are far from clear. The fact that Nizan was attempting to disclose the significance of the events of February 1934 *in their immediate aftermath* cannot be overemphasised. He was, in other words, writing history as it was being made. The risks for the political novelist are self-evident.

The epic tone of the narrative, clearly signalled in the title of the novel itself, a title eventually preferred to the more immediately evocative but less morally uplifting *Le Jour de la colère*, is consequently not the product of casual imitation of Soviet socialist realist models. It is a narrative tone that coincides precisely with the sense of moral and political regeneration that the events of February had appeared to have sparked off, and which seemed to be sweeping the country before it in a Popular Front crusade.

The fundamental shift in historical perspective accomplished in *Le Cheval de Troie* has implications beyond mere narrative tone, however. The focusing of attention on the contemporary struggle in its unfolding produces a marked attenuation of the voice of omniscient historical narration legislating a definitive Marxist interpretation of events, the legislating voice itself becoming part of the process of History in the making. This is an important point since it highlights the significance of the material presence of the communist party in this particular novel. Unlike *Antoine Bloyé*, where the depoliticised consciousness of the central character, and the material absence of the communist party itself, created an ideological space in the novel which was ceaselessly filled by the voice of an omniscient communist narrator, a disembodied discourse at a distance from the concrete social relations depicted in the text, the ideological presence of communism in *Le Cheval de Troie* is guaranteed by the physical presence of communist miliants. The thoughts, emotions, words and deeds of the party activists become the natural expression of communist ideology organically linked to the theme and structure of the narrative. The ideological content of the novel is therefore predominantly communicated to the reader by the social actors themselves.

The transformed historical perspective in *Le Cheval de Troie* also produces a movement away from the examination of individual characters as exemplifications of the life-style of a particular class, towards the description of class conflict at a moment of political and social realignment. Specifically, whereas *Antoine Bloyé* was centred on the situation of one individual progressively ensnared in the serial relations of the petty bourgeoisie, *Le Cheval de Troie* seeks to capture the defining characteristics of a communist group at a moment of intense political activity. In *Antoine Bloyé* the focus was the *analysis* of a given life, in *Le Cheval de Troie* the focus becomes the *description* of a conflictual political event.

This development is reflected in the epigraphs that Nizan selects for the two novels. For *Antoine Bloyé* an extract from Marx's *German Ideology*, locating the root cause of bourgeois alienation and proletarian oppression in the work process itself, gives pre-eminence to a Marxist discourse aimed at disclosing the underlying causes of class conflict. For *Le Cheval de Troie*, by contrast, an extract from a worker's letter addressed to the editorial committee of *Iskra*, Lenin's revolutionary newspaper, requesting assistance in the search to understand the processes of living and dying within the class struggle, gives pre-eminence to a communist discourse aimed at describing the problems and actions of men and women directly implicated in class conflict.

The centre of the novel is consequently no longer the distant voice of history dispassionately recording the alienation and death lodged at the heart of an oppressive class. It becomes the ideologically charged description of the social, moral and emotional predicament of the members of two opposed classes at a moment of political confrontation. The challenge issued by one class to another constitutes an act of social and moral regeneration. The challenge itself is the narrative centre of *Le Cheval de Troie*.

History

The events recorded in *Le Cheval de Troie* take place in June 1934 in the town of Villefranche.[31] The novel begins one Sunday afternoon amidst the relaxed and peaceful atmosphere of a country setting just outside the town, and ends the following Sunday afternoon amidst an atmosphere of violence and polarised class conflict inside the town itself. The stark contrast between the opening scene depicting docile workers slumbering in the bosom of nature, and the concluding scenes depicting militant workers struggling in the heart of the city is pointedly symbolic. The journey in text, time and space, from initial to final chapter, from one Sunday to the next, from country to town, is a journey of deepening political and social awareness.

The division of the novel into two distinct parts, the first recording the gradual build-up of events during an entire week beginning in the peace and calm of an initial Sunday afternoon, the second recording the explosive street-fighting of the subsequent Sunday afternoon, is a structural reflection of this progressive conscientisation of the working class. In the first part, the various social actors are presented to the reader within their own specific living and working environments. Each distinctly separate group of social actors is situated within a global economic, political and cultural hierarchy which regulates the town. In the second part, the stultifyingly predictable social existence of the town is shattered. The town's principal actors are involved in a dramatic and dynamic performance of class conflict set in the public square, suitably and ironically named 'La place du théâtre'. Years of pent-up resentment and anger explode violently in the June sunlight. In a festival of confrontation, the injustice and oppression of the town's political and social hierarchies are publicly denounced.

The extent to which this fictionalised movement from social and political stasis described in part 1 to dynamic fusion and growing working-class consciousness described in part 2 reflects an ideological movement from sectarianism to popular frontism can be gauged by an assessment of the evolution of the communist discourse within the narrative itself.

A sectarian discourse is clearly visible in the opening pages of the novel. The initial scene of relaxation in the countryside serves several purposes. Not only does it function as a peaceful counterpoint to the subsequent violence. It also acts as an effective means of presenting the communist group to the reader. In this introductory ceremony the communist militants are described at a moment of respite when they are briefly withdrawn from the front-line of an endless political battle. The image of the group projected in this opening sequence is that of an isolated sect, surrounded on all sides by powerful political enemies, and locked in a desperate life and death struggle against the forces of Darkness:

They were men and women who lived all their lives in a world of anxiety and struggle. They were familiar with factories, workshops, the police. They lived in a world which was divided and torn apart, a world resembling the background of those pictures by painters of the Middle Ages, separated into celestial and infernal divisions, a conflict between heaven and hell. They were at war with their town, with their own lives, in a struggle which had not yet been lit up by heroic explosions and where there had been only isolated deaths; but it was a battle in which they had little protection, in which the blows aimed against them usually found their mark.

For them, hunger, homelessness, prison, the destruction of love, incurable diseases, were not monstrous fables but merely misfortunes which they had escaped for the time being. The future appeared to them as an awesome and pitiless snare.[32]

What is striking in this passage is not only the extent to which this fundamentally manichean image of the communist group as besieged and isolated coincides with the reality of a sectarian French communist party during the late 1920s, but also the extent to which it plays down the possibility of epic events at this juncture in the narrative. On this initial Sunday afternoon in June 1934 there is as yet no premonition of the imminent political explosion that is about to detonate Villefranche. The communist group is described simply as committed to pursuing its bitter struggle, with little hope of major success in the foreseeable future.

It is significant, in fact, that the concluding pages of the opening chapter focus on the setbacks and failures of the past as recollected by individual members of the communist group. The conversations between the militants, centred as they are on the development of the labour movement since the outbreak of the First World War, enable historical assessments to emerge organically from the fictional situation itself. Although buoyed by distant memories of anarchist rebellion in 1910 and 1911, there is no attempt at self-delusion. It is recognised that after 1920 the working class entered a historical phase of division and disenchantment. The only beacon of hope on the horizon was the possibility that the political consciousness of the labour movement might be reactivated by the growing world economic crisis.

The tragic communist discourse in which the voice of sectarianism takes stock of the oppressed and isolated existence of the working class in general and the communist group in particular is, nonetheless, progressively abandoned in the course of the narrative and replaced by a more optimistic, occasionally euphoric discourse climaxing in the concluding explosive confrontation.

A significant moment of transition occurs at the point at which the threat of fascism is introduced. Mid-way through the first half of the novel the enemy is clearly signalled. Posters announcing a fascist meeting to be held the following Sunday inject into the text the catalyst of working-class solidarity. The communist narrator reacts immediately, shifting the emphasis from division and defeatism to the imminent struggle against fascism.

Things were beginning to stir in France.

On Sundays, in town squares which had known centuries of tranquillity, squares which had occasionally not even observed the passing shadows of revolutions, of wars and of invasions, where the inhabitants had for generations not experienced a quickening of their heart-beat, hostile groups were confronting one another. The French had for a long time lived in their own isolated little world; Europe was seething around this rock of France, and all the while the French continued to look upon Germany, Italy, Spain, all their neighbours, with the detached gaze of spectators. . . . Then suddenly, on these same squares, stones were being hurled, horses were galloping, truncheons were crashing down on heads, and guns were being fired. In every town secret meetings were being held, hatred and anger were growing more intense. People were getting to know hunger and privation at first hand. Despair was assuming an explosive potency. It was a period which called to mind the beginning of the religious wars, when the barns of Protestants went up in flames and men took to the highways to fight.[33]

The epic tone of this passage in which the forthcoming conflict is likened to a religious war, stands in marked contrast to the tone of the opening pages of the novel where emphasis was placed on a more mundane struggle for existence. Nonetheless, despite a clear recognition that the advent of fascism has fundamentally transformed the political and social situation, attention at this stage is focused primarily on the brutal emergence of conflict and violence in the political sphere, rather than on popular front opposition to fascism itself. It is significant, in fact, that there is no global co-ordination of political strategy in the first half of the novel. Each political party acts independently, holding separate meetings to devise individual responses to the fascist threat. Although a popular front strategy is doubtless implied, it comes into existence only at the moment of the counter-demonstration itself when communists, socialists, radicals, trade-unionists, the unemployed, unite spontaneously to form a coherent and unified group facing a common enemy.

The sense of burgeoning political consciousness conveyed in the novel occasionally borders on the apocalyptic. Segments of the narrative which project a violent and courageous political stance based on heroism in the face of death are doubtless the product of a residual anarchism in Nizan's personality, so clearly visible in the early and violently iconoclastic text, *Aden Arabie*.

The presence of such violent epic discourse within *Le Cheval de Troie* can also be explained organically, however, as an expression of the anarchist tendencies of the working-class characters portrayed in the novel. So deep-rooted, in fact, are the anarchist traditions in this region that the workers of Villefranche are described as bearing a resemblance on occasions to 'sectarian, orthodox Protestants', capable of experiencing fervently religious emotions at the thought of a general strike.[34] In this sense, the violently ethical discourse which functions primarily as a direct appeal to the reader to support the anti-fascist struggle, does nonetheless arise naturally from the fictional situation itself.

Although the appeal to support the anti-fascist struggle is clearly located at the political centre of the novel, the emergence of the fascist threat is paradoxically presented not only as a moment of impending catastrophe, but also as a moment of political opportunity. Above all, the communist discourse presents fascism as the catalysing agent which unmasks the democratic pretensions of bourgeois society, forces the working class into political self-consciousness, and in the process rejuvenates a previously isolated communist party.

The presentation of fascism within the narrative is, in other words, ideologically motivated. *Le Cheval de Troie* is not a democratic, anti-fascist text. It is a strategic narrative which aims at analysing the fascist phenomenom from a Marxist perspective in order to re-situate the French communist party at the centre of the political arena.

The strategic nature of the presentation of fascism is clearly visible in the bourgeois dinner party sequence located towards the end of the first half of the novel. Leaving aside the highly idiosyncratic contribution of Lange, the dialogue between these representatives of bourgeois law and order is a narrative pretext designed primarily to disclose the underlying economic contradictions of fascism threatening the continued stability of bourgeois democracy. The industrialist, Provost-Livet, informs both the dinner party guests and the reader in an implacably cynical voice that despite his personal ideological attraction to fascism, economically it is a dangerous and misguided ideology. Once the demagogic economic promises of fascism have proved to be illusory, he asserts, the consequent social disorder unleashed will become uncontrollable and the only remaining solution will be war.

This dialogue illuminates the fact that fascism simultaneously threatens the social stability of the bourgeoisie and activates the political rebellion of the working class. It is consequently not fascism as such which is the subject of this novel. It is rather the twin effects that fascism itself produces: on the one hand, the disruption of the bourgeois state, on the other, the politicisation of the proletariat. The second half of the novel, although centred on an anti-fascist counter-demonstration, is in reality a festival of liberation in which a fascist meeting is exploited as a means of exploding the law and order of the bourgeoisie and of celebrating the political activism of the working class.

It is quite clear at the end of the novel that the significance of the events themselves is not primarily the struggle against fascism but the rebirth of working-class political consciousness:

> The political significance of the day was perhaps simply that thousands of men had at long last given vent to their anger. Resistance and militancy, fundamental values of the working class, had once again entered into their lives with a certainty and clarity which exalted them.[35]

Fascism is opposed in the novel. But the overriding teleology of the novel is to designate the working class as politically active after a long period of docility. Significantly, fascism disappears from the conclusion of the novel which is dominated by images of the political re-awakening of the labour movement.

The transitional moment of production of the novel is consequently reflected in the progressive development of the communist discourse in the narrative. Throughout, there is a sustained tension between a sectarian and a popular front strategy. Initially sectarian and defensive, the narrative adopts a progressively more combative stance with the emergence of fascism, climaxing in the popular front fusion of the anti-fascist counter-demonstration. However, fascism recedes into the distance in the conclusion where attention is focused on the rebirth of working-class political consciousness and militancy. At the same time the entire narrative is bathed in a persistent anarchist tone, echoing Nizan's early iconoclasm, the political culture of the workers portrayed, and the anti-authoritarian, undisciplined quality of the counter-demonstration itself.

From a purely political and historical perspective, therefore, *Le Cheval de Troie* resists classification as an archetypal exemplification of Zhdanovite socialist realism. A secondary, existential discourse adds a further dimension to such resistance.

Existence

Death is an inescapable presence in *Le Cheval de Troie*. Death is not an external, supernatural phenomenom that descends upon the world unexpectedly. Death is a deadly poison which enters into the pores of life at birth, relentlessly corrodes the body fabric of the living, and is secreted only at the moment of dying. This ceaseless flow of death in life's bloodstream is the metaphysical centre of *Le Cheval de Troie*.

Death refuses to recognise class boundaries. The revolution does not banish the fears that death instils in the minds of men and women. Nizan's bitter realisation that even the Soviet revolutionary state ultimately did not protect its citizens from an anguished confrontation with death is never far from the surface of the narrative of *Le Cheval de Troie*. Unlike *Antoine Bloyé*, where death was for the most part presented as the defining characteristic of the existence of an oppressive class, in this second novel men and women on both sides of the class divide are equally tormented by death, although in different ways.

The clear-cut distinction between a deathly bourgeois existence and a dynamic communist existence is nonetheless retained in *Le Cheval de Troie*. An explicit comparison is made between the burgeoning, life-giving existence of the communist militants on the one hand, and the dead, oppressive life-style of the bourgeois teaching profession on the other. Bloyé's professional colleagues are described as frightened, ghostly figures, desperately seeking ways of masking the emptiness of their lives and the inevitability of their death. Their existence is dismissed as a cowardly pretence, a life sentence in which genuine human relations have been abandoned in a sadistic teaching environment dominated by mindless, self-deluding petty-bourgeois careerism.

The links between death and the bourgeoisie, the central theme of *Antoine Bloyé*, are analysed in a more deeply metaphysical vein, however, in *Le Cheval de Troie*. The character of Lange, exploited in the narrative to symbolise the deathly void at the heart of bourgeois existence, graphically exemplifies the intricate interweaving between the metaphysical and the political in the novel.

Lange is presented as an extreme example of petty-bourgeois alienation, a man who inhabits a ghostly, shadowy world, and whose thoughts centre morbidly on death and the production of a book describing the desolation of a solitary individual exploring the death-filled landscape of an urban environment. There is a haunting intensity in the description of Lange's nocturnal prowling in the town which reaches beyond the limitations of stereotypical socialist realist literature. Lange, Roquentin and Sartre become merged in the deathly twilight existence of Villefranche.

The highly metaphysical presence of Lange is, however, not gratuitous to the political message. As well as offering a hallucinating example of the aberrations of petty-bourgeois alienation in an extreme form, the character of Lange also functions as an integral part of the global ideological thesis that emerges from the novel. In the dinner party sequence Lange's metaphysical anguish appears naïve compared to the cynical economic views of the industrialist Provost-Livet. Yet the strategic objective of the dialogue itself is to highlight the imminent bankruptcy of the bourgeoisie not only politically and economically (Provost-Livet), but also spiritually and ethically (Lange). The alienated voice of Lange communicates to the reader the desolate conclusion that the only surviving values in bourgeois society are the values of death. Lange projects the deathly spiritual void at the heart of bourgeois society and in the process completes a picture of total bourgeois degeneration.

The figure of Lange consequently poses the more general problem of the regeneration of spiritual and ethical values in a society defined by death. Lange's final response, aligning himself with fascism at the moment of the street confrontation, is not merely aimed at highlighting the need to progress beyond sterile intellectual masturbation and engage in political action. It is also pointedly symbolic of the need articulated generally in the novel to search for a response to a wider ethical problem. Although the narrative of *Le Cheval de Troie* makes it abundantly clear that Lange's response is misguided, and that the solution is to be found on the other side of the class divide in the ranks of the communist militants, none the less the importance of this character resides primarily in his expression of the death, decay and disintegration of the entire value-system of bourgeois society. Metaphysics in this instance lends effective support to politics.

It is symbolic that whereas the descriptions of the bourgeoisie evoke images of death that are linked primarily to the sterile and anesthetised process of *living*, the descriptions of the working class evoke images of death that are centred primarily on the heroic and painful moment of *dying*. Beyond the general exploitation of the death theme to symbolise the oppressive living and working environment of the communist militants, the process and the act of dying are together exploited to project a specific ideological message.

Two deaths in the narrative are effectively orchestrated to serve the ideological objectives of the novel itself: the deaths of Catherine and Paul. Catherine dies totally alone, bleeding to death after an abortion. Paul dies in the company of communist comrades, hit by a stray bullet during the street fighting. The reader is given little insight into the personality of either of these characters. The strained marital relationship between Albert and Catherine is briefly sketched but the overriding objective is to explain the tensions and emotional problems of private life as the inevitable product of a society which makes back-street abortions necessary. Paul remains a totally anonymous figure, an unknown militant who comes to symbolise the essential qualities of the political struggle itself.

Catherine dies almost without a struggle, at the precise moment when the militant cries of working-class protest are ringing through the streets of Villefranche. She dies of a haemorrhage, her life blood streaming from her as she secretes her own death. This harrowing episode, which interrupts the narrative flow of the street-fighting, is strategically placed. The reader, confronted by the sickening description of a young woman dying in a pool of blood, unaided, helpless, too weak to resist, is forced to reflect not only on the injustice of one particular death, but also on the inescapable presence of death in life. For a brief moment, the narrative subsumes the dominant political thesis beneath broader metaphysical concerns, before pointing a finger of accusation at the society of unequal chances which makes such a death possible.

This process of fusion between the political and the metaphysical is prominent in the narrative exploitation of the death of Paul. Compared to the meticulous description of the moment of Catherine's death, Paul's moment of dying is but briefly described. Yet this death in the heat of the street battle prompts the articulation of the global political/metaphysical message of the novel.

Dying alone and at a distance from the struggle, Catherine dies a pointless, insignificant death. Her death merely highlights the waste of an entire existence. Hers can only be a negative exemplary tale. Dying for the party in the midst of the struggle, by contrast, Paul dies a heroic, exemplary death. His death comes to symbolise a victory not only over political enemies but also over death itself: 'Either lead a fearful life of anguish, or risk death in order to conquer life itself', notes Bloyé towards the end of the novel,[36] highlighting a fundamental choice to be made between defensive, *angst*-ridden acquiescence and militant, risk-taking combat. Such a conclusion not only foregrounds the twin struggle against death and the bourgeoisie, it also signals a synthesis between two discourses, existential and communist, within the narrative itself.

The existential discourse encoded in the narrative, although enmeshed inextricably in communist ideology, does nonetheless occasionally strike a different chord. Segments of the narrative drift tantalisingly close to metaphysical speculation devoid of ideological ballast. Certain passages depicting Lange's metaphysical *angst*, certain aspects of the description of Catherine's death cannot be entirely subsumed within the communist framework. Likewise, the concluding pages of the novel contain elements which attach an importance to the metaphysical oppression of death which transcends orthodox communist ideology:

> For years at a time we do not think about death. We simply have sudden brief intimations of its existence in the midst of our lives, although there are people who think of it more often than most: they are born like that. Death passes nearby, a cloud poisoning the earth upon which its shadow falls, and our spirit is caught by fear. Then we recover, and begin again to live as though we were immortal; we continue to play the game of cheating death, we take medicines and follow diets or indulge in passionate pursuits. But still it appears again. However much we try, we cannot forget the army of men who die each second, the vast cavalcade of funerals proceeding towards all the cemeteries of the earth. We need only see the mangled body of a cat lying on the shiny surface of a road to realise that death may come and that our hearts may stop.[37]

The principal foe here is death, not political oppression. The paradox of *Le Cheval de Troie* is revealed in these lines. This text, which is the most visibly politicised of Nizan's novels, is at the same time the most deeply metaphysical. Politics and metaphysics collide in a kaleidoscopic confrontation.

Ideology and Form

The formal structure of *Le Cheval de Troie* reflects the global political, metaphysical and cultural position that Nizan had reached during 1934 and 1935. His political perception had been transformed by the events of February 1934. His cultural views had been influenced by

the Soviet Writers' Congress of the same year. His sense of metaphysical alienation had been heightened not only by his realisation that death remained a formidable presence even in the revolutionary Soviet state, but doubtless also by his close contact with André
· Malraux in the Soviet Union. *Le Cheval de Troie* is consequently a formal synthesis of a global ideological development which represents a clear development from *Antoine Bloyé*.

The ideological view that emerges from *Le Cheval de Troie* is inherently more problematical than the view that is presented in *Antoine Bloyé*. Whereas in *Antoine Bloyé* the implication of the narrative was that avoidance of a deathly existence could be achieved by breaking with an oppressive bourgeois class and entering the dynamic, living existence of the working class, in *Le Cheval de Troie* it is apparent that death is a metaphysical presence which even encroaches upon the lives of the communist party militants. The consequences of this all-pervading presence of death in *Le Cheval de Troie* is a fusion between the collective effort of all the communist militants to struggle against the oppression of a deathly class enemy, and the individual effort of each communist militant to struggle against the oppressive presence of death itself. This revised ideological view inevitably has implications for the formal structure of the novel itself.

Most strikingly, the material presence of the party in *Le Cheval de Troie* facilitates the organic emergence of communist ideology from within the text. The uneasy presence of abstract segments of narrative in *Antoine Bloyé*, where an omniscient communist narrator legislates the significance of historical developments, is replaced by the voices of the communist militants themselves expressing their own political convictions in the context of their living environment.

Occasionally, such dialogue sequences are not entirely convincing. Specific utterances do not ring true, sounding more like the unmediated slogans of the party than the ideas of the individuals voicing them. Yet for the most part, this technical device is skilfully handled and enables the effective integration of communist ideology into the narrative.

The structural division of the narrative is also ideologically significant. The first half of the text, a series of separate tableaux depicting the hierarchical divisions and class distinctions in the town, constitutes an analytical phase in which the social actors are introduced, and the reader is allowed time to reflect upon the established economic and political order. The second half of the text, by contrast, depicting the violent confrontation and fusion of the various social groups in conflict, conjures up vivid images of political struggle, and propels the reader relentlessly to the concluding synthesis of the narrative. The individual characters soon fade from the reader's mind. What remains is the memory of a powerfully evoked scene of political confrontation which reinforces through its emotional intensity the comparisons previously made between two classes, two lifestyles, two social and political orders. This enduring memory of class division, class conflict and class consciousness is the ultimate proof of the ideological potency of this novel.

This ideological potency is also greatly enhanced by a more effective use of images evoking natural settings and the passage of time. Unlike *Antoine Bloyé* where the naturalising effect of such images tends to subvert the potency of the historical dimension of the novel, images of time and nature in *Le Cheval de Troie* work to the ideological advantage of the text.

The time-scale is limited to one week. The reader's thoughts are consequently focused on immediate practical action, not the irretrievable passage of time as in *Antoine Bloyé*. The reader's attention, in other words, is not diverted from the passage of *historical* time by a sad lament on the passage of time *in general*. Images of nature are also exploited in a more effective, contrastive fashion. Whereas in *Antoine Bloyé* images of natural settings tend to mask the realities of urban existence, in *Le Cheval de Troie* nature is presented as the image of a counter-culture in opposition to the town, a refuge from oppression, a place to breathe freely. This contrastive technique ultimately reinforces the ideological message of the novel aimed at disclosing the oppressiveness of working-class living conditions in the town.

Ultimately, however, the most important aspect of the narrative technique is the merging of the communist and existential discourses within the text itself, a merging which reflects the intimate relationship that Nizan perceived at this stage in his ideological development between the political struggle against the oppression of a hated class and the metaphysical struggle against the oppression of death itself. It is precisely the extra dimension given to this text by the existential discourse woven into the fabric of the narrative that enables the effective insinuation of ideology into the reader's mind.

This strategic merging of communist and existential discourses not only releases *Le Cheval de Troie* from the authoritarian grip of Zhdanovite socialist realism. It is also the crucial factor explaining

Nizan's success in achieving a fine balance between artistic means and ideological ends. More than fifty years after its moment of production, *Le Cheval de Troie* remains a powerfully evocative and mobilising image of a group in fusion, a vivid illustration of the leap from acquiescence and seriality to rebellion and authenticity.

(iii) *LA CONSPIRATION*, 1938: POST-MORTEM OF A GENERATION

Emotional, intellectual and political adolescence is the subject matter of *La Conspiration*. Centred on the lives of five students in the late 1920s, this novel represents a mercilessly demystifying account of the delusions and traumas experienced by the sons of the bourgeoisie in their attempts to make the painful transition from immaturity to manhood.

The moment of production of *La Conspiration* is crucial. Published in 1938, the novel is a product of the Popular Front experience. Unlike *Le Cheval de Troie*, produced in 1934 and 1935 at a historical moment when the realities of the transformed political and ideological climate were temporarily masked by a crusading, heroic rhetoric, itself a distillation of sectarian mythology and civil war anarchy, *La Conspiration* originated in the political developments that took place between 1936 and 1938. The subject matter, tone and style of this novel are consequently a mediated reflection of the historical realities of popular front co-operation.

By 1937 and 1938, when Nizan was writing *La Conspiration*, it had become clear that the heroic, civil war scenario that he had proposed in *Le Cheval de Troie* was no longer on the political agenda. The epic struggle, seemingly predicted by the events of February 1934, had not materialised and had been replaced by the more prosaic, daily struggle of popular front politics. This fundamental shift in perspective from the heroic to the prosaic, expressed symbolically in *Histoire de Thésée*,[38] is the ideological force motivating *La Conspiration*.

When Nizan speaks ironically of the immaturity and political delusions of a generation of students in the late 1920s, he is at the same time speaking in a guarded manner of the immaturity and irrelevance of sectarian politics and civil war scenarios in post-1936 France. Given that the underlying theme of *La Conspiration* is the painful transition from an immature to a mature politics, this novel is an indictment not only of the *uncertainty* of pre-communist alienation, but also of the *certainty* of sectarian communist simplicity. It is, in other words, an account of a passage to manhood at two levels, at two different historical moments. The complexity, the density, the opacity, the elusiveness of the world, apparent in 1937 and 1938, had been masked not only in the late 1920s by the problems of adolescence, but also in the early 1930s by the rhetorical illusions of sectarian politics:

> They did not yet know how massive, how formless the world is, how little it resembles a wall that can be knocked down in order to build another that is more impressive, but rather a gelatinous mass with neither head nor tail, a kind of enormous jellyfish with well hidden organs.[39]

This dual historical reasonance is the ideological secret of *La Conspiration*. Too frequently, this novel is interpreted as a fictional reflection of Nizan's growing disillusionment with communism which was to culminate in his exit from the party in 1939. This is merely liberal wishful thinking. *La Conspiration* does not contain within it an implicit abandonment of communist ideology. On the contrary, this novel is a mature communist assessment of both an immature, pre-communist adolescent phase, and an immature, communist sectarian phase.

The subject matter of the novel itself corroborates this view since it comprises an amalgamation of two different historical periods. Although at one level Nizan draws on his own pre-communist student experiences in 1924 and 1925, specifically exploiting his involvement in the 'Philosophies' group, he chooses by contrast to situate the novel in 1928 and 1929 at a moment when he himself was already a member of a French communist party isolated in its pursuit of sectarian politics. This amalgamation of pre-communist and sectarian communist attitudes sets this novel apart from *Antoine Bloyé*, a 'balance-sheet' novel, and *Le Cheval de Troie*, a 'problem-centred' novel. *La Conspiration* is unusual to the extent that it is both balance sheet and problem. The balance sheet records the mystifications of the late 1920s. The problem centres on the nature of revolutionary politics in post-1936 France.

With few exceptions, *La Conspiration* was greeted with enthusiastic critical approval on its publication.[40] In December 1938 Nizan was awarded the Prix Interallié for this, his third novel. It seemed at the time that the maturity of political viewpoint implicitly recorded in

La Conspiration had finally been matched by a maturity of literary expression.

History

Although far more complex than *Antoine Bloyé*, *La Conspiration* is a similar experiment in the novel of apprenticeship. Unlike Nizan's first novel, however, in which a single character functioned as the symbol of a negative apprenticeship, *La Conspiration* records with varying degrees of depth and complexity, a series of concurrent apprenticeships, some concluding negatively, others concluding at the threshold of possible solutions.

The plot is focused on the lives of five students, Rosenthal, Laforgue, Bloyé, Jurien and Pluvinage, and events take place between July 1928 and December 1929. The narrative is divided into three unequal parts. The first centres on the political activities of the student group ranging from the setting up of a revolutionary journal entitled *La Guerre civile*, to involvement in industrial and military espionage for the benefit of the French communist party, the second on a love affair between Rosenthal and sister-in-law Catherine, and the third on the betrayal by Pluvinage of a leading member of the central committee of the PCF.

The ideological dimension of the narrative reveals itself both seriously and ironically. As in the two previous novels, the communist discourse appears in its full ideological seriousness in order to direct the reader, frequently diverted by a massively present existential discourse, towards a correct interpretation of events. At the same time, however, this serious discourse is supplemented by an ironic communist discourse which situates the narrative voice itself at a mid-way position between judgement and empathy. The characters are criticised from the outside, but their actions are also explained as the consequences of a given social environment, and their failings and weaknesses are on occasions articulated from the inside.

It is this capacity not only to puncture illusions but also to locate the social origins of the illusions that constitutes the maturity of the ironic narrative voice itself. Such narrative maturity is not to be understood as a sign of ideological uncertainty, but rather as a willingness to recognise the existence of very real obstacles impeding progress to a correct ideological vision.

This ironic communist discourse asserts its presence at the very outset of the novel where the five students are introduced to the reader in a manner that fulfils a demystifying function and at the same time exhibits a residual allegiance to the problems of youth. The ideas and projects of Rosenthal, Laforgue, Bloyé, Jurien and Pluvinage are presented as no more than a series of inconsequential gestures arising from the unstable situation of young men marking time in a transition period between childhood and manhood, young men whose dependent student status ultimately places them at the periphery of social activity and deprives them of seriousness and credibility. 'We are planning a journal and having high-minded conversations because we have neither women nor money; there's nothing to get excited about', notes Bloyé, articulating the ironic view of the communist narrator.[41]

At the same time, however, this mature, retrospective view is in no sense a betrayal of the genuine anger expressed seven years previously in *Aden Arabie* when Nizan had unceremoniously denounced the mystifications manufactured for the youth of the bourgeoisie by their elders. The burning hostility to the platitudinous deceptions of the middle-aged seeking to delude young people with romantic images of youth remains in *La Conspiration*. 'When you are twenty years old, you go to sleep every single night in that state of angry uncertainty and disorientation that arises from missed opportunities.'[42]

This residual hostility to the mystifications of an elder generation comfortably ensconced in complacency, is echoed in a sustained critical analysis of family life, itself the locus of parental authority. The children of the bourgeoisie, although ridiculed for their fatuous and unrealistic life-style, are perceived ultimately as prisoners trapped in a claustrophobic bourgeois family cage. For some, such as Laforgue and Bloyé, social experiences outside the family circle will lead to rebellion and liberation. For others, however, such as Rosenthal and Pluvinage, imprisoned within the overpoweringly oppressive traditions of family life, escape is impossible. The logic of their family situation leads irreversibly to suicide and betrayal. Globally, the ironic tone of the entire narrative, fluctuating between scepticism and empathy, implicates both narrator and reader more intimately in the flow of events. This unique distillation of ironic judgement and allegiance evokes a sense of critical empathy which both instructs and fascinates the reader intrigued by the spectacle of a communist narrator retrospectively involved in the adolescent problems of the central characters of the novel itself.

All is not ironical in *La Conspiration*, however. Segments of the narrative are evidently not written tongue-in-cheek. They carry the full weight of ideological seriousness and fulfil the essential role of clarifying doctrinal implications for the benefit of the reader. The ideological seriousness is most clearly visible when attention is focused on either the working class or the French communist party. The first shared political memory of the student group, for example, the transferral of the body of Jaurès to the Panthéon in 1924, is exploited not only to foreground the unity and strength of a mass rally expressing popular support for a symbolic left-wing personality, but also to indicate unequivocally to the reader the communist narrator's belief in the truth and justice of the revolutionary rallying calls of the working class.

Initially, however, the ideological dimension of the novel is signalled to the reader by means of extra-textual information. A note at the end of the original edition of *La Conspiration* indicates that a sequel was planned in which Laforgue would enter the ranks of the French communist party. To draw attention to a future communist solution to the problems outlined in *La Conspiration* is to invite the reader to make sense of this novel in a given ideological way. The reader is expected, in other words, to interpret the actions of the characters in *La Conspiration* in the light of a subsequent allegiance to the communist cause by both Laforgue and Bloyé.

Extra-textual and intra-textual factors are consequently significant when assessing the ideological weight of *La Conspiration*. Not only is there a clear indication that Laforgue is destined to join the party in a subsequent novel (extra-textual indicator); it is also apparent to any reader conversant with Nizan's novels that Bloyé is destined for the same route, his political activities having already been narrated in *Le Cheval de Troie* (intra-textual indicator).

Laforgue and Bloyé also fulfil a highly significant ideological function in *La Conspiration* itself, insofar as they constitute a potentially orthodox counterweight to the more alienated political views of both Rosenthal and Pluvinage. It is noticeable that although Laforgue and Bloyé are criticised generally for their participation in the adolescent activities of the student group, Laforgue's immature sexuality being highlighted in particular, none the less throughout the narrative both characters articulate serious misgivings regarding the viability of Rosenthal's more exotic political ideas. Such reservations which serve the purpose of contrasting not only the leisured existence of bourgeois students with the oppressed existence of the working class, but also the illusory political activities of the student group with the realistic political activites of the communist party, inevitably encourage the reader to speculate on the future ideological development of these two characters, and, as a consequence, on the global ideological significance of the novel itself. Laforgue's transition to manhood at the conclusion of the novel, symbolic of a future allegiance to communism, is merely the final clue prompting the reader to interpret the novel in a communist perspective.

The extent to which this text is ultimately beckoning the reader towards a communist vision can also be gauged by the importance that membership of the PCF assumes in the eyes of the very character who betrays the party to the police authorities. 'This small group of men gave me the only insight that I shall ever have of a genuine human community. You do not get over communism once you have experienced it', notes Pluvinage bitterly.[43] The comradeship, vitality and warmth that Pluvinage encounters for the first time in his life within the party contrasts dramatically with the deathly oppression of his family origins and the alienating abstraction of the student group. This third section of the novel centred on Pluvinage is exploited by the communist narrator not only to situate a pathology of betrayal, but also to sanctify the party in the eyes of the reader. To explain the processes whereby the party was betrayed at a critically desperate moment in its development is to elicit a degree of understanding, if not sympathy, for both victims, Pluvinage and the PCF. There is a negative exemplary quality in the tale of Pluvinage which ultimately serves the ideological ends of the novel by highlighting the truth and justice of the communist cause in the face of great adversity.

The core of the doctrinal message in *La Conspiration*, however, is located in the figure of Carré, the exemplary communist militant. Although Carré occupies very little space in the narrative, his presence is vital since it posits a mature communist vision at the outer limits of the consciousness of the other fictional characters struggling to reach communist authenticity. The moment at which Carré articulates the significance of his allegiance to communism is the moment when the reader is confronted by a mature communist discourse that enables him/her to make sense of the hesitating and uncertain political development of the student group:

I have been a communist since the Congress of Tours for many reasons, but none is more important than being able to answer this question: with whom can I live? I can live with communists. With socialists I cannot. Socialists meet, talk politics and elections, and that's as far as it goes. Their allegiance does not determine their very breathing, their private life, their personal loyalties, their idea of death and of the future. They are citizens. They are not men. A communist always has the absolute ambition to be a man, even though his efforts might be tactless, tentative, unsuccessful. . . . It is true that some days, some nights, I have said to myself: the party is wrong, its assessment is not correct. I have said it out loud. I have been told that I was wrong, when perhaps I was right. Was that a reason to defend the principle of critical freedom against the interests of my very being? Loyalty has always appeared to me to be of far greater importance than the victory, at the cost of a possible break, of any of my political positions of a given moment. We do not live our lives from day to day according to minor truths, but according to a global relationship with other men.[44]

The voice of Carré coincides in this passage with the voice of the communist narrator. What emerges here is a global ethical commitment to communism which echoes Nizan's own position in 1937 and 1938. Beyond differences of tactics and policy, there is an all-embracing moral dimension to the communist cause which makes allegiance to the party essential. In the final analysis, it is clear that the ideological thrust of *La Conspiration* is aimed at highlighting the problems encountered by a generation of young bourgeois intellectuals in the late 1920s struggling to reach the mature communist vision symbolised by Carré.

Existence

La Conspiration overflows in existential discourses, not only because it is centred on the alienated lives of a group of students struggling to make the painful transition from adolescence to manhood, but also, and perhaps more significantly, because the communist narrator ironically recording events is less preoccupied with confronting deviant ideological positions head-on, and more interested in understanding the personal and social origins of alienation itself, with the result that greater freedom of expression is granted to deviant non-communist and pre-communist ideas and life-styles.

Unlike Nizan's two previous novels, in which the voice of communist orthodoxy retained relatively tight control over alien discourses introduced into the narrative, the alien discourses in this particular text are far more prominent. The uncertain, self-preoccupied voice of youth, the equivocating voice of liberal intellectualism, even the treacherous voice of betrayal are allowed scope to exist autonomously in *La Conspiration*, not because they are perceived as having any particular credibility *per se*, but rather because it is finally considered strategically more effective both artistically and ideologically, to foreground these alienated existential discourses in order to demonstrate the capacity of the communist novel to reflect intelligently on problems of alienation, and to highlight at the same time the inadequacy of these alienated discourses when compared to a mature communist vision.

La Conspiration is consequently a liberating text in so far as the communist narrator no longer considers it necessary to curb the expression of unorthodox discourses previously kept in check in *Antoine Bloyé* and *Le Cheval de Troie*. The self-confidence of the ideological dimension of this novel enables the articulation of a series of alienated existential discourses within a global communist framework that itself remains discreetly distant. Each of these alienated existential views is consequently granted autonomy in the text in order to allow the reader greater insight into the complex reality of a specific mode of existence and to invite him/her to reflect upon its credibility in the light of a potential communist alternative.

Doubtless the dominant existential discourse in *La Conspiration* is that of alienated youth, distracted momentarily from the serious world of work and politics by an endless preoccupation with individual sexual and intellectual development: 'It is easy to underestimate the distracted psychological state of young men discovering both books and women for the first time', notes the communist narrator.[45] Throughout the entire text there is a foregrounding of the discourse of personal, emotional development, whether it be the sexual adventures of Laforgue and Simon, the romantic conquests of Rosenthal, or the morbid self-obsessions of Pluvinage, a foregrounding which places the ideological dimension of the novel at a distance.

The alienated discourse of Pluvinage is the most nakedly existential in the narrative. The themes of death, oppression and betrayal combine to form a composite picture of existential anguish that is explicitly contrasted with the moral authenticity of communist militancy.

Pluvinage, like Rosenthal, is presented as a victim of an impossible childhood situation. Unlike Rosenthal, however, who fails to escape from his upper-middle-class, Jewish origins, Pluvinage remains scarred for life by the deathly environment in which he was born. 'I grew up in an environment where the principal concern was the removal of city scum and the registration of private disasters', he recalls, referring to his upbringing by a father who was chief clerk for burials in the Préfecture de la Seine.[46] Close proximity to cemeteries, mortuaries and death at an early age fostered in him a deep sense of humiliation and resentment at his lowly social situation. As a student, Pluvinage experienced both shame and inferiority in the presence of Rosenthal and Laforgue, both of whom were perceived as emanating from socially 'superior' family backgrounds. Paradoxically, Pluvinage's need to erase the memory of his deathly origins led him initially to membership of the PCF, a surrogate family, and finally to betrayal of the PCF, when he became convinced that the party itself was about to be obliterated by the forces of law and order. 'People like me are only capable of being loyal to winners', he confesses.[47] Pluvinage, a loser by birth, could not remain loyal to a party of losers.

What is perhaps most striking in this extended existential analysis is the extent to which the detailed account of the traumatic emotional and intellectual difficulties experienced by Pluvinage succeeds not only in presenting a convincing picture of an individual character, but also in linking an autonomous existential problem to the global ideological dimension of the novel itself. The narrative exploitation of the themes of inferiority, oppression, comradeship, loyalty and betrayal establishes a symbiotic relationship between the personal dilemma of Pluvinage and the social dilemma of the PCF.

Although the alienated discourse of Pluvinage is exceptional through its extremism, it is not unique in its success in linking a genuinely autonomous existential perception of a given character to the ideological dimension of the novel itself. The sophisticated, if equivocating, discourse of the middle-aged writer, François Régnier, fulfils the same function in relation to the authentic communist discourse of the militant Carré.

At one level, Régnier is revealed as a complex personality reflecting on the fundamental differences between his own generation, formed amidst the brutal reality of the First World War, and the subsequent generation of Rosenthal and Laforgue, luxuriating in exotic and totally unreal political adventures. At another level, he reveals himself as an ineffectual liberal, incapable of understanding the nature of Carré's commitment to the PCF, unable to grasp the significance of the qualitative change in existence that membership of the PCF brings about.

Despite important examples of the intermeshing between existential and communist discourses in *La Conspiration*, however, large sections of the narrative are conspicuously detached from any overt ideological significance, none more so than the entire episode recording the relationship between Rosenthal and Catherine. Arguably, it could be maintained that the ironic criticism of Rosenthal's conception of love as conquest, a means of revenge on an oppressive family, is at the same time a discreet criticism of a sectarian view of politics as conquest and revenge. However, such an interpretation should not be overstated since the entirety of this second section of the novel does not accede to the political sphere, rooted as it is in interpersonal and family relations.

The political dimension of the novel as encoded in the conspiracy to engage in military and industrial espionage for the PCF is completely forgotten by Rosenthal in his emotional pursuit of his sister-in-law Catherine. The love story itself, which is as much an analysis of upper-middle-class French family life as an account of the psychological development of the two characters involved, progressively distances the reader from political events and dramatically highlights the escapist option that was hinted at in *Antoine Bloyé*.

It is a curious fact that the possibility of genuine authentic relations between men and women is almost inevitably linked in Nizan's narratives with a form of escapism. Bernard and Catherine literally escape into each others' arms and away from the oppression of society and the family. The distinctly Stendhalian quality of the discourse recording the progressive stages of Bernard's love for Catherine is symptomatic of a fundamental shift in perspective that relocates the centre of gravity of this section of the novel in interpersonal and psychological dramas rather than in political and social events.

There is a hedonism in this escapist solution which is echoed in the narrative style itself. Nothing could be further removed from the omniscient historical narration of *Antoine Bloyé* or the epic narrative tone of *Le Cheval de Troie* than the textual pleasure evoked by the following passage describing a country setting in Greece removed from the political and social struggle:

The landscape was a completely autonomous and self-defining

whole; it possessed within itself its own justification; The awesome magnitude of the earth was entirely absent. . . . nothing seemed to age or change within a world which was replicated from second to second in an identical series in the same way that a great work of art is ceaselessly reproduced. It was enough to take your breath away with surprise and happiness; you were integrated in this world which was totally self-sufficient, where the past and the future had ceased to exist, where the passage of time and death seemed suspended; you were caught up in the great imaginary adventure of the repetition of eternal moments.[48]

In this extract, history, time, politics, oppression, death, all are denied. The conflictual reality of the world is transformed briefly into a perfectly balanced natural setting where individual happiness becomes a genuine possibility. Such moments are rare in Nizan's work. It is nonetheless a fact that in this third novel hedonistic tendencies become more pronounced.

Ideology and Form

The formal complexity of *La Conspiration* stands in marked contrast to the one-dimensional, linear structure of *Antoine Bloyé* and the taut cohesiveness of *Le Cheval de Troie*. The discreet presence of communist ideology throughout the narrative, explained substantively as a reflection of the pre-communist mentality of the central characters portrayed, leads inevitably to a degree of formal flexibility and experimentation absent from previous novels. The focusing of the narrative on the problems of adolescence, the growing prominence of distinctly existential themes, the retrospective, ironic quality of the ideological perspective, all project the novel towards a more libertarian form. *La Conspiration* is a multi-faceted text in which a variety of alienated discourses are allowed scope to develop freely within a global framework that nonetheless remains resolutely communist.

This increased formal suppleness is signalled most clearly to the reader by the shifting narrative perspectives within the novel itself. There is constant movement in the text between omniscient narration, subjective narration, and omniscient narration in the guise of subjective narration. At times, an omniscient narrator intrudes to legislate a communist viewpoint, either seriously or ironically. At other times, the subjective experiences of individual characters are articulated directly and authentically. Then again, however, the discourse of specific characters is colonised by the communist narrator in order to project a specific ideological view more advantageously. The overall effect is consequently a series of interactive discourses which slide tantalisingly between autonomous self expression and ideological manipulation.

This sophistication of narrative technique in *La Conspiration* is enhanced by the extensive exploitation of letters (Rosenthal, Laforgue), private journals and notebooks (Régnier, Pluvinage). Such exploitation not only disrupts the more conventional structure adopted in previous novels, but also makes possible a far wider range of narrative perspectives within the text itself. The autonomous expression of an alienated viewpoint becomes legitimate because manifestly signposted as the product of an alienated consciousness. The reader is expected to interpret letters and private journals as genuine expressions of alienation. And yet this notionally genuine expression of alienation remains at heart ideologically motivated. Letters and private journals are exploited by the communist narrator at one level to introduce orthodox ideological opinions surreptitiously into the narrative, and at another level to invest the text with alternative visions of other characters in the novel, visions emanating directly from the consciousness of the author of a given letter or private journal. Rosenthal and Laforgue, for example, speak critically of Régnier, Régnier of Rosenthal, Rosenthal of Pluvinage, Pluvinage of Rosenthal and Laforgue, and so on.

The result is a perpetual criss-crossing of value-judgements which both convinces the reader of the realism of the narrative, the complexity of the text mirroring the complexity of reality, and at the same time relativises the views of all the characters in the novel, with the sole exception of the authentic communist militant, Carré. At the end of the novel, only communism as embodied in the personality of Carré remains an absolute pole of attraction, above and beyond the equivocating uncertainties of an endless series of mutually critical alienated discourses.

The complexity of the novel is also compounded by the fracturing of the narrative into three unequal parts, consecutively entitled 'La Conspiration', 'Serge' and 'Catherine'. Although each of the three parts is organically linked to the other in so far as each narrates an aspect of the personal and political dilemmas of one or more of the principal characters, there is a sense in which it is possible to speak of the autonomous existence of three distinct narrative units, each

one possessing a specific set of thematic and structural characteristics
Each one reveals a highly original configuration of the communist
and existential discourses encoded within its textual fabric.

Focused on the existential dilemmas of the student group, the first
narrative unit is nonetheless dominated by a communist discourse
fluctuating between the ironic and the serious. On occasions, the
omniscient voice of historical narration that speaks volumes in
Antoine Bloyé, but which is virtually silenced in *Le Cheval de Troie*,
returns. The retrospective, authoritarian voice of history recording
the origins and social development of the Rosenthal and Simon
families, for example, reasserts itself and brooks no contradiction.
At other times, the ironic tone of the communist narrator ceaselessly
deflating the adolescent pretensions of the luckless student group
comes to the fore. This critical, retrospective communist view is
further supplemented by the occasionally cynical voices of Laforgue
and Bloyé themselves undercutting the seriousness of their own
personal and political activities. Hence, overall, although there is a
massive foregrounding of existential problems at the thematic level
in this first narrative unit, the existential problems themselves are
articulated exclusively through a communist discourse whose primary
task is the demystification of the illusions of youth.

In the second narrative unit, by contrast, the ideological dimension
of the novel is dissolved. The personal and familial problems of
Bernard and Catherine are foregrounded in a manner that grants
pre-eminence to an existential discourse centred on hedonistic
escapism, interpersonal relations, emotional states, family tensions,
and individual alienation culminating in suicide. What is perhaps
most striking in this second narrative unit is that the existential
dimension of the text is heightened not merely by the predominance
of a specific type of discourse associated with problems of personal
angst and individual self-fulfilment, but more significantly by the
increased importance attached to characterisation. The depth and
autonomy of the character of Rosenthal in particular is such that the
existential dimension of the novel is no longer located in fragmentary
segments of narrative, but in the consciousness of a specific individual
reflecting upon the significance of his own life. This second narrative
unit consequently represents a major development of the existential
aspect of Nizan's writing technique. History, politics and ideology
are temporarily forgotten in the quest for individual happiness.

The third narrative unit, however, centred on Pluvinage's act of
betrayal, redirects attention towards the political, ideological sphere.

Although in many ways the most dramatically existential part of the entire novel, this third section witnesses a sustained attempt to link personal and ideological themes. As in the second narrative unit, there is a distinct shift of emphasis in terms of characterisation. The individual character of Pluvinage emerges as evocatively as that of Rosenthal. However, this third narrative unit differs from the second to the extent that the psychological problems of the central character are intimately connected with the political problems of the PCF through the act of betrayal of the communist militant, Carré.

Existential and communist discourses are consequently merged in the final narrative unit of the novel in order not only to highlight the impossibility of all efforts to suspend or dissolve the reality of social and political oppression, but also to refocus the reader's attention on the global ideological thrust of the novel itself. The concluding section of the third narrative unit, in which Laforgue reflects upon the global significance of the events recorded in *La Conspiration*, and invites the reader to speculate on the likelihood of his future allegiance to the communist cause, is made possible precisely through the prior narration of Pluvinage's act of betrayal. It is unquestionably the detailed account of Pluvinage's treachery which accomplishes the task of re-situating the narrative in the political domain, following the temporary suspension of politics and history during the highly charged emotional events involving Bernard and Catherine in the central narrative unit.

La Conspiration is consequently a novel which exhibits a strange configuration of existential and communist discourses. During an initial phase, a communist discourse that fluctuates between the serious and the ironic dominates. This communist discourse is subsequently superseded in a second phase by a powerful existential discourse recording the emotional relationship between two central characters. During a third and final phase, a desperately morbid existential discourse is paradoxically linked to political themes, a linkage which ultimately propels the reader towards a greater understanding of the communist ideological viewpoint that regulates the entire narrative.

The potency of Nizan's third novel resides above all else in its effective foregrounding of acute existential problems within a global ideological framework that remains resolutely communist. The fascination and residual appeal that *La Conspiration* continues to exercise over the contemporary reader is explained principally by the narrative fusion of existential *angst* and discreet, though ultimately dominant, communist ideology. This complex novel, which records the problems and dilemmas of the youth of a previous epoch struggling to make the painful transition to adulthood, continues to catalyse the emotional and political sensibilities of the youth of today.

(iv) *LA SOIRÉE À SOMOSIERRA*, 1940: DEAD-END HAPPINESS

The sequel to *La Conspiration*, entitled *La Soirée à Somosierra*, was to be set in the years 1936 and 1937 against the background of the Spanish Civil War. Philippe Laforgue was destined to continued his narrative existence in the role of communist journalist involved initially in the events in Spain and subsequently in a love affair with Catherine. With the exception of one small fragment,[49] the manuscript of this novel was lost, buried near Dunkirk, and never recovered.

Nizan's war correspondence indicates that *La Soirée à Somosierra* was to be the second volume of three, *La Conspiration* being the first, the third and final volume to be centred on events leading to the Second World War. This second volume was itself divided into two parts. The first part, 'Les Amours de septembre', had been completely written by October 1939. Nizan was doubtless working intermittently on the second part of the novel until his death in May 1940.

In December 1938, following the award of the Prix Interallié for *La Conspiration*, Nizan was insistent that although the beginning of *La Soirée à Somosierra* was to be located in Spain during the spring of 1936, the global theme of the novel was not the Spanish Civil War, but 'happiness'.[50] The centring of 'Les Amours de septembre' on the relationship between Laforgue and Catherine would appear to support this view, although the Spanish dimension cannot be entirely ruled out. In August 1936, at the moment of the battle of Somosierra, the importance of the events in Spain has been brought home to Nizan in a conversation with President Azana. Azana's conviction that the destiny of France was linked directly to the outcome of the events in Spain almost certainly figured in the broader political design of the book.[51] However, the eventual Republican defeat in Spain, would unquestionably have rendered problematical the status of the civil war in the narrative, and this doubtless explains in some measure the personal rather than political gloss that Nizan gives to his description of the novel.

Nizan was involved in the production of *La Soirée à Somosierra* from the autumn of 1938 until his death in May 1940. The general plan was evidently sketched out as early as December 1938. His war correspondence reveals that certain chapters were written in August 1939 in Corsica just prior to his resignation from the party, and that by October 1939 he had completed 'Les Amours de septembre'. By the beginning of February 1940, however, his political isolation and emotional depression had led to a growing disillusionment with the novel,[52] and on 8 April he confessed that he was writing very little.[53]

Nizan's forebodings concerning the consequences of his resignation from the party undoubtedly had a debilitating effect on him psychologically and creatively. In a letter dated 28 March 1940, he contrasts the apparent serenity with which Sartre was continuing to write during the Phoney War, with his own emotional distress and loss of interest in writing.[54] The unpredictability of the war situation and, above all, his exit from the party had left him in state of tension and anxiety that was reminiscent of his disorientation in the mid 1920s prior to his entry to the PCF.

The rhythm of Nizan's writing practice had been interrupted by the flow of history. Trapped in a historical situation with apparently no solution, the writing project itself seemed to lose all significance. Writing, in Nizan's eyes, had been linked to the political and moral crusade of the French communist party. Once this link had snapped, the project became meaningless. Nizan sensed that he was writing in a void. His final novel remained unfinished, a novel on happiness that terminated in a dead-end.

8

Obituary

'Can a communist write a novel?' asked Sartre rhetorically in 1938.[1]
The sceptical conclusion that Sartre himself reached was more a
reflection of his own idiosyncratic conception of the novel than a
definitive assessment of Nizan's achievements as a novelist. *Antoine
Bloyé*, *Le Cheval de Troie* and *La Conspiration* together constitute a
trilogy of communist novels whose originality and continuing topicality challenge the stereotypical view that literature and ideology
do not mix. The fine balance between technical means and ideological
ends displayed in Nizan's three experiments in the novel is a telling
testimony not only to Nizan's undoubted talent as a political novelist
but also to the genuine possibility of a successful union between
ideological belief and literary form.

The effectiveness of Nizan's communist novels resides principally
in the interlocking of two distinctive but complementary discourses,
one politically motivated and centred on problems of an ideological
and social nature, the other existentially motivated and centred on
problems of a metaphysical and personal nature. The injection of
interactive communist and existential discourses within the narrative
fabric of each of the novels enables Nizan to avoid the twin pitfalls of
ideological predictability and literary irresponsibility. The presence
of a clearly articulated communist discourse is the narrative guarantee that the reader's gaze will not be diverted too long from issues of
a political and social nature. At the same time, the presence of a
clearly articulated existential discourse is the narrative guarantee
that the reader will not lose sight of the individual problems and
dilemmas of ordinary men and women struggling to face up to life
and death in an oppressive political and social order. This dual-
edged quality of Nizan's fictional technique, an evolving configuration of communist and existential discourses, is the secret of Nizan's
success as a political novelist.

The three novels do not achieve success in equal measure, however. Critical opinion is for the most part politely unimpressed by
the residual naturalism of *Antoine Bloyé*, neglectful or dismissive of
the ideological assertiveness of *Le Cheval de Troie*, but generally

supportive of the literary maturity and technical sophistication of *La Conspiration*. Although any process of evaluation is a patently subjective and ideological act which ultimately reduces criticism to personal preferences, self-indulgence of this kind is nevertheless legitimate at this stage in the argument.

The enthusiasm for *La Conspiration* manifested by liberal criticism is motivated as much by ideological as by formal considerations. The technical complexity of Nizan's final novel, allied to the more discreet presence of communist ideology, corresponds more closely to a traditional bourgeois view of literature. The fact that this final novel is also frequently, and erroneously, interpreted as a reflection of Nizan's loss of faith in communism merely adds to its attractiveness in the eyes of the liberal critic. By contrast, *Antoine Bloyé*, although praised for its poetic imagery, is criticised from a liberal perspective for its failure to integrate (read obliterate) communist ideology within the fabric of the narrative. Predictably, the overtly ideological slant of *Le Cheval de Troie* is dismissed as misguided socialist realism.

A more satisfactory critical evaluation, however, would appear to be based on an assessment of the global ideological/aesthetic effect of each text, the extent, in other words, to which Nizan succeeds in exploiting the formal structure of the novel to ideological ends, the degree to which a balance is achieved between communist and existential discourses in the narrative itself. Critical evaluation based on criteria which focus on the relationship between ideological objectives and technical means results in a quite different assessment of the three novels.

By these criteria, the textual potency of *Antoine Bloyé*, for example, is reduced not by an excessively visible communist discourse insufficiently integrated within the narrative, but rather by an over-usage of conventional metaphors and symbols, residual vestiges of a bourgeois literary tradition, which serve the purpose of dissolving the political and historical dimension of the novel amidst a naturalising literary rhetoric. In similar vein, the global effectiveness of *La Conspiration* is arguably attenuated, not enhanced, by its formal sophistication and ideological discretion. The dispersed and fractured quality of the narrative inevitably undermines the ideological certainty normally attributable to a communist novel, and ultimately produces a slightly enigmatic text which disorientates as much as it intrigues. Only in *Le Cheval de Troie* do ideological ends and technical means appear to cohere. This notionally socialist realist novel in which the epic struggle of the communist group is mirrored in the solitary existential *angst* of each communist militant, is a classic illustration of the successful fusion of ideological belief and literary form.

More important, however, than elevating one text above another is to envisage all three novels as a process of experimentation in the linkages to be made between literature and ideology. In this sense, both the successes and the failures are equally instructive for the contemporary writer engaged in the production of militant literature. Nizan's trilogy of communist novels, a graphic illustration of the ideological and technical problems encountered in the attempt to fuse politics and aesthetics, are essential reading matter for the contemporary novelist even in the transformed historical situation of the postwar period.

From a critical perspective, the most significant aspect of the evaluation process of Nizan's novels is the necessary recognition of the need to root analysis in the historical moment of production of each text. To detach the novels of a writer of Nizan's calibre from their moment of production would be an act of ideological heresy which would deny the very premises on which the novels themselves were written. The textual configuration of each of the three novels is a mediated reflection of a highly specific moment of production.

Antoine Bloyé, produced between 1931 and 1933, is a refracted image of the sectarian communist isolationism of the late 1920s and early 1930s. *Le Cheval de Troie*, produced in 1934 and 1935, mirrors the moment of transition from sectarian to co-operative politics. *La Conspiration*, produced between 1936 and 1938, is a fragmented reflection of popular front historical developments. The formal configuration of the discourses in each of Nizan's three novels can ultimately be explained only by reference to the historical moment of production which engendered the formal configuration itself. To deny this is to emasculate the literary and critical process. 'Literature', notes Gramsci, 'does not generate literature'. It is generated 'by the intervention of the "male" element, history, that is to say new social relations'.[2]

This need to focus on the historical moment of production in critical evaluation is further highlighted in Nizan's case by his communist allegiances. At a time of massive disaffection from the French communist party in the late 1980s, when the credibility of the communist militant, the communist intellectual and the communist writer is seriously questioned, it is essential to place Nizan's communist itinerary in the context of the 1930s. During the 1930s it was still possible to retain a belief in the political and moral status of the PCF. Such times have long since passed. The unique opportunity of Nizan was to have lived at a moment when a genuine commitment to a revolutionary left-wing cause functioned as the political and moral driving force of an individual writing practice. During the 1930s Nizan produced three exemplary novels which constitute not only a vivid evocation of the political, moral and intellectual history of the period, but also a unique distillation of authentic ideological belief and rich literary talent.

From the vantage point of the 1980s, it is necessary not only initially to understand Nizan's literary production in the context of his time, when communism had a big stake in political and moral righteousness, but also subsequently to reflect on the chastening thought that communist novels of the quality produced by Nizan might never be duplicated. In the post-industrial society of contemporary France, where culture is dominated by technology, and where the PCF has lost all claim to political and moral credibility, the possibilities for authentic communist literature appear remote. Nizan's communist novels are destined in all probability to remain as symbols of the unfulfilled communist potential of a departed epoch, rather than as catalysts for the rejuvenation of contemporary communist literary production.

The destiny of Nizan's communist novels consequently remains uncertain. Whether, as is probable, *La Conspiration* alone will survive as a marginally acceptable text on the periphery of a dominant bourgeois literary tradition, or whether, as is less likely, Nizan's trilogy of novels continue their narrative existence as an instructive model of the formal and ideological problems confronting the contemporary left-wing novelist, cannot be predicted with any certainty.

The real significance of Paul Nizan, however, is not to be located exclusively in the production of isolated literary texts. His is rather a broader, symbolic significance. 'A man is nothing unless he questions the established order', noted Sartre in 1968.[3] Beyond all else, Nizan's life and work are a testimony to radical protest and constructive political beliefs. His words and his acts constitute a refusal to acquiesce to oppression, a commitment to work towards revolutionary political objectives, a desperate attempt to give meaning to the desolation of death. There is no greater lesson for the contemporary writer.

Here lies Paul Nizan. Long may he symbolise the struggle.

English Translation of the Principal Titles Cited in French

WORKS BY NIZAN

Les Acharniens	*The Acharnians*
Aden Arabie	*Aden Arabia*
Les Amours de septembre	*September Love*
Antoine Bloyé	*Anthony Bloyé*
Le Cheval de Troie	*Trojan Horse*
Les Chiens de garde	*The Watchdogs*
Chronique de septembre	*September Chronicle*
'Les Conséquences du refus'	'The Consequences of Refusal'
La Conspiration	*The Conspiracy*
'L'Ennemi public n° 1'	'Public Enemy no. 1'
La Guerre civile	*Civil War*
Le Jour de la colère	*Day of Wrath*
'Littérature révolutionnaire en France'	'Revolutionary Literature in France'
Les Matérialistes de l'antiquité	*The Ancient Materialists*
Morceaux choisis de Marx	*Selected Extracts of Marx*
'Notes-programme sur la philosophie'	'Programmatic Notes on Philosophy'
La Soirée à Somosierra	*Evening at Somosierra*
'Sur l'humanisme'	'On Humanism'
Visages de la France	*Images of France*

WORKS BY SARTRE

Les Chemins de la liberté	*The Roads to Freedom*
'Drôle d'amitié'	'An Odd Friendship'
L'Enfance d'un chef	*Childhood of a Leader*
Les Mains sales	*Dirty Hands*
Les Mots	*Words*
Préface: Aden Arabie	*Preface: Aden Arabia*

'La Semence et le scaphandre'   'The Seed and the Diving Suit'

GENERAL

Paul Nizan: intellectuel   *Paul Nizan: Communist*
  communiste   *Intellectual*
Paul Nizan: pour une nouvelle   *Paul Nizan: Towards a New*
  culture   *Culture*

Notes and References

ABBREVIATIONS

The place of publication of all works cited is Paris unless otherwise indicated.

Works by Nizan

AA	*Aden Arabie* (Rieder, 1931).
AB	*Antoine Bloyé* (Grasset, 1933).
CG	*Les Chiens de garde* (Rieder, 1932).
CO	*La Conspiration* (Gallimard, 1938).
CS	*Chronique de septembre* (Gallimard, 1939).
CT	*Le Cheval de Troie* (Gallimard, 1935).

Works by Sartre

PAA	*Préface: Aden Arabie* (François Maspero, 1960).
SIT I, II, IV, VI, VII, X	*Situations I* (Gallimard, 1947); *II* (1948); *IV* (1964); *VI* (1964); *VII* (1965); *X* (1976).

General

ATO	'Paul Nizan', *Atoll*, 1 (Nov–Dec 1967–Jan 1968): contributions by Y. Buin, L. Martin-Chauffier, B. Besnier, J. Leiner, J.-J. Brochier, A. Ginsbourg, C. Malraux, J.-P. Barou, H. Nizan.
PIC	*Paul Nizan: intellectuel communiste 1926–1940*, ed. J.-J Brochier (François Maspero, 1967).
NOC	*Paul Nizan: pour une nouvelle culture*, ed. S. Suleiman (Grasset, 1971).

Notes to Chapter 1: Problems and Method

1. J. Leiner, 'Un portrait pirandellien', in *ATO*, p. 41.
2. J.-P. Sartre, '*La Conspiration* par Paul Nizan', in *SIT* I, pp. 25–8.
3. A. Ulmann, 'Avec Paul Nizan: Prix Interallié', *Vendredi*, 8 Dec 1938, p. 5.

4. The biographies written by Pascal Ory, *Nizan: Destin d'un révolté* (Ramsay, 1980) and Annie Cohen-Solal and Henriette Nizan, *Paul Nizan, communiste impossible* (Grasset, 1980) have already accomplished this task.

5. Nizan was awarded the Prix Interallié for *La Conspiration* in 1938. The manuscript of his partially written fourth novel, *La Soirée à Somosierra*, was buried near Dunkirk and never recovered despite extensive searches.

6. P. Nizan, *'Pour un réalisme socialiste* par Aragon', *L'Humanité*, 12 Aug 1935; reprinted in *NOC*, pp. 176–7.

Part One   Paul Nizan: Novel Communist

Note to the Introduction

1. For an account of biography as a process of cultural reproduction, see my *Sartre's Existential Biographies* (London: Macmillan, 1984).

Notes to Chapter 2: Enter the Party

1. P. Nizan, 'Notes-programme sur la philosophie', *Bifur*, 7 Dec 1930; reprinted in *PIC*, p. 207.

2. J.-P. Sartre, 'Un entretien avec Jean-Paul Sartre', *Le Monde*, 14 May 1971, p. 20.

3. P. Nizan, 'Secrets de famille', *Monde*, 14 Mar 1931, p. 4

4. Ibid.

5. Ibid.

6. *PAA*, pp. 29–30.

7. J.-P. Sartre, *Les Mots* (Gallimard, 1964) p. 190.

8. In a critical review of the work of Dickens, published in *Ce Soir*, 9 Mar 1939, Nizan unequivocally proclaimed his allegiance to a manichean view of the world.

9. Nizan, 'Lettre à une amie', July 1925, published *in extenso* in A. Cohen-Solal and H. Nizan, *Paul Nizan, communiste impossible* (Grasset, 1980) pp. 42–3. Further evidence of Nizan's public disdain for 'losers' is provided in the original manuscript of an early novel written in 1923–4 by Jean-Paul Sartre, entitled *La Semence et le scaphandre* and centred on the Sartre–Nizan friendship. Nizan/ Lucelles is described in the following terms: 'Pity was totally unknown to him. I have never seen him commiserate with those worse off than himself. He used to refer to them as "losers"' (*Le Magazine littéraire*, 59 (Dec 1971) p. 62).

10. Even as late as 1924, Nizan was actively seeking to rehabilitate his father's name. Cohen-Solal records that Nizan had enlisted Raymond Aron's well-connected family to intercede on his father's behalf. Aron, however, is quite categorical in confirming the railway

company's version of events: Pierre Nizan had been disciplined for professional incompetence, he asserts. See Cohen-Solal and Nizan, *Paul Nizan, communiste impossible*, pp. 38–9.

11. This driving ambition to succeed, so clearly visible in the personality of the adolescent Nizan, is doubtless a manifestation of what Emmanuel Todd, Nizan's own grandson, refers to as the competitive and highly individualist ideology of the French petty bourgeoisie ensnared in the brutally aggressive and egoistic social relations of contemporary French capitalism. See E. Todd, *Le Fou et le prolétaire* (Laffont, 1979) pp. 231–5.

12. P. Nizan, 'Mort de la morale bourgeoise par Emmanuel Berl', *Europe*, 15 July 1930; reprinted in *NOC*, p. 27.

13. For a detailed account of Nizan's academic achievements between 1917 and 1924, see A. Ginsbourg, *Paul Nizan* (Editions Universitaires, 1966) pp. 5–6.

14. Nizan first met Sartre in the academic year 1916–17. Sartre spent the years 1917–18, 1918–19 and 1919–20 in the lycée in La Rochelle. He returned to Henri IV in 1920 and became a close friend of Nizan. Between 1920 and 1926, the year of Nizan's departure for Aden, the two friends were inseparable. Sartre's early autobiographical novel, *La Semence et le scaphandre*, is essentially an account of the Sartre–Nizan friendship as experienced in the early 1920s, whereas his preface to *Aden Arabie* comprises a retrospective view of their relationship between 1920 and 1926. The concluding pages of *Les Mots*, Sartre's autobiography, include an account of Sartre's first encounter with Nizan in 1916–17.

15. *PAA*, p. 30.

16. 'Lettre à Henriette Alphen', 7 Mar 1927; cited in A. King, *Paul Nizan, Écrivain* (Didier, 1976) p. 12. See also J. Leiner, 'Un portrait pirandellien', *ATO*, pp. 32–3: 'As a child he adored his father, but when he went to the École Normale there occurred a split in their relationship.'

17. *CO*, p. 46.

18. Nizan, 'Secrets de famille', p. 4.

19. Nizan, 'Lettre à une amie', pp. 41–3.

20. The precise dates of Nizan's membership of *Le Faisceau* are not known. What is clear is that his membership was of very short duration. Ory's estimate of two to three months in late 1925 and early 1926 is probably correct. It needs to be stressed, first that Valois's movement initially lacked ideological clarity – Raymond Aron describes it as a 'semi left-wing movement' (Cohen-Solal and Nizan, *Paul Nizan, communiste impossible*, p. 46) – and secondly, that Nizan rapidly became disenchanted with its aims and objectives, turning his attentions to the French communist party.

21. The precise date of Nizan's entry to the PCF is similarly not clearly established. J. Leiner pinpoints the entry data as 'late 1927, early 1928' (*Le Destin littéraire de Paul Nizan* (Klincksieck, 1970) p. 265); C. Prévost as 'late 1927' (*Les Intellectuels et le PCF* (Cahiers de l'Institut Maurice Thorez, 1976) p. 52).

22. This role-playing activity in which the objective is to affirm one's

presence in the world by means of disguise (ideological, emotional or vestimentary) doubtless finds its clearest expression in Nizan's cult of the dandy. His flirtation with fascism may in many ways be understood as a product of the exhibitionism and self-affirmation associated with the dandy. When Merleau-Ponty describes Nizan returning to Louis-le-Grand dressed in the blue of Valois, self-affirmation through disguise reaches its climax. Disguised in the ideological and vestimentary uniform of Valois's fascist group, Nizan masks his inner turmoil beneath a reassuring cloak of certainty. See M. Merleau-Ponty, *Signes* (Gallimard, 1960) pp. 35–6.

23. For a detailed account of the wide-ranging literary styles in Nizan's juvenilia, see Leiner, *Le Destin littéraire de Paul Nizan*, pp. 25–35.
24. In early to mid-1926 Nizan became somewhat disillusioned with literature and turned his attentions to the cinema.
25. P. Nizan, Correspondance d'Aden', in *PIC*; pp. 73–97.
26. Ibid., p. 84.
27. Ibid., p. 85
28. Ibid., p. 87.
29. P. Nizan, 'Lettre à Henriette Alphen', 18 Aug 1926; cited in Cohen-Solal and Nizan, *Paul Nizan, communiste impossible*, p. 52.
30. P. Nizan, 'Lettre à Henriette Alphen', Apr 1927; cited in P. Ory, *Paul Nizan: Destin d'un révolté* (Ramsay, 1980) p. 72.
31. Nizan, 'Correspondance d'Aden', in *PIC*, p. 91.
32. *PIC*, pp. 94–5.
33. Nizan's celebrated car accident, alluded to in a letter of 2 May 1927 (*PIC*, pp. 96–7), described by Sartre as an attempted suicide (*PAA*, pp. 36–7), and supported in this interpretation by Merleau-Ponty (*Signes*, p. 36), occurred at about the same time that he was debating the entrepreneurial solution, just prior to his return to France. Arguably, this event can be understood as a final dramatic manifestation of Nizan's highly charged emotional state of the time, following which the political solution in France became progressively more dominant. Alternatively, the alleged suicide can be interpreted as pure myth-making on Sartre's part. André Besse, Nizan's tutee in Aden, is adamant, for example, that suicide can 'definitely be ruled out'. (See A. King, *Paul Nizan, écrivain* (Didier, 1976) p. 20.)
34. Nizan, 'Secrets de famille', p. 4.
35. Merleau-Ponty, *Signes*, p. 42.
36. E. Todd, *Le Fou et le prolétaire* (Laffont, 1979) pp. 231–65.
37. Ibid., p. 236.
38. D. Caute, *Communism and the French Intellectuals, 1914–1960* (London: André Deutsch, 1964) p. 98.
39. *CT*, p. 119.
40. See G. Cogniot, *L'Internationale communiste* (Editions Sociales, 1969) p. 100.
41. See, for example, D. Tartakowsky, 'Le tournant des années trente', in *Le PCF: étapes et problèmes, 1920–1972* (Editions sociales, 1981), and G. Cogniot, 'L'Internationale devant la crise économique des pays

capitalistes et la montée du fascisme (1929–1933)', in *L'Internationale communiste*.

42.   According to G. Cogniot, Thorez was highly supportive of the Amsterdam Congress held in August 1932. In November and December 1932 Duclos was outspoken in his attacks on sectarian politics which he judged to be undermining the party's appeal to the masses (see Cogniot, *L'Internationale communiste*, pp. 111–15). J. Touchard, by contrast, is of the view that both Thorez and Duclos remained committed to the 'class against class' strategy until February 1934 (see J. Touchard, 'Le Parti communiste français et les intellectuels', *Revue française de science politique*, 17 June 1967, pp. 468–83).

43.   *AA*, p. 155.

44.   It is a curious fact that both Nizan and Sartre were fatally attracted to the communist party during highly sectarian phases when the party itself felt under siege in a hostile environment Nizan between 1927 and 1933, Sartre between 1950 and 1955 at the height of the Cold War.

45.   Nizan married Henriette Alphen on 24 December 1927.

46.   Cohen-Solal and Nizan, *Paul Nizan, communiste impossible*, pp. 272–3.

47.   P. Nizan, 'Notes-programme sur la philosophie', *Bifur*, 7 Dec 1930; reprinted in *PIC*, p. 212.

48.   *AA*, pp. 154–5.

49.   *CG*, p. 123.

50.   See R. Garmy, 'Les Livres: *Les Chiens de garde*', *L'Humanité*, 6 Sep 1932, p. 4.

51.   Apart from Nizan, Politzer and Rappoport, the other members of the editorial board of *La Revue marxiste* were H. Lefebvre, N. Guterman and P. Morange. For an account of the '*Revue marxiste*' episode, see H. Lefebvre, *La Somme et le reste* (La Nef de Paris, 1959) pp. 425–35.

52.   For an account of this incident and the quite bitter personal relationship that existed between Nizan and Barbusse, see Cohen-Solal and Nizan, *Paul Nizan, communiste impossible*, pp. 93–102 and 275–82.

53.   At the first round of the elections on 1 May 1932, Nizan gained 338 votes (3 per cent). At the second round on 8 May, his score was 80 votes.

54.   *Le Courrier de l'Ain* and *Le Journal de l'Ain* demanded that Nizan, 'the red Messiah', be immediately removed from his post as philosophy teacher in the Lycée Lalande.

55.   P. Nizan, 'Les Conséquences du refus', *La Nouvelle Revue française*, Dec 1932; reprinted in *PIC*, p. 239.

56.   Nizan spent twelve months in the Soviet Union. He arrived in January 1934 and departed in January 1935. Apart from a trip to central Asia, he was for the most part resident in Moscow working at the Marx–Engels Institute in his capacity as French editor of the journal *La Littérature internationale*. During the Soviet Writers' Congress held in August of that year, Nizan was given responsibility for welcoming foreign 'fellow-travelling' writers and artists.

57.   S. de Beauvoir, *La Force de l'âge* (Gallimard, 1960) p. 237.

58.   Cited in Leiner, *Le Destin littéraire de Paul Nizan*, p. 196.

59. C. Malraux, 'Le Voyage à Moscou', *ATO*, p. 64.
60. Although it is clearly the case that between 1928 and 1933 Nizan's understanding of the Soviet Union progressed considerably, in no small measure due to his translation in 1933 of L. Fischer's *Les Soviets dans les affaires mondiales* (Gallimard, 1933), nevertheless Nizan's quest for moral integrity, allied to the generally simplified view of the world purveyed by the PCF during this sectarian phase, encouraged him to opt for an abstract Soviet Utopia, the site of moral justice and sublimated *angst*. It is worth mentioning in this context Nizan's translation of T. Dreiser's *L'Amérique tragique*, published similarly in 1933, which substantially increased Nizan's knowledge of America.
61. Malraux, 'Le Voyage à Moscou', p. 64.
62. P. Nizan, 'Le Tombeau de Timour', *Vendredi*, 22 Jan 1937, p. 11; and 'Sindobod Toçikiston', *Europe*, 15 May 1935, pp. 73–99, reprinted in *PIC*, pp. 175–96.
63. The extent of their mutual dislike can be gauged by Barbusse's description of Nizan as a 'petty-bourgeois careerist, a parasite on the working class destined to become a parasite on the bourgeois state' (*Monde*, Sep 1932, quoted in A. Cohen-Solal and H. Nizan, *Paul Nizan communiste impossible* (Grasset, 1980) p. 102).
64. P. Nizan, 'André Gide', *La Littérature internationale*, 3 (1934) pp. 126–33; reprinted in *PIC*, pp. 107–20.
65. Cohen-Solal and Nizan, *Paul Nizan, communiste impossible*, pp. 145–7.
66. P. Nizan, 'Sur l'humanisme', *Europe*, July 1935, pp. 453–7; reprinted in *PIC*, p. 230.
67. See Nizan, 'André Gide' (*PIC*, pp. 107–20); 'Sur l'humanisme', (*PIC*, pp. 226–31); 'Nous te tendons la main, catholique . . . *Catholicisme et communisme* par Robert Honnert', *L'Humanité*, 3 Apr 1937; reprinted in *NOC*, pp. 254–9.
68. *L'Humanité*, 7 Mar 1936.
69. Ibid.
70. Ibid., 9 Nov 1936.
71. A. Gide, *Retour de l'URSS* (Gallimard, 1936).
72. P. Nizan, 'Un esprit non prévenu: *Retour de l'URSS* par André Gide', *Vendredi*, 29 Jan 1937; reprinted in *NOC*, pp. 240–9.
73. Ibid., *NOC*, p. 244.
74. Ibid., *NOC*, p. 243.
75. Ibid., *NOC*, p. 245.
76. P. Nizan, *De la Sainte Russie à l'URSS* par Georges Friedmann', *Commune*, May 1938, pp. 1123–5.
77. King, *Paul Nizan, Écrivain* p. 41.
78. Nizan, *De la Sainte Russie à l'URSS* par Georges Friedmann'.
79. Ibid., p. 1125.
80. P. Nizan, 'L'Ennemi public numéro un', *Regards*, 61 (14 Mar 1935); reprinted in *PIC*, pp. 246–50.
81. Ibid., *PIC*, p. 247.
82. Ibid., *PIC*, pp. 249–50.
83. P. Nizan, La France trahie', *Ce Soir*, 19–23 July 1939.

84. Ibid., 19 July 1939.
85. Whilst at *L'Humanité*, Nizan worked under the direction of Gabriel Péri, the foreign-affairs spokesman for the PCF parliamentary group. When Nizan moved to *Ce Soir*, he assumed full responsibility for foreign affairs.
86. *L'Humanité*, 5 Aug 1935.
87. Ibid., 16 Mar 1936.
88. Ibid., 29 Sep 1935.
89. Ibid., 22, 24, 25, 30 July 1935; 7, 19–22 Aug 1935.
90. Ibid.
91. Ibid., 20, 21, 23 July 1935; 4, 5, 8, 13 Aug 1935; 29 Sep 1935; 14, 17, 21, 26 Oct 1935; 2, 24, 25 Nov 1935; 10, 14, 22 Dec 1935.
92. Ibid., 17 Oct 1935.
93. Ibid.
94. Ibid., 2 Nov 1935.
95. Ibid., 30 Dec 1935.
96. Ibid.
97. J. Leiner, 'Un portrait pirandellien', *ATO*, p. 39.
98. Ibid.
99. *L'Humanité*, 4 Jan 1936.
100. Ibid., 16 Feb 1936.
101. Ibid., 18 Feb 1936.
102. Ibid., 20, 25 Apr 1936; 20, 22 July 1936.
103. P. Nizan, 'Secrets de l'Espagne', *La Correspondance internationale*, 13 June–11 July 1936.
104. Ibid., 20 June 1936, p. 758.
105. P. Nizan, 'Renaissance de l'Espagne', *Commune*, Sep 1936, pp. 10–13.
106. *L'Humanité*, 5 Aug 1936.
107. Ibid., 15 Nov 1936.
108. Ibid., 23–31 Jan 1937.
109. Ibid., 29 Aug 1936.
110. Ibid., 14 June 1936.
111. Ibid., 4 Jan 1937.
112. See G. Péri, 'Laissera-t-on l'armée de Mussolini conquérir l'Espagne?', ibid., 12 Mar 1937.
113. *Ce Soir*, 7 May 1937.
114. The Second International Congress of Writers for the Defence of Culture was held from 5–18 July 1937 at Valencia, Madrid, Barcelona and finally Paris. See *Ce Soir*, 5, 9, 11 and 18 July 1937.
115. See ibid., 28 July, 2 and 10 Aug 1937.
116. O. Todd, *Préface: Chronique de septembre* (Gallimard, 1978) p. v.
117. *CS*, pp. 192–4.
118. *Ce Soir*, 29 Mar 1939.
119. Ibid., 26 Mar 1939.
120. Ibid., 1 Apr 1939.
121. Ibid., 22–4 May 1939.
122. See J. Elleinstein, *Staline* (Fayard, 1984) pp. 241–65.
123. *Ce Soir*, 1 July 1939.

124. Ibid., 11 July 1939.
125. Nizan, 'La France trahie'.
126. Ibid., 15 July 1939.
127. S. de Beauvoir, *La Force de l'âge* (Gallimard, 1960) p. 429.
128. Merleau-Ponty, *Signes*, pp. 41–2.
129. *Ce Soir*, 7 Aug 1939.

Notes to Chapter 3: Exit the Party

1. For an account of the signing of the Nazi–Soviet pact, see J. Elleinstein, *Staline* (Fayard, 1984) pp. 241–65.
2. J.-P. Sartre, 'Drôle d'amitié', in *Oeuvres romanesques*, Bibliothèque de la Pléiade (Gallimard, 1981) p. 1481.
3. For an account of Nizan's psychological state following the pact and his decision to resign from the party, see: Nizan, 'Correspondance de guerre: septembre 1939–avril 1940', in *PIC*, pp. 251–8; L. Martin-Chauffier, 'Nizan n'était pas un délateur', in *ATO*, pp. 10–13; J. Leiner, 'Un portrait pirandellien', in *ATO*, pp. 31–41.
4. Henriette Nizan asserts that following the announcement of the pact, '(Péri) had had doubts. He and Nizan were kindred spirits' (Annie Cohen-Solal and Henriette Nizan, *Paul Nizan, communiste impossible* (Grasset, 1980) p. 247).
5. For an account of Thorez's disorientation after the pact, see P. Robrieux, *Maurice Thorez* (Fayard, 1975) pp. 243–8.
6. *L'Humanité*, 3 Dec 1935.
7. *Ce Soir*, 5 May 1939.
8. See Nizan, 'Correspondance de guerre: septembre 1939–avril 1940', in *PIC*, p. 261.
9. Ibid.
10. 'M. Paul Nizan quitte le parti communiste', *L'Oeuvre*, 25 Sep 1939.
11. For an account of this transition, see G. Willard, 'Le PCF et la Deuxième Guerre mondiale', in *Le PCF: étapes et problèmes, 1920–1972* (Editions sociales, 1981) pp. 199–231.
12. *Ce Soir*, 24 Aug 1939.
13. *Ce Soir*, 23 Aug 1939.
14. *Ce Soir*, 25 Aug 1939.
15. See Elleinstein, *Staline*, pp. 250–1.
16. Nizan, 'Correspondance de guerre: septembre 1939–avril 1940', in *PIC*, p. 256.
17. Ibid., p. 272.
18. Ibid., p. 257.
19. Ibid., p. 261.
20. Ibid., p. 268.
21. *CT*, p. 204.
22. Nizan, 'Correspondance de guerre: septembre 1939–avril 1940', in *PIC*, p. 266.
23. Ibid., pp. 271–2.
24. M. Thorez, 'The Traitors in the Pillory', *The Communist International*,

3 (Mar 1940) pp. 171–8.

25. Ibid., p. 174. Two days after the banning of *L'Humanité* on 25 Aug 1939, Nizan had advocated communist collaboration on non-communist newspapers.
26. Ibid., p. 176.
27. H. Lefebvre, *L'Existentialisme* (Sagittaire, 1946) pp. 16–18.
28. Ibid.
29. The extent of communist hostility to Nizan and the general unwillingness on the part of the PCF to make any concessions in the immediate postwar period can be gauged by the following two reactions quoted by C. Connolly in 'The Nizan Case', *Horizon*, June 1947, pp. 305–9. (a) '[Nizan's] public repudiation of his Party and his comrades, at the moment when they were persecuted and in danger, filled me with disgust. He reserved his announcement of this event for *Temps*, the organ of the Comité des Forges, and for *L'Oeuvre*, run by Marcel Déat. A man of good faith would have remained silent' (*Les Lettres Françaises*, Apr 1947;) (b) 'Nizan left [the PCF] with a great deal of noise, surrounding his gesture with ostentation, immediately participating in the abominable campaign of calumny which was let loose against the most far-seeing and courageous citizens of France. . . . Traitor to his Party, he became by the same action a traitor to France because his public pronouncements helped such men as Daladier and Bonnet – against whom he had been writing on the eve of his decision – and the whole fifth column in their criminal political activities. Can we believe that this attitude was anything but the development of previous activity?' (*L'Humanité*, Apr 1947).
30. L. Aragon, *Les Communistes 1: février–septembre 1939* (La Bibliothèque française, 1949) pp. 152–72.
31. S. Téry, *Beaux enfants qui n'hésitez pas* (Editeurs français réunis, 1957).
32. Ory records that on 15 April 1955 Gallimard decided to pulp 405 unsold copies of *Le Cheval de Troie*. See P. Ory, *Nizan: Destin d'un révolté* (Ramsay, 1980) p. 254.
33. J.-P. Sartre and Michel Contat, 'Autoportrait à soixante-dix ans', *Le Nouvel observateur*, 7–13 July 1975, p. 70; reprinted in *SIT X*, pp. 133–226.
34. S. de Beauvoir, *Entretiens avec Jean-Paul Sartre* (Gallimard, 1981) p. 352.
35. J.-P. Sartre 'La Semence et le scaphandre', *Le Magazine littéraire*, 59 (Dec 1971) pp. 29 and 59–64.
36. Ory, *Nizan: Destin d'un révolté*, pp. 255–6.
37. 'Les Communistes et la paix (I et II)', *Les Temps modernes*, 81 (July 1952) pp. 1–50; 84–5 (Oct–Nov 1952) pp. 695–763; reprinted in *SIT VI*. 'Les Communistes et la Paix (III)' was published in *Les Temps modernes* 101 (Apr 1954,) pp. 1731–1819; reprinted in *SIT VI*.
38. For an account of Sartre's involvement in the RDR and his ensuing collaboration with the PCF, see M.-A Burnier, *Les Existentialistes et la politique* (Gallimard, 1966).
39. J.-P. Sartre, *L'Affaire Henri Martin* (Gallimard, 1953).
40. 'Les impressions de Jean-Paul Sartre sur son voyage en URSS', *Libération*, 15–20 July 1954.

41. J.-P. Sartre, *Nekrassov* (Gallimard, 1956).
42. 'Le Fantôme de Staline', *Les Temps modernes*, 129–31 (Nov 1956–Jan 1957) pp. 577–697; reprinted in *SIT VII*.
43. H. Lefebvre, *La Somme et le reste* (La Nef de Paris, 1959).
44. de Beauvoir, *Entretiens avec Jean-Paul Sartre* pp. 333 and 352.
45. 'Autoportrait à 70 ans par Jean-Paul Sartre', *Le Nouvel observateur*, 7–13 July 1975, p. 70.
46. 'L'imagination au pouvoir: Entretien de Jean-Paul Sartre avec Daniel Cohn-Bendit', *Le Nouvel observateur*, 20 May 1968.
47. 'Les Bastilles de Raymond Aron', *Le Nouvel observateur*, 19–25 June 1968.
48. J.-P. Sartre, *Les Communistes ont peur de la révolution* (Editions John Didier, 1969).
49. See E. Todd, *La Chute finale, essai sur la décomposition de la sphère soviétique* (Laffont, 1976).
50. See Cohen-Solal and Nizan, *Paul Nizan, communiste impossible*.
51. S. de Beauvoir *La Cérémonie des adieux* (Gallimard, 1981) p. 159.

Notes to Chapter 4: Autopsy

1. P. Nizan, 'Correspondance de guerre: septembre 1939–avril 1940', in *PIC*, p. 261.
2. P. Nizan, 'Un esprit non prévenu: *Retour de l'URSS* par André Gide', *Vendredi*, 29 Jan 1937; reprinted in *NOC*, pp. 246–7.
3. A. Cohen-Solal and H. Nizan, *Paul Nizan, communiste impossible* (Grasset, 1980) pp. 217–18.
4. E. Todd, *Le Fou et le prolétaire* (Laffont, 1979) pp. 259–61.
5. *L'Express*, 10 Sep 1959; reprinted in M. Contat and M. Rybalka (eds), *Sartre: un théâtre de situations* (Gallimard, 1973) p. 315.
6. J.-P. Sartre, *Saint Genet comédien et martyr* (Gallimard, 1952) p. 212.

Part Two Paul Nizan: Communist Novelist

Notes to the Introduction

1. For example, at one extreme, Henri Lefebvre's Stalinist rejection of *La Conspiration* as 'a harsh and hard-hearted distortion' (*L'Existentialisme* (Sagittaire, 1946) p. 17); at another, Sartre's proselytising description of *Antoine Bloyé* as 'the finest, the most lyrical of funeral orations' (*PAA*, p. 49).

Notes to Chapter 5: Cultural Politics

1. 'Radioscopie: Roland Barthes', interview with J. Chancel, 17 Feb

1975; published in J. Chancel, *Radioscopie* (Laffont, 1976) p. 256.

2. Barbusse joined the PCF in 1923. In 1926 he became literary editor of *L'Humanité*.

3. Nizan publicly denounced *Monde* as a 'group of traitors' who 'sheltering behind the name of Barbusse, have for years been pursuing a strategy that is very close to a betrayal of the revolution' ('Littérature révolutionnaire en France', *La Revue des vivants*, Sep–Oct 1932; reprinted in *NOC*, p. 40).

4. 'Résolution sur les questions de la littérature prolétarienne et révolutionnaire en France', *L'Humanité*, 28 Oct and 3 Nov 1931.

5. See L. Aragon, *Pour un réalisme socialiste* (Denoël et Steele, 1935) pp. 15–17.

6. P. Nizan, 'Les Violents par Ramon Fernandez', *Monde*, 1 Aug 1935; reprinted in *NOC*, pp. 172–4.

7. P. Nizan, *'Mort de la morale bourgeoise* par Emmanuel Berl', *Europe*, July 1930; reprinted in *NOC*, p. 31.

8. P. Nizan, 'L'URSS et la culture', *L'Humanité*, 9 Nov 1936.

9. P. Nizan, 'Sur l'humanisme', *Europe*, 15 July 1935; reprinted in *NOC*, pp. 164–71.

10. 'Nous te tendons la main catholique. . . . *Catholicisme et communisme* par Robert Honnert', *L'Humanité*, 3 Apr 1937. See also '*Catholicisme et communisme* par Robert Honnert', *L'Humanité* 25 Mar 1937.

11. It is important to differentiate between Nizan's sectarian attack on the idealist philosophy of the French university system in 1932, and his defence of the teaching profession as a bulwark against fascism in 1935. Régis Debray, although undoubtedly correct in highlighting the anachronism of *Les Chiens de garde* (described as 'one of the greatest mediological blunders of our time') in the technological society of today where relations between Marxism and the university system have been transformed by the media revolution, is unjustified not only in his criticism of Nizan's alleged inability to recognise in 1932 that the real enemy was not bourgeois philosophy but fascism, but also in his failure to acknowledge the significant historical role played by a text such as *Les Chiens de garde* when reproduced in the cultural context of May 1968. See R. Debray, *Le Pouvoir intellectuel en France* (Ramsay, 1979) pp. 70–3.

12. P. Nizan, 'Correspondance d'Aden', 4 Jan 1927, in *PIC*, p. 88.

13. L. Goldmann, *Pour une sociologie du roman* (Gallimard, 1964) pp. 273–5.

Notes to Chapter 6: Interwar Socialist Realism

1. T. Eagleton, *Marxism and Literary Criticism* (London: Methuen, 1976) p. 38.

2. The gradual loss of credibility of the Zhdanov line in France culminated in the resolution adopted by the Central Committee of the French Communist Party in 1966, in which there appeared a denunciation of 'any dogmatic conception of culture and education'. See 'Résolution sur les problèmes idéologiques et culturels' (Comité

central d'Argenteuil du PCF, 13 Mar 1966) in *Les Intellectuels et le parti communiste français: L'alliance dans l'histoire* (Cahiers d'histoire de l'Institut Maurice Thorez, 15 (1976)) pp. 149–60.

3. For a global account of these developments, see D. Laing, *The Marxist Theory of Art* (Brighton: Harvester Press, 1978) pp. 81–104.

4. For a detailed analysis of French socialist realism, see J.-P. Bernard, *Le Parti communiste français et la question littéraire* (Grenoble: Presses universitaires de Grenoble, 1973); D. Caute, *Communism and the French Intellectuals, 1914–1960* (London: André Deutsch, 1964); J. E. Flower, *Literature and the Left in France* (London: Macmillan, 1983).

5. L. Aragon, *Pour un réalisme socialiste* (Denoël et Steele, 1935).

6. Ibid. The text consists of five lectures delivered between April and June 1935.

7. M. Gorky *et al.*, *Soviet Writers' Congress 1934: The Debate on Socialist Realism and Modernism in the Soviet Union,* (London: Lawrence and Wishart, 1977) p. 57.

8. In Aragon's case, the colonial expedition of the 'Guerre du Rif' (1925) was the turning-point in his move to communism. It is interesting to note that Nizan was similarly converted to communism as a result of direct experience of British colonialism in Aden (1926).

9. Aragon, *Pour un réalisme socialiste*, p. 27.

10. This failure by Aragon to theorise, or at least offer a rigorous definition of socialist realism is symptomatic of the relatively liberal climate of the time, global statements allowing maximum scope for interpretation being preferred to rigorous doctrinal clarity.

11. Aragon, *Pour un réalisme socialiste*, pp. 82–7.

12. P. Nizan, '*Pour un réalisme socialiste* par Aragon', *L'Humanité*, 12 Aug 1935; reprinted in *NOC*, pp. 175–9.

13. G. Lukács, *The Meaning of Contemporary Realism* (London: Merlin Press, 1963) pp. 101–2.

14. For an account of the proceedings of the Congress, see Gorky *et al.*, *Soviet Writers' Congress 1934*.

15. Bernard, *Le Parti communiste français et la question littéraire*, pp. 127–8.

16. The example of the non-communist writers Bloch, Malraux and Gide, all of whom attended the 1934 Writers' Congress in the company of party members Aragon, Nizan and Pozner, is instructive in this respect. Not only were Bloch and Malraux allowed to voice serious misgivings on the artistic implications of socialist realism at the Congress itself, but their reservations were also published in *Commune* (Sep–Oct 1934) and *Europe* (Sep 1934). Aragon himself conducted an interview with Malraux on his return from Moscow which was published in *L'Humanité* (18 Sep 1934). Nizan was allocated the task of carrying out the ideological rehabilitation of Gide in order to publicise the latter's commitment to the anti-fascist, pro-Soviet cause. This he did with some success and no lack of intellectual ingenuity, (*Vendredi*, 8 Nov 1935), only to see his handiwork undermined a few months later when Gide reversed his originally positive views of the Soviet experiment and published his highly critical *Retour de l'URSS* (Gallimard, 1936).

17. For details of individual speeches, see Gorky *et al.*, *Soviet Writers' Congress 1934*.

18. J.-P. Bernard, for example, argues that in 1934 Zhdanov's significance was minimal. Only from 1936, with the eradication of Radek and Bukharin, and the death of Gorky, did he gain pre-eminence in cultural affairs (see Bernard, *Le PCF et la question littéraire*, pp. 127–8).

19. It is doubtless significant that Nizan refers in extremely favourable terms to Bukharin's contribution to the debate on socialist realism (see *L'Année des Vaincus* par André Chamson', *Monde*, 15 Feb 1935; reprinted in *NOC*, p. 92).

20. Gorky *et al.*, *Soviet Writers' Congress 1934*, p. 210.

21. Ibid., pp. 273–9.

22. Ibid., p. 21.

23. Karl Radek, 'James Joyce or Socialist Realism', Ibid., pp. 150–62. Not surprisingly, Radek is renowned above all else for his scathing comments on the work of James Joyce which he describes as 'a heap of dung, crawling with worms, photographed by a cinema apparatus through a microscope'.

24. Ibid., p. 74.

25. Ibid., p. 112. 'January 30 1933 – the date when the German fascists came to power – and the March days of 1933, when German and World literature was consigned to the bonfire on the square before the University of Berlin – this was the last test which the world set bourgeois literature, this was the last challenge issued to it by history' (K. Radek).

26. Ibid., p. 94.

27. See, in particular, Georg Lukács, 'Critical Realism and Socialist Realism', in his *The Meaning of Contemporary Realism* (London: Merlin Press, 1963) pp. 93–135.

28. G. Lukács, *Writer and Critic* (London: Merlin Press, 1978) p. 9. Whether or not this is an accurate description of Lukács's critical work in the 1930s and 1940s is open to debate. Dave Laing, for example, argues that during this period 'Lukács was carrying out a parallel policy to that of the Moscow "realists", to rid the cultural left of "deviationists"' (D. Laing, *The Marxist Theory of Art* (Brighton: Harvester Press, 1978) p. 48).

29. Ibid., pp. 103–9.

30. Lukács, *The Meaning of Contemporary Realism*, p. 103.

31. Ibid., p. 93.

32. Ibid., p. 108.

33. It is not appropriate in this context to extend this critical review of socialist realism since such a review would go beyond the scope of this study. Nevertheless, it is instructive to draw attention to three key critical responses which echo the hostile views outlined above. First, Sartre's polemical and predictably dramatic account of what he views as the utter incompatibility between the writer's allegiance to literature on the one hand, and his/her allegiance to the French communist party on the other (*Situations II: Qu'est-ce que la littérature?*

(Gallimard, 1948) pp. 277–89). When Sartre asserts that 'the politics of Stalinist communism are incompatible with the honest practice of the literary profession' (p. 280), he simply dramatises his view that the 'heretical' nature of literature, its subversive, dissident quality has been obliterated in communist circles under the influence of Stalinism. Secondly, Barthes offers an equally critical view, although from a more specifically literary perspective ('Ecriture et révolution', in *Le Degré zéro de l'écriture* (Seuil, 1953) pp. 49–53). Paradoxically, Barthes argues, socialist realist writing has not only failed to develop its own specifically revolutionary writing style, but has, on the contrary, adopted a method of realist writing abandoned many years previously by the traditional bourgeois writer as obsolete. Thirdly, and finally, an anonymous article printed in *L'Esprit* in Feburary 1959 (pp. 335–67), entitled simply 'Le Réalisme socialiste', and subsequently attributed to the Soviet writer Andrei Sinyavsky. Sinyavsky offers a cogent and uncompromisingly acerbic account of the inadequacies of Soviet socialist realism, essentially corroborating the ideas outlined in Lukács's 1956 essay, 'Critical realism and socialist realism', and arguing that the vibrancy of the original movement, stifled by the 'seriousness' of an ossified structure, ultimately degenerated into a new 'classicism'.

34. P. Nizan, 'Littérature révolutionnaire en France', *La Revue des vivants*, Sep–Oct 1932; reprinted in *NOC*, p. 34.
35. *NOC*, p. 92.
36. L. Aragon, 'Paul Nizan – *Antoine Bloyé*', *Commune*, Mar–Apr 1934, pp. 824–6.
37. It is interesting to note, however, that by 1940, after his resignation from the PCF, Nizan becomes disillusioned with the quality of Aragon's novels. 'Aragon's novel is becoming damned boring', he notes, referring to *Les Voyageurs de l'impériale*, in 'Correspondance de guerre: septembre 1939–avril 1940', *PIC*, p. 283.
38. '*Naissance d'une culture* par Jean-Richard Bloch', *Commune*, Feb 1937; reprinted in *NOC*, pp. 250–3.
39. Ibid., p. 251.
40. P. Nizan, '*Mes Songes que voici* par André Maurois', *L'Humanité*, 10 Mar 1933; reprinted in *NOC*, pp. 66–7; P. Nizan, '*Sentiments et Coutumes* par André Maurois', *Monde*, 1 Mar 1935; reprinted in *NOC*, pp. 101–6.
41. P. Nizan, '*Années d'espérance (Les Hauts-Ponts, t.III)* par Jacques de Lacretelle', *Monde*, 12 Apr 1935; reprinted in *NOC*, pp. 148–52.
42. P. Nizan, '*Journal* de Julien Green', *Ce Soir*, 7 July 1939; reprinted in *NOC*, pp. 312–13.
43. P. Nizan, 'Une Utopie paysanne, *Le Poids du ciel* par Jean Giono', *L'Humanité*, 17 Nov 1938; reprinted in *NOC*, pp. 286–90. It is worth recording that in 1935 Nizan's view of Giono was more favourable. See '*Que ma joie demeure* par Jean Giono', *Monde*, 16 May 1935; reprinted in *NOC* pp. 153–7.
44. Nizan is particularly critical of populist literature which he describes as a 'new form of exoticism', a means of presenting an extremely

partial and selctive image of the private life of the working class. See *NOC*, pp. 138–41.

45. P. Nizan, '*Fantomas* par P. Souvestre et M. Allain', *L'Humanité*, 24 Mar 1933; reprinted in *NOC*, pp. 68–70.

46. P. Nizan, '*Le Temps du mépris* par André Malraux', *Monde*, 6 June 1935; reprinted in *NOC*, pp. 158–63; P. Nizan, '*L'Espoir*, un roman d'André Malraux', *Ce Soir*, 13 Jan 1938; reprinted in *NOC*, pp. 283–4.

47. P. Nizan, '*Pour un réalisme socialiste* par Aragon', *L'Humanité*, 12 Aug 1935; reprinted in *NOC*, pp. 175–9.

48. P. Nizan, '*Bonsoir Thérèse* par Elsa Triolet', *Ce Soir*, 15 Dec 1938; reprinted in *NOC*, pp. 291–3.

49. P. Nizan, '*Tu seras ouvrier* par Georgette Guéguen-Dreyfus', *Monde*, 15 Mar 1935; reprinted in *NOC*, pp. 138–41.

50. P. Nizan, 'L'Oeuvre d'Eugène Dabit, *Trains de vie*', *L'Humanité*, 6 Sep 1936; reprinted in *NOC*, pp. 211–6.

51. P. Nizan, 'De la vérité au mensonge, *L'Acier* par André Philippe; *Rêveuse bourgeoisie, Avec Doriot* par Drieu la Rochelle', *L'Humanité*, 7 Aug 1937; reprinted in *NOC*, pp. 270–4.

52. P. Nizan, 'Images de l'Amérique. *Le Petit arpent du bon dieu* par Erskine Caldwell', *L'Humanité*, 18 Oct 1936; reprinted in *NOC*, pp. 217–21.

53. P. Nizan, '*Des souris et des hommes* par John Steinbeck', *Ce Soir*, 22 June 1939; reprinted in *NOC*, pp. 310–11. By contrast, the literature of the American Nobel Prize winner, Eugene O'Neill, is criticised by Nizan as a symbolist aberration. See P. Nizan, 'Eugène O'Neill: Prix Nobel 1936', *L'Humanité* 26 Nov 1936; reprinted in *NOC*, pp. 222–7.

54. P. Nizan, '*Barnaby Rudge* par Charles Dickens', *Ce Soir*, 9 Mar 1939; reprinted in *NOC*, pp. 304–6.

55. Ibid., p. 306.

56. For Gide, compare Nizan's (a) 'André Gide' (*La Littérature internationale*, 5 Mar 1934; reprinted in *PIC*, pp. 107–20) and (b) 'Un esprit non prévenu: *Retour de l'URSS* par André Gide' (*Vendredi*, 29 Jan 1937; reprinted in *NOC*, pp. 240–9). For Giono, compare (a) '*Que ma joie demeure* par Jean Giono' (*Monde*, 16 May 1935; reprinted in *NOC*, pp. 153–7) and (b) 'Une utopie paysanne, *Le Poids du ciel* par Jean Giono' (*L'Humanité*, 17 Nov 1938; reprinted in *NOC*, pp. 286–90). For Mauriac, compare (a) 'François Mauriac, *La Fin de la nuit*' (*Monde*, 1 Feb 1935; reprinted in *NOC*, pp. 76–8) and (b) 'Un roman de la sainteté: *Les Anges noirs* par François Mauriac' (*L'Humanité*, 22 Mar 1936; reprinted in *NOC*, pp. 196–9).

57. For Mauriac, see note 56 above. For Drieu la Rochelle, see Nizan's (a) '*Socialisme fasciste: Journal d'un homme trompé*, deux livres de Drieu la Rochelle' (*Monde*, 25 Jan 1935; reprinted in *NOC*, pp. 71–5), (b) 'Drieu la Rochelle' (*Vendredi*, 13 Dec 1935; reprinted in *NOC*, pp. 184–7) and (c) 'De la vérité au mensonge. *L'Acier* par André Philippe, *Rêveuse bourgeoisie, Avec Doriot*, par Drieu la Rochelle' (*L'Humanité*, 7 Aug 1937; reprinted in *NOC*, pp. 270–4). For Céline, see (a) '*Voyage au bout de la nuit* par L.-F. Céline' (*L'Humanité*, 9 Dec 1932; reprinted in *NOC*, pp. 44–5) and (b) 'Pour le Cinquantenaire du symbolisme, *Mort à crédit* par

Louis-Ferdinand Céline' (*L'Humanité*, 15 Jul 1936; reprinted in *NOC*, pp. 205–10).

58. P. Nizan, 'Renaissance de la tragédie', *L'Humanité*, 1 Mar 1936; reprinted in *NOC*, pp. 189–90.
59. P. Nizan, 'Ambition du roman moderne', *Cahiers de la jeunesse*, 5 Apr 1939; reprinted in *PIC*, pp. 101–4.
60. Ibid., p. 104.
61. Nizan, *'Le Temps du mépris* par André Malraux', *NOC*, p. 162.
62. Nizan, 'L'Oeuvre d'Eugène Dabit, *Trains de vie*', *NOC*, p. 212.
63. P. Nizan, *'Eté 1914* par Roger Martin du Gard', *La Nouvelle Revue française*, Jan 1937; reprinted in *NOC*, pp. 229–34.
64. Ibid., p. 231.
65. Nizan, 'Ambition du roman moderne', *PIC*, p. 102.
66. The influence of Malraux on Nizan's thinking is clearly visible here. For Nizan's assessment of Malraux, see (a) *'Le Temps du mépris* par André Malraux', *NOC*, pp. 158–63; (b) *'L'Espoir*, un roman d'André Malraux', *NOC*, pp. 283–4.
67. J.-P. Sartre, *'La Conspiration* de Paul Nizan', *La Nouvelle Revue française*, Nov 1938; reprinted in *SIT I*, pp. 25–8.
68. It is worth recording the fact that Nizan was constantly preoccupied in his critical writings with the problem of producing literature of lasting value. It was clearly a matter of great importance in Nizan's eyes to devise the technical means necessary to combine the short-term ideological objectives of the novel with more long-term artistic objectives.
69. Nizan, *'Le Temps du mépris* par André Malraux', *NOC*, p. 161.
70. Nizan, 'L'Oeuvre d'Eugène Dabit, *Trains de vie*', *NOC*, p. 213.
71. P. Nizan, *'L'Adolescent* par Dostoievsky', *Monde*, 29 Mar 1935; reprinted in *NOC*, p. 144.
72. Nizan, *'L'Année des vaincus* par André Chamson'.

Notes to Chapter 7: Nizan's Communist Novels

1. P. Nizan, *'L'Année des vaincus* par André Chamson', *Monde*, 8 Feb 1935; reprinted in *NOC*, pp. 87–92. Nizan's assertion in 1930 that proletarian culture 'needs neither novels nor sonnets', amounts to no more than sectarian rhetoric. See P. Nizan, *'Mort de la morale bourgeoise* par Emmanuel Berl', *Europe*, July 1930; reprinted in *NOC*, pp. 25–32.
2. A. Ulmann, 'Avec Paul Nizan: Prix Interallié', *Vendredi*, 8 Dec 1938, p. 5.
3. P. Nizan, *'Les Violents* par Ramon Fernandez', *Monde*, 1 Aug 1935; reprinted in *NOC*, pp. 172–4.
4. J. Fréville, *'Antoine Bloyé*', *L'Humanité*, 18 Dec 1933.
5. L. Aragon, 'Paul Nizan: *Antoine Bloyé*', *Commune*, Mar–Apr 1934, pp. 824–6.
6. 'Le Prix Goncourt vu par les candidats', *Le Rempart*, 16 Nov 1933.
7. *Antoine Bloyé* gained one vote, that of Lucien Descaves, in the ballot

for the Prix Goncourt in 1933. This literary prize was eventually awarded to André Malraux for *La Condition humaine*.

8. 'Le Prix Goncourt vu par les candidats'.
9. *AB*, p. 308.
10. Ibid., p. 167.
11. Ibid., pp. 137–8.
12. Ibid., p. 280.
13. Ibid., p. 30.
14. Aragon, 'Paul Nizan: *Antoine Bloyé*'.
15. *AB*, p. 207.
16. Ibid., p. 290.
17. Ibid., p. 53.
18. Ibid., p. 65.
19. Ibid., pp. 232–3.
20. Ibid.
21. Ibid., p. 109.
22. Ibid., pp. 142–5.
23. Ibid., p. 261.
24. Ibid., pp. 282–3.
25. Ibid., pp. 309–10.
26. A. Cohen-Solal and H. Nizan, *Paul Nizan, communiste impossible* (Grasset, 1980) p. 187.
27. S. Suleiman, *Authoritarian Fictions: The Ideological Novel as a Literary Genre* (New York: Columbia University Press, 1983) p. 103.
28. J.-P. Sartre, *Situations II: Qu'est-ce que la littérature?* (Gallimard, 1948) pp. 277–89.
29. S. de Beauvoir, *La Force de l'âge* (Gallimard, 1960) p. 272. Nizan is alleged to have told Sartre that the model for Lange was Brice-Parain.
30. Nizan, '*Les Violents* par Ramon Fernandez'.
31. Villefranche is almost certainly a fictionalised version of the towns of Bourg and Vienne which Nizan knew well following his year of grass-roots political activity in Bourg in 1931 and 1932. Nizan's global understanding of the political, social and cultural dynamics of this town is articulated in an analytical piece 'Présentation d'une ville', which was published in *La Littérature internationale*, 4 (1934) (reprinted in *PIC*, pp. 124–68), and which doubtless served as the basis of the descriptions of the town and its inhabitants in *Le Cheval de Troie*
32. *CT*, p. 17.
33. Ibid., pp. 68–9.
34. Ibid., pp. 89–90.
35. Ibid., p. 189.
36. Ibid., p. 211.
37. Ibid., p. 205.
38. P. Nizan, *Histoire de Thésée*, a short story published in *Commune* in November 1937 (pp. 306–12), constitutes an elusive but undeniable recognition on Nizan's part of the irretrievable loss of heroic, epic values in modern society.

39. *CO*, p. 30.
40. Only Léon G. Marcantonato struck a discordant note, arguing that *La Conspiration* was no more than a pale imitation of *Les Thibault*, and that the award of the Prix Interallié to Nizan was ultimately an indirect tribute to Roger Martin du Gard (see 'Roger Martin du Gard et le Prix Interallié', *Cahiers du Sud*, June 1939, pp. 515–21). Sartre, in his review of *La Conspiration*, although sceptical of the possibility of amalgamating communism and the novel, was nonetheless globally positive. It is worth recording the literary and critical interaction between Sartre and Nizan at this time. Nizan had enthusiastically reviewed *La Nausée* in May 1938, concluding that Sartre's talents as a social satirist would lead him inevitably to greater political commitment (*Ce Soir*, 16 May 1938). January 1939 witnessed the publication of Sartre's *L'Enfance d'un chef*, in which the appearance of a General Nizan was doubtless a fictional allusion to the presence of a Major Sartre in *La Conspiration*.
41. *CO*, p. 14.
42. Ibid., p. 26.
43. Ibid., p. 283.
44. Ibid., pp. 212–13.
45. Ibid., p. 57.
46. Ibid., p. 268.
47. Ibid., p. 288.
48. Ibid., p. 144.
49. One short document relating to *La Soirée à Somosierra* was published in the appendices to P. Ory's *Nizan: Destin d'un révolté* (Ramsay, 1980) p. 288.
50. Ulmann, 'Avec Paul Nizan: Prix Interallié'.
51. *L'Humanité*, 5 Aug 1936.
52. 'Correspondance de guerre: septembre 1939–avril 1940', in *PIC*, p. 272.
53. Ibid., p. 280.
54. Ibid., p. 283.

Notes to Chapter 8: Obituary

1. *SIT I*, p. 28.
2. A. Gramsci, *Letterature e Vita Nazionale: Quaderni del Carcere 5* (Turin: Einaudi, 1974) p. 11.
3. J.-P. Sartre, 'Les Bastilles de Raymond Aron', *Le Nouvel observateur*, 19–25 June 1968.

Bibliography

The bibliography is in three parts. The first and second parts constitute the primary and secondary sources relevant to Nizan's political and literary evolution. The third part comprises a list of theoretical, ideological and historical texts which have been instrumental in the formulation of the specific critical viewpoint adopted in this book. For a more comprehensive account of Nizan's work and Nizan criticism in general, the reader is referred to the following three texts which contain extensive bibliographical references:

Brochier, J.-J. (ed.), *Paul Nizan, intellectuel communiste 1926–1940* (François Maspero, 1967).
Leiner, J., *Le Destin littéraire de Paul Nizan* (Klincksieck, 1970).
Suleiman, S (ed.), *Paul Nizan: Pour une nouvelle culture* (Grasset, 1971).

PRIMARY SOURCES: SELECTED BIBLIOGRAPHY OF THE WORKS OF PAUL NIZAN

Essays

Aden Arabie (Rieder, 1931); preface by J.-P. Sartre (François Maspero, 1960).
Les Chiens de garde (Rieder, 1932; François Maspero, 1960).

Novels

Antoine Bloyé (Grasset, 1933, 1960).
Le Cheval de Troie (Gallimard, 1935, 1969).
La Conspiration (Gallimard, 1938, 1968).

Narrative

Hécate, ou la méprise sentimentale in *La Revue sans titre*, 2 (1923–4) pp. 7–10; reprinted by Spectres Familiers (1982) pp. 39–71.
Complainte du carabin qui disséqua sa petite amie en fumant deux paquets de Maryland in *La Revue sans titre*, 4 (1923–4) reprinted by Spectres Familiers (1982) pp. 11–37.
L'Eglise dans la ville in *Commune*, 1 (1 July 1933) pp. 58–63.

Présentation d'une ville in *La Littérature internationale*, 4 (1934) pp. 3–36; reprinted in J.-J. Brochier (ed.), *Paul Nizan, intellectuel communiste* (François Maspero, 1967) pp. 124–68.

Histoire de Thésée, in *Commune*, Nov 1937, pp. 306–12; reprinted in J.-J. Brochier (ed.), *Paul Nizan, intellectuel communiste*, pp. 169–74.

Le Marché, in *Le Point*, 15 (June 1938); pp. 126–9.

History

Chronique de septembre (Gallimard, 1939, 1978).

Film

Visages de la France (1937); film script by P. Nizan and A. Wurmser.

Adaptation

Aristophanes, *Les Acharniens* (Editions sociales internationales, 1937).

Translations

Dreiser, T., *L'Amérique tragique* (Rieder, 1933).
Fisher, L., *Les Soviets dans les affaires mondiales* (Gallimard, 1933).

Edited Texts

Les Matérialistes de l'antiquité (Démocrite, Epicure, Lucrèce) (Editions sociales internationales, 1938; François Maspero, 1965).

Morceaux choisis de Marx, introduction by H. Lefebvre and N. Guterman (Gallimard, 1934).

Preface

Lefebvre, H., *Le Nationalisme contre les nations* (Editions sociales internationales, 1937) pp. 7–9.

SECONDARY SOURCES

'Paul Nizan', *Atoll*, 1 (Nov–Dec 1967–Jan 1968) 80 pages. Contributions by Y. Buin, L. Martin-Chauffier, B. Besnier, J. Leiner, J.-J. Brochier, A. Ginsbourg, C. Malraux, J.-P. Barou and H. Nizan. Details appear below under these authors' names.

Anon., *'Les Matérialistes de l'antiquité'*, *The Times Literary Supplement*, 30 Sep 1965, p. 883.

Aragon, L., *Les Communistes: 1 (février–septembre 1939), 2 (septembre–novembre 1939)* (La Bibliothèque française, 1949).

——, 'Paul Nizan – *Antoine Bloyé*', *Commune*, Mar–Apr 1934, pp. 824–6.

——, 'Le Roman terrible', *Europe*, 15 Dec 1938, pp. 433–52.

Arland, M., '*Antoine Bloyé, La Nouvelle revue française*, 1 Dec 1933, pp. 903–4.
Ascherson, N., 'High on Guilt', *New York Review of Books*, 1 Aug 1968, pp. 20–2.
Barou, J.-P., 'Mort et vie d'un romancier', *Atoll*, 1 (Nov–Dec 1967–Jan 1968) pp. 66–77.
Beauvoir, S. de, *La Cérémonie des adieux* (Gallimard, 1981).
——, *La Force de l'âge* (Gallimard, 1960).
——, *La Force des choses* (Gallimard, 1963).
——, *Mémoires d'une jeune fille rangée* (Gallimard, 1958).
Bédé, J.-A., 'Paul Nizan par Ariel Ginsbourg', *Romanic Review*, LVIII, 4 (Dec 1967) pp. 310–13.
Berl, E., 'Deux contemporains', *L'Express*, 9 June 1960, pp. 36–7.
Besnier, B., 'Modus vivendi', *Atoll*, 1 (Nov–Dec 1967–Jan 1968) pp. 14–30.
Blanzat, J., '*Le Cheval de Troie*', *Europe*, 15 Jan 1936, pp. 135–6.
Brochier, J.-J., 'La Critique comme arme', *Le Magazine littéraire*, 59 (Dec 1971) pp. 28–9.
——, 'Fonction du traître', *Atoll*, 1 (Nov-Dec 1967–Jan 1968) pp. 44–7.
——, (ed.), *Paul Nizan, intellectuel communiste, 1926–1940* (François Maspero, 1967).
Bruhat, J., 'Une Oeuvre de Paul Nizan: *La Conspiration*', *L'Humanité*, 25 Oct 1938, p. 7.
——, 'Le Prix Interallié est attribué à Paul Nizan pour son roman *La Conspiration*', *L'Humanité*, 7 Dec 1938, p. 2.
Buin, Y., 'Nizan ou le malaise', *Atoll*, 1 (Nov-Dec 1967–Jan 1968) pp. 2–9.
Burnier, M.-A., 'Nizan philosophe', *Le Magazine littéraire*, 59 (Dec 1971) pp. 26–7.
Camus, A., 'La Conspiration par Paul Nizan', *Alger-Républicain*, 11 Nov 1938, p. 5.
Carile, P., 'Paul Nizan', *I Contemporanei. Letteratura Francese*, 1977, pp. 565–82.
Cassou, J., '*La Conspiration* de Paul Nizan', *Commune*, Jan 1939, pp. 67–9.
Catesson, J., 'Un Roman et ses personnages: *La Conspiration*', *Cahiers du Sud*, Mar 1939, pp. 221–9.
Cheronnet, L., 'Les Visages de la France', *L'Humanité*, 17 Nov 1937, p. 4.
Cohen-Solal, A., *Sartre: 1905–1980* (Gallimard, 1985).
——, and H. Nizan, *Paul Nizan: communiste impossible* (Grasset, 1980).
Connolly, C., 'The Nizan Case', *Horizon*, June 1947, pp. 305–9.
Contat, M. and M. Rybalka, *Les Ecrits de Sartre* (Gallimard, 1970).
Deharme, L., *Les Années perdues: journal (1939–1949)* (Plon, 1961).
Dupeyron, G., 'Paul Nizan – *Antoine Bloyé*', *Europe*, 15 Jan 1934, pp. 147–8.
Etiemble, R, 'D'André Chénier à Paul Nizan', in *Hygiène des lettres* (Gallimard, 1952) pp. 97–124.
Faye, J.-P., 'Aden Arabie', *Esprit*, 3 (1961) pp. 522–3.
Fe, F., *Paul Nizan, un intelletuale communista* (Rome: La Nuova Sinistra, 1973).
Friedmann, G., '*Aden Arabie*', *Cahiers du Sud*, July 1931, pp. 386–7.
Garaudy, R., 'L'Erreur de Roger Garaudy', *Le Nouvel observateur*, 12–18 Nov 1979, p. 54.
——, 'Garaudy, celui qui ne regrette rien', *Le Nouvel observateur*, 29 Oct–4 Nov

1979, pp. 111–153.

Garmy, R., 'Les Livres: *Les Chiens de garde*', *L'Humanité*, 6 Sep 1932, p. 4.

Ginsbourg, A., *Paul Nizan* (Editions Universitaires, 1966).

——, 'Une Promenade politique avec Paul Nizan', *Atoll*, 1 (Nov–Dec 1967–Jan 1968) pp. 48–62.

Guiliano, Z., 'La Riscoperta di Paul Nizan', *Nuova Rivista Storica*, 64 (5–6) (1980) pp. 635–65.

Ishaghpour, Y., *Paul Nizan: une figure mythique et son temps* (Le Sycomore, 1980).

Juquin, P., 'Critiques sans bases', *La Nouvelle Critique*, 118 (1960) pp. 109–30.

King. A., *Paul Nizan Écrivain* (Didier, 1976).

Lanteri-Laura, G., 'Nizan et Politzer quarante ans après', *Critique*, Aug–Sept 1968, pp. 772–89.

Laude, A., 'Paul Nizan: le jeune homme révolté', *Le Temps des hommes*, Oct–Dec 1960, pp. 7–10.

Leiner, J., '*Aden Arabie*: Etude d'une structure autobiographique ou des équivoques du langage', *Studi Francesi*, xx (1976) pp. 286–92.

——, *Le Destin littéraire de Paul Nizan* (Klincksieck, 1970).

——, 'La Part de l'actuel dans l'oeuvre de P.-Y. Nizan', *Revue des sciences humaines*, Jan–Mar 1968, pp. 107–24.

——, 'Paul Nizan: *Aden Arabie*, *Les Chiens de garde*, *Antoine Bloyé*, *Les Matérialistes de l'antiquité*', *French Review*, xli (1 Oct 1967) pp. 167–71.

——, 'Un Portrait pirandellien: Nizan vu par ses contemporains', *Atoll*, 1 (Nov–Dec 1967–Jan 1968) pp. 31–41.

Malraux, C., 'Le Voyage à Moscou', *Atoll*, 1 (Nov–Dec 1967–Jan 1968) pp. 63–5.

Marion, D., '*Aden Arabie*', *La Nouvelle Revue française*, 1 May 1931, pp. 753–5.

Martin-Chauffier, L., 'Nizan n'était pas un délateur', *Atoll*, 1 (Nov–Dec 1967–Jan 1968) pp. 10–13; originally published in *Caliban*, 15 May 1947.

——, 'Portrait animé de Paul Nizan', *Vendredi*, 18 June 1937, p.5.

Marcantonato, L. G., 'Roger Martin du Gard et le Prix Interallié', *Cahiers du Sud*, June 1939, pp. 515–21.

Maublanc, R., 'Épicure et Lucrèce: *Les Matérialistes de l'antiquité*', *L'Humanité*, 16 Aug 1936, p. 8.

Merleau-Ponty, M., *Signes* (Gallimard, 1960).

Montanari, F., 'Ritratti critici di contemporanei: Paul Nizan', *Belfagor*, 38 (6) (1983) pp. 669–82.

Moussinac, L., *Le Radeau de la Méduse: journal d'un prisonnier politique, 1940–1941* (Editions Hier et Aujourd'hui, 1945).

Nadeau, M., 'Paul Nizan: deux fois mort et ressuscité', *L'Observateur littéraire*, 30 June 1960, pp. 17–18.

Nizan, H., 'Lettre ouverte', *Atoll*, 1 (Nov–Dec 1967–Jan 1968) pp. 78–80.

——, 'Madame Nizan répond à Roger Garaudy', *Le Nouvel observateur*, 5–11 Nov 1979, p. 53.

——, 'Une Lettre d'Henriette Nizan', *L'Express*, 6 Oct 1960, p. 36.

Ory, P., *Nizan: Destin d'un révolté, 1905–1940* (Ramsay, 1980).

Pierre-Quint, L., 'Orientation des nouvelles générations: *La Conspiration* par Paul Nizan', *Les Volontaires*, 1 Dec 1938, pp. 93–6.

Queneau, R., '*Les Chiens de garde*', *La Critique sociale*, 6 Sep 1932, p. 272.

Redfern, W. D., 'A Vigorous Corpse: Paul Nizan and *La Conspiration*', *Romanic Review*, 4 (Dec 1968) pp. 278–95.

——, 'Nizan: a matter of death and life', in S. Williams (ed.), *Socialism in France from Jaurès to Mitterrand* (London, Frances Pinter: 1983), pp. 57–63.

——, *Paul Nizan: Committed Literature in a Conspiratorial World* (Princeton, N.J.: Princeton University Press, 1972).

Sartre, J.-P., '*La Conspiration* par Paul Nizan', in *SIT I* (Gallimard, 1947) pp. 25–8.

——, 'Drôle d'amitié', in *Oeuvres romanesques*, Bibliothèque de la Pléiade (Gallimard, 1981) pp. 1461–1534.

——, *Les Mots* (Gallimard, 1964).

——, *Préface: Aden Arabie* (François Maspero, 1960); reprinted in *SIT IV* (Gallimard, 1964) pp. 130–88.

——, 'La Semence et le scaphandre', *Le Magazine littéraire*, 59 (Dec 1971) pp. 29 and 59–64.

Schalk, D. L., 'Professors as Watchdogs: Paul Nizan's theory of the intellectual and politics'. *Journal of the History of Ideas*, xxxiv (1973) pp. 79–96.

——, *The Spectrum of Political Engagement: Mounier, Benda, Nizan, Brasillach, Sartre* (Princeton, N. J.: Princeton University Press, 1979).

Sénart, P., 'Sartre et Nizan', *Combat*, 2 July 1964, p. 7.

Sigaux, G., 'Il paraît', *Preuves*, 113 (1960) pp. 87–90.

Simon, P.-H., 'Le Désenchantement de Jean-Paul Sartre', *Le Monde*, 27 July 1960.

Sudaka, J., 'Figures juives ou les crimes de la littérature', *Histoire H*, Nov 1979, pp. 263–79.

Suleiman, S. R., 'History as Myth: Nizan's *Le Cheval de Troie*', in her *Authoritarian Fictions: The Ideological Novel as a Literary Genre* (New York: Columbia University Press, 1983) pp. 102–18.

—— (ed.), *Paul Nizan: pour une nouvelle culture* (Grasset, 1971).

Téry, S., *Beaux enfants qui n'hésitez pas* (Editeurs français réunis, 1957).

Thomas, E., 'Le Cas Nizan', *La Quinzaine Littéraire*, 1–15 Jan 1968, pp. 11–12.

Thorez, M., 'Les Traîtres au pilori', *Die Welt*, 21 Mar 1940; published as 'The Traitors in the Pillory', in *The Communist International*, Mar 1940, pp. 170–8.

Todd, O., 'Paul Nizan: an Appraisal', *Time and Tide*, 42 (30 Mar 1961) p. 524.

——, *Préface: Chronique de septembre* (Gallimard, 1978).

Ulmann, A., 'Avec Paul Nizan: Prix Interallié', *Vendredi*, 8 Dec 1938, p. 5.

Vaudal, J., '*Le Cheval de Troie*', *La Nouvelle Revue française*, Feb 1936, pp. 276–8.

Vernoy, S., 'Nous avons offert *Visages de la France* à l'Union soviétique', *La Russie d 'aujourd'hui*, 69 (Dec 1937) p. 12.

Weightman, J., 'France My Enemy', *Observer Review*, 16 June 1968, p. 25.

CRITICAL THEORY, IDEOLOGY AND HISTORY

Andreu, P., 'Les Idées politiques de la jeunesse intellectuelle de 1927 à la guerre', *Revue des travaux de l'Académie des sciences morales et politiques*,

1957, pp. 17–35.

Anissimov, I., 'Le Réalisme socialiste dans la littérature mondiale', *La Nouvelle Critique*, Jan 1955, pp. 82–108.

Anon., 'Le Réalisme socialiste', *Esprit*, Feb 1959, pp. 335–67.

Aragon, L., *Pour un réalisme socialiste* (Denoël et Steele, 1935).

Aron, R., *Marxismes imaginaires* (Gallimard, 1970).

——, *Mémoires*, (Julliard, 1983).

Barbéris, P., *Lectures du réel* (Editions sociales, 1973).

Barbusse, H., *Manifeste aux intellectuels* (Les Ecrivains réunis, 1927).

Berl, E., *Mort de la morale bourgeoise* (Gallimard, 1929; reprinted Jean-Jacques Pauvert, 1965).

——, *Mort de la pensée bourgeoise* (Grasset, 1929).

Bernard, J.-P. A., *Le Parti communiste français et la question littéraire: 1921–1939* (Grenoble: Presses universitaires de Grenoble, 1972).

——, 'Le Parti communiste français et les problèmes littéraires (1920–1939)', *Revue française de science politique*, 17 (June 1967) pp. 520–44.

Biro, B., 'Bukharin and Socialist Realism', *Marxist Studies*, 2 (1) (1970) pp. 26–30.

Bloch, J. R., 'Paroles à un congrès soviétique', *Europe*, 15 Sep 1934, pp. 102–6.

Borland, H., *Soviet Literary Theory and Practice during the First Five Year Plan: 1928–1932* (New York: King's Crown Press, 1950).

Bourderon, R., *et alia*, *Le PCF: étapes et problèmes, 1920–1972* (Editions sociales, 1981).

Brewster, B., 'The Soviet State, the Communist Party and the Arts, 1917–1936', *Red Letters*, 3 (1976) pp. 3–9.

Buin, Y. (ed.), *Que peut la littérature?* (Union générale d'éditions, 1965).

Casanova, L., *Le Communisme, la pensée et l'art* (Editions du parti communiste français, 1947).

——, *Le Parti communiste, les intellectuels et la nation* (Editions sociales, 1949).

Caute, D., *Communism and the French Intellectuals: 1914–1960* (London: André Deutsch, 1964).

——, *The Fellow Travellers* (London: Quartet, 1977).

Cogniot, G. (ed.), *Les Intellectuels et le parti communiste français: l'alliance dans l'histoire*, Cahiers d'histoire de l'institut Maurice Thorez, 15 (1976).

——, *L'Internationale communiste* (Editions sociales, 1969).

Courtois, S., *Le PCF dans la guerre* (Ramsay, 1980).

Debray, R., *Le Pouvoir intellectuel en France* (Ramsay, 1979).

Duquesne, J., 'Pourquoi le PC voit rouge', *Le Point*, 667 (1 July 1985) pp. 36–44.

Eagleton, T., *The Function of Criticism* (London: Verso, 1984).

Elleinstein, J., *Staline* (Arthème Fayard, 1984).

Ellul, J., *Propagandes* (Armand Colin, 1962).

Fauvet, J., *Histoire du parti communiste français* (Fayard, 1964).

Fischer, E., *Art against Ideology* (New York: George Braziller 1969).

——, *The Necessity of Art: A Marxist Approach* (Harmondsworth: Penguin, 1963).

Flower, J. E., *Literature and the Left in France* (London: Macmillan, 1983).

——, *Writers and Politics in Modern France* (London: Hodder and Stoughton, 1977).

Folhen, C., *La France de l'entre-deux guerres (1917–1939)* (Casterman, 1966).

Garaudy, R., *D'un réalisme sans rivages* (Plon, 1963).
——, *L'Itinéraire d'Aragon: du surréalisme au monde réel* (Gallimard, 1961).
——, *Literature of the Graveyard* (New York: International Publishers, 1948).
Gide, A., *Journal (1881–1939)* (Pléiade, 1951).
——, *Littérature engagée* (Gallimard, 1950).
——, *Retour de l'URSS* (Gallimard, 1936).
Goriély, B., 'Contribution à l'histoire de la littérature prolétarienne', *Avant-Poste*, June 1933, pp. 40–7.
Gorky, M., K. Radek, N. Bukharin, and A. Zhdanov, *Soviet Writers' Congress 1934* (London: Lawrence and Wishart, 1977).
Gramsci, A., *Letteratura e Vita Nazionale* (Turin: Einaudi, 1974).
——, *Selections from the Prison Notebooks* (London: Lawrence and Wishart, 1971).
Howe, I., *Politics and the Novel* (New York: Horizon Press, 1957).
James, C. V. (ed.), *Socialist Realism in Literature and Art* (Moscow: Progress Publishers, 1971).
——, *Soviet Socialist Realism: Origins and Theory* (London: Macmillan, 1973).
Jameson, F., *Marxism and Form: Twentieth-century Dialectical Theories of Literature* (Princeton, N. J.: Princeton University Press, 1974).
Jean, R., 'Marxisme et littérature: l'exemple de Gramsci', in *Littérature et société*, ed. J. Onimus and A.-M. Rousseau (Desclée de Brouwer, 1973) pp. 365–70.
Kanapa, J., *Critique de la culture 1: Situation de l'intellectuel* (Editions sociales, 1957).
——, *Critique de la culture 2: Socialisme et culture* (Editions sociales, 1957).
Kelly, M., *Modern French Marxism* (Oxford: Basil Blackwell, 1982).
Kriegel, A., *Les Communistes français* (Seuil, 1968).
——, 'Naissance du mouvement Clarté', *Le Mouvement social*, Jan–Mar 1963, pp. 117–35.
——, 'Le Parti communiste français (1920–1939): Evolution de ses effectifs', *Revue française de science politique*, Feb 1966, pp. 5–35.
Laing, D., *The Marxist Theory of Art* (Brighton: Harvester Press, 1978).
Lefebvre, H., *L'Existentialisme* (Le Sagittaire, 1946).
——, 'Faire jaillir les forces vives de la négativité – Entretien: Henri Lefebvre et Jean Duvignaud', *Les Lettres nouvelles*, May 1959, pp. 45–7.
——, *La Somme et le reste* (La Nef de Paris, 1959).
Lefebvre, R., *La Révolution ou la mort* (Editions Clarté, 1920).
Lenin, V. I., *On Culture and Cultural Revolution* (Moscow: Progress Publishers, 1970).
——, *On Literature and Art* (Lawrence and Wishart, 1967).
——, *What Is to Be Done?* (Moscow: Progress Publishers, 1967).
Lifshitz, M., *The Philosophy of Art of Karl Marx* (London: Pluto Press, 1973).
Lukács, G., *Lenin: A Study on the Unity of his Thought* (London: New Left Books, 1970).
——, *The Meaning of Contemporary Realism* (London: Merlin Press, 1963).
Mander, J., *The Writer and Commitment* (London: Secker and Warburg, 1961).
Morawski, S., 'Les Péripéties de la théorie du réalisme socialiste', *Diogène*, Oct–Dec 1961, pp. 120–42.

Mouffe, C. (ed.), *Gramsci and Marxist Theory* (London: Routledge and Kegan Paul, 1979).

Naudy, M., *PCF: le suicide* (Michel Albin, 1986).

O'Connell, D., 'Eugène Dabit: a Working-Class Novelist', *Research Studies*, 41 (4) (Dec 1973) pp. 217–33.

Orwell, G., 'Literature and the Left', *Tribune*, 4 June 1943.

——, 'Literature and Totalitarianism', *The Listener*, 19 June 1941.

——, 'The Proletarian Writer', *The Listener*, 19 Dec 1940.

Ory, P., 'Front populaire et création artistique', *Bulletin de la société d'histoire moderne*, 8 (1975) pp. 5–21.

Péri, G., *Gabriel Péri: une vie de combat pour la paix et la sécurité de la France* (Editions sociales, 1947).

Plékhanov, G., *L'Art et la vie sociale* (Editions sociales, 1975).

Politzer, G., *Fin d'une parade philosophique* (Jean-Jacques Pauvert, 1968).

——, *Révolution et contre révolution au XXème siècle* (Editions sociales, 1947).

Poster, M., *Existential Marxism in Postwar France: From Sartre to Althusser* (Princeton, N. J.: Princeton University Press, 1975).

Racine, N., 'L'Association des écrivains et artistes révolutionnaires (A.E.A.R.)', *Le Mouvement social*, 54 (Jan–Mar 1966) pp. 29–47.

——, 'Une revue d'intellectuels communistes dans les années vingt: *Clarté* (1921–1928)', *Revue française de science politique*, 17 (June 1967) pp. 484–519.

Robin, R. *Le Réalisme socialiste* (Payot, 1986).

Robrieux, P., *Histoire intérieure du parti communiste* (Fayard, 1981).

——, *Maurice Thorez: vie secrète et vie publique* (Fayard, 1975).

Rossi, A., *Les Communistes français pendant la drôle de guerre* (Les Iles d'or, 1951).

——, *Physiologie du parti communiste français* (Editions Self, 1948).

Sartre, J.-P., *Situations I: essais critiques* (Gallimard, 1947).

——, *Situations II: qu'est-ce que la littérature?* (Gallimard, 1948).

——, *Situations IV: portraits* (Gallimard, 1964).

——, *Situations VI: problèmes du marxisme 1* (Gallimard, 1964).

——, *Situations VII: problèmes du marxisme 2* (Gallimard, 1965).

——, *Situations VIII: autour de mai '68* (Gallimard, 1972).

——, *Situations X: politique et autobiographie* (Gallimard, 1976).

——, 'Socialism in One Country', *New Left Review*, 100 (Nov 1976–Jan 1977) pp. 138–63.

Scriven, M., 'Comparative Perspectives on the Popular Front Experiences of France and Spain (1936–1986)', *Quinquereme*, 9 (2) (July 1986) pp. 190–3.

——, *Sartre's Existential Biographies* (London: Macmillan, 1984).

Serge, V., *Mémoires d'un révolutionnaire: 1901–1941* (Le Seuil, 1951).

Solomon, M. (ed.), *Marxism and Art* (Brighton: Harvester Press, 1979).

Stil, A., *Vers le réalisme socialiste* (Editions de la Nouvelle Critique, 1952).

Suleiman, S. R., *Authoritarian Fictions: The Ideological Novel as a Literary Genre* (New York: Columbia University Press, 1983).

Swingewood, A., 'Literature and Praxis: a Sociological Commentary', *New Literary History*, V(1) (Autumn 1973) pp. 169–76.

——, *The Novel and Revolution* (London: Macmillan, 1975).

Tartakowsky, D., *Une histoire du PCF* (Presses universitaires de France, 1982).

Thibaudeau, J., *Socialisme, avant-garde, littérature* (Editions sociales, 1972).

Tison-Braun, M., *La Crise de l'humanisme: le conflit de l'individu et de la société dans la littérature française moderne: tome II (1914–1939)* (Nizet, 1967).

Todd, E., *La Chute finale: essai sur la décomposition de la sphère soviétique* (Laffont, 1976).

——, *Le Fou et le prolétaire* (Laffont, 1979).

Touchard, J., 'Le Parti communiste français et les intellectuels (1920–1939)', *Revue française de science politique*, 17 June 1967, pp. 468–83.

Trotsky, L., *Class and Art: Problems of Culture under the Dictatorship of the Proletariat* (London: New Park Publications, 1974).

——, *Literature and Revolution* (Ann Arbor, Mich.: University of Michigan Press, 1960).

——, *On Literature and Art* (New York: Merit, 1970).

Wilson, E., *To the Finland Station* (London: Fontana, 1974).

Wohl, R., *French Communism in the Making: 1914–1924* (Stanford, Cal.: Stanford University Press, 1966).

Zhdanov, A. A., *On Literature, Music and Philosophy* (London: Lawrence and Wishart, 1950).

Index

The most important discussions of a topic are indicated by page numbers in bold type.